PENGUIN CLASSICS

THEAETETUS

PLATO (c. 427–347 B.C.) stands with Socrates and Aristotle as one of the shapers of the whole intellectual tradition of the West. He came from a family that had long played a prominent part in Athenian politics, and it would have been natural for him to follow the same course. He declined to do so, however, disgusted by the violence and corruption of Athenian political life, and sickened especially by the execution in 399 of his friend and teacher, Socrates. Inspired by Socrates' inquiries into the nature of ethical standards, Plato sought a cure for the ills of society not in politics but in philosophy, and arrived at his fundamental and lasting conviction that those ills would never cease until philosophers became rulers or rulers philosophers. At an uncertain date in the early fourth century B.C. he founded in Athens the Academy, the first permanent institution devoted to philosophical research and teaching, and the prototype of all western universities. He travelled extensively, notably to Sicily as political adviser to Dionysius II, ruler of Syracuse.

Plato wrote over twenty philosophical dialogues, and there are also extant under his name thirteen letters, whose genuineness is keenly disputed. His literary activity extended over perhaps half a century; few other writers have exploited so effectively the grace and precision, the flexibility and power, of Greek prose.

ROBIN ANTHONY HERSCHEL WATERFIELD was born in Oxfordshire in 1952 and was educated at Shrewsbury School, University College School, the University of Manchester and King's College, Cambridge. He taught for several years at the universities of Newcastle upon Tyne and St Andrews. There then followed a spell as a copy-editor for Penguin Books and he is now a freelance writer and editor. His main academic interests are in Greek philosophy and he has also translated for Penguin Classics Plato's *Philebus* and (in the volume *Early Socratic Dialogues*) *Hippias Major*, *Hip̄p̄ias Minor* and *Euthydemus*. He has worked in an ad̄v̄̄ this series.

PLATO

THEAETETUS

TRANSLATED WITH AN ESSAY BY
ROBIN A. H. WATERFIELD

PENGUIN BOOKS

Penguin Books Ltd, Harmondsworth, Middlesex, England
Viking Penguin Inc., 40 West 23rd Street, New York, New York 10010, U.S.A.
Penguin Books Australia Ltd, Ringwood, Victoria, Australia
Penguin Books Canada Limited, 2801 John Street, Markham, Ontario, Canada L3R 1B4
Penguin Books (N.Z.) Ltd, 182–190 Wairau Road, Auckland 10, New Zealand

This translation first published 1987

Made and printed in Great Britain by
Richard Clay Ltd, Bungay, Suffolk
Typeset in 10 on 12½ pt Photina

FOR BRIJI

ἐν χάριτος μέρει καὶ δωρείας

Contents

PREFACE   9

MAP   12

THEAETETUS   13

ESSAY   132

BIBLIOGRAPHY   247

PREFACE

Theaetetus is often hailed as 'Plato's most sustained study of epistemology' or the like – and this is true, but it is also misleading. It is misleading because it makes it sound as though epistemology was an established subject, which Plato was addressing. It wasn't. His philosophical predecessors had occasionally made remarks which we would classify as concerned with the problem of knowledge, and so had Plato himself, more systematically, in earlier dialogues; but it is closer to the truth to say that *Theaetetus* establishes the study of knowledge as a branch of philosophy in its own right, distinct from, especially, ontology. Consider, then, how remarkable it is that two and a half thousand years later it is still worth reading and discussing, for its philosophical interest as well as for its literary merits. Indeed, it is one of the few Platonic dialogues which consistently appears in modern works and courses on philosophy.

This alone is enough to justify the inclusion of an essay on the dialogue in a volume whose first aim is to translate it. To make such an inclusion is not to suggest that the dialogue cannot be appreciated by a lay reader, but to acknowledge its importance and the fact that, as the virtual inventor of the subject, Plato's discussion lacks technical vocabulary and precise distinctions, and therefore occasionally requires elucidation. In fact, *Theaetetus* is a philosophical work *par excellence* – accessible to the layman, yet leading one ever deeper into philosophical areas.

An anecdote may indicate a further reason for the necessity of exploration of this (and of any) Platonic dialogue. I well remember how, on first reading *Theaetetus* as an undergraduate, I was entranced by the clarity of the writing and the confidence of the arguments into believing almost everything Plato said. This is a trap which I am sure Plato himself would have wanted us to avoid: he wrote philosophy to stimulate thought rather than acceptance.

So much for justifying the inclusion of the essay on the dialogue. It will be noticed that I have broken with common practice and put this essay after the translation, rather than as an introduction: this is to indicate that the text needs reading first. The essay, it should finally be noted, falls far short of a thorough scholarly commentary on the dialogue, but is intended to alert the reader to the major issues which should be confronted if reading the dialogue develops into study of it.

As for the translation, my policy has been to try to reproduce the Greek both fluently and literally. Where these two aims clashed, I have preferred fluency to literalness, except where to do so would gloss over some important ambiguity. I chose not to break up the rhythm of the dialogue with the type of running commentary which is popular among translators of Plato; but I have added footnotes on minor points of explication or interest.

The Greek text used is that of J. Burnet (*Platonis Opera*, Volume 1, Oxford, 1900). Any divergences from this text have been mentioned in footnotes. The numbers and letters which appear in the margins are the standard means of precise reference to Plato; they refer to the pages and sections of pages of the edition of Plato by Henri Estienne, or Stephanus (Geneva, 1578).

Plato's *Theaetetus* has been very intensively studied, particularly by recent scholars. The bibliography may be taken to express my acknowledgements to written work. I also have two further academic acknowledgements to make: I attended a series of lectures on the dialogue by Myles Burnyeat in Cambridge in late 1976, and at much the same time was participating in the late Gwil Owen's seminars on the dialogue.

I would also like to thank Glyn Davies for many Socratic discussions on philosophy in general and knowledge in particular, Diana Pulvermacher for a thorough reading of the first draft of the typescript, Hugh Lawson-Tancred for several improvements, and Christine Collins for intelligent and observant editing. The book is dedicated to my wife Briji, for far more than simply checking the translation.

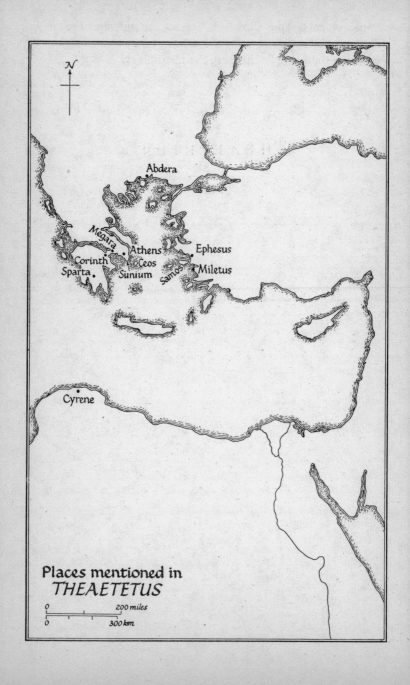

Places mentioned in
THEAETETUS

THEAETETUS

EUCLID: Hello, Terpsion. Been in town long, or have you
just arrived?

TERPSION: I've been here a while. In fact, I was looking
for you in the agora – I was surprised not to find you.

EUCLID: I was out of town.

TERPSION: Where?

EUCLID: I was on my way down to the port when I came
across Theaetetus being brought back to Athens after active
duty at Corinth.

TERPSION: Alive or dead?

EUCLID: Alive – but only just. He sustained some wounds, *b*
but he also caught the epidemic that's broken out in the
army, and that has weakened him more than the wounds.

TERPSION: Is it dysentery?

EUCLID: Yes.

TERPSION: What a person to be on the danger list!

EUCLID: Yes, he's a fine man, Terpsion. Why, only just
now I overheard some people praising him highly for his part
in the battle.

TERPSION: That doesn't surprise me; I'd be far more
surprised to hear anything else of him. But how come he
didn't stay here in Megara? *c*

EUCLID: He was in a hurry to get home. I kept asking him
and advising him to stay, but he didn't want to. So I saw him
on his way. As I was returning, I remembered with astonish-
ment how Socrates had predicted Theaetetus' future particularly accurately. It was shortly before Socrates' death,
I think, that he met Theaetetus, who was just a boy
then, spent some time in conversation with him, and was
very favourably impressed with his natural abilities. When
I was in Athens, he recounted their remarkable discus- *d*
sion for me, and he commented that without a doubt

Theaetetus would become well known, if he lived long enough.[1]

TERPSION: Events seem to have proved him right. But what was this discussion? Are you in a position to go through it?

EUCLID: Well, that would be quite out of the question if I
143a was unprepared, but I made notes as soon as I got home on that occasion, and later, when I had the time, I wrote it out from memory; and whenever I went to Athens, I used to ask Socrates about the bits I didn't remember, and then come back here and make corrections. So I think I've got almost all of it written out now.

TERPSION: Oh, yes: I've heard you mention it before, and, you know, I always meant to ask you to show it to me, but I never got around to it. But what's to stop us going through it now? I don't know about you, but I could certainly do with a rest after my journey from the country.

b   EUCLID: Well, in fact, I accompanied Theaetetus as far as Erineon,[2] so a rest would be welcome for me too. So that's settled; my slave will read to us while we take a rest together.

TERPSION: Good idea.[3]

EUCLID: Here's what I wrote, Terpsion. I didn't write the discussion down in the form in which Socrates repeated it to me, with him doing all the talking, but as a dialogue between him and those who he said took part in the discussion – who were the geometer Theodorus and Theaetetus, he said. I
c   wanted to avoid the nuisance of all the bits which Socrates had to insert about himself for explanation, like 'And I said' or 'And I remarked', or about the interlocutor, like 'He agreed' or 'He disagreed'; so I omitted all that kind of stuff and wrote it down as a dialogue between them.

TERPSION: That sounds very sensible, Euclid.

1. This does not imply that Theaetetus is young at the time of the prologue; early death was always a possibility to be taken into account in the ancient world.

2. Presumably a village near Megara.

3. A few minutes pass while the slave goes to fetch the scrolls.

EUCLID: All right, boy, take the book and read to us.

SOCRATES: If Cyrene were uppermost in my mind, Theodorus, I would ask you about events there, to find out *d* whether there's any interest in geometry or any other branch of philosophy among the Cyrenian young men. But as it is, I am less concerned about them than the local lads; I've a greater desire to know which of *our* young men are likely to turn out well.[1] I investigate this myself as much as I can, and I ask other people whose company I see they seek out. Now, *you* attract quite a crowd – which is as it should be, given your knowledge, of geometry especially. So I'd be glad *e* to know if you've met anyone worth mentioning.

THEODORUS: As it happens, Socrates, there *is* a young Athenian I've come across who is well worth my telling you about – though if he were good-looking I would hesitate to be too enthusiastic, in case anyone thought I fancied him![2] But as it is – and I hope you'll take this in good part – he isn't good-looking, but he looks like you! He's snub-nosed and his eyes bulge, though not as much as yours.[3] I know you won't mind the comparison, because you should know that *144a* of all the people I've met – and that's no inconsiderable number – I have never yet seen anyone with such incredible talents. For someone to be remarkably intelligent and yet exceptionally unassuming, and moreover to have courage that would bear comparison with anyone's – well, I would not have credited it. It's not a phenomenon that I've seen before: such quickness, acuity and retentiveness usually go hand in hand with emotional instability – the image of un-ballasted ships being tossed about comes to mind – and lack of control, rather than courage. On the other hand, the *b*

1. On Socrates' parochialism, see especially *Apology* 28a–31c, 37e–38a, and *Crito* 52a–53a, with Kraut ([69] Chapters 7 and 8).

2. Homosexuality was a fact of life in the upper strata of Athenian society.

3. On Socrates' appearance, see also *Symposium* 215b, *Meno* 80a, and Xenophon, *Symposium* 5.

steadier ones tend to approach intellectual matters somewhat sluggishly, and their ballast is forgetfulness. But this lad
tackles his lessons and research so calmly and precisely and
efficiently, and in such an unassuming manner – like a
soundless stream of liquid oil – that it's amazing to find one
so young setting about them like that.[1]

SOCRATES: That *is* good news. And whose son is he?

THEODORUS: Somebody told me, but I've forgotten. Never
c mind – he's the one in the centre of the group coming up to
us now. He and these friends of his were just oiling themselves
in the portico outside, and now, I suppose, they've finished
and are on their way here. So you see if you know him.

SOCRATES: Yes, I do. He's the son of Euphronius of
Sunium, who was just as you have described his son to be,
and well respected too; *and* he left quite a large estate. But I
don't know the boy's name.

d   THEODORUS: It's Theaetetus, Socrates. By the way, I think
some of the trustees have squandered the estate. Despite that,
however, another one of his remarkable characteristics is
financial generosity, Socrates.

SOCRATES: You are describing a person of good breeding.
Please ask him to come and sit down here.

THEODORUS: All right. Theaetetus, come and be with
Socrates.

SOCRATES: Yes, do, Theaetetus. I want to examine the
cast of my own features. I mean, Theodorus claims that we
e are alike. But if we each had a lyre, and he said that they
were similarly tuned, would we just take his word for it, or
would we first see whether his statement was backed by
musical knowledge?

THEAETETUS: The latter.

SOCRATES: And our belief or disbelief would depend on
whether or not we found him to be a musician?

THEAETETUS: Right.

SOCRATES: In the present instance, if we were bothered

1. Theodorus' praise of Theaetetus resembles Plato's list of qualities essential to a philosopher at *Republic* 503c.

about whether our features were similar, I suppose we should
see whether or not he speaks with the authority of being an 145*a*
artist.

THEAETETUS: I think so.

SOCRATES: Is Theodorus an artist?

THEAETETUS: Not as far as I know.

SOCRATES: He's a *geometer*, isn't he?

THEAETETUS: Absolutely, Socrates.

SOCRATES: And does he know about astronomy, mathematics, music and other educational subjects?

THEAETETUS: I think so.

SOCRATES: So if he says that we have physical similarities
– whether or not he finds them commendable – we have no
particular reason to listen to him.

THEAETETUS: I suppose not.

SOCRATES: But what if he were to praise one or the other *b*
of us for mental attainments and cleverness? Whoever he
was talking *to* ought to do his best to examine whoever he
was talking *about*, who in turn should do his best to prove
himself, don't you think?

THEAETETUS: Yes, Socrates.

SOCRATES: Now is the time, then, my dear Theaetetus, for
you to do the proving and for me to do the examining. I must
tell you that Theodorus, who has often praised both Athe-
nians and others to me before, has never praised anyone as
he did you just now.

THEAETETUS: That's all very well, Socrates, but are you
sure he wasn't joking? *c*

SOCRATES: That's not his style. Now, don't you try to
duck out of our agreement by pretending that he was joking.
Otherwise he'll have to give evidence under duress; I mean,
there's absolutely no chance of anyone accusing him of
perjury and making him take an oath. But don't give up:
abide by our agreement.

THEAETETUS: All right, if you say so.

SOCRATES: So tell me: you learn some geometry from
Theodorus, I imagine, don't you?

THEAETETUS: I do.

d   SOCRATES: And what is relevant to astronomy, harmony and calculation?

THEAETETUS: I do my best.

SOCRATES: So do I, my boy, when I learn from him and from anyone else who I think has any understanding of these subjects. But although I get on fairly well in these subjects on the whole, there's a minor issue[1] which puzzles me and which I'd like to look into, with the help of you and your friends here. Tell me: isn't learning becoming wiser about the subject one is learning?

THEAETETUS: Of course.

SOCRATES: And it is *wisdom* that makes people wise?

THEAETETUS: Yes.

e   SOCRATES: Is this different from knowledge?

THEAETETUS: What?

SOCRATES: Wisdom. If you know something, aren't you also wise about it?

THEAETETUS: Certainly.

SOCRATES: So knowledge is the same as wisdom?[2]

THEAETETUS: Yes.

SOCRATES: Well, now we're at the heart of what puzzles me and what I cannot satisfactorily grasp on my own – what knowledge in fact is. Are we in a position to give an account of

146*a* it? What do you all think? Which of us should have a go first? If he misses the mark – and the same goes for anyone who misses the mark at any time – then he'll sit down and be the 'donkey', as children say in their ball-game. But anyone who comes through without making a mistake will be our 'king', and it'll be *his* turn to set us to answer any questions he likes.

Why doesn't someone say something? Surely, Theodorus, it's not ill-mannered of me to enjoy discussions so much that I am trying to get us talking and to be on friendly and familiar terms?

1. Socrates not infrequently calls his concerns, which provoke whole dialogues, 'minor issues' or the like.

2. The two words are in fact often equivalent in Greek: *sophia* (wisdom) also means 'cleverness', 'technical expertise', etc.

THEODORUS: No, that could never be considered ill- *b* mannered, Socrates. But you must address yourself to the young men. I'm not used to this way of carrying on a discussion, and besides, I'm too old to form the habit now. But it'd be just the thing for them, and they'll get far more out of it. There's always further to go when you're young, and that's a fact. Why don't you carry on as you started? Don't let Theaetetus off the hook: ask *him* your questions.

SOCRATES: Theaetetus, you have heard Theodorus, and I'm sure you'll do as he says; indeed, when a wise man gives *c* an order in such matters, the only proper course of action for a younger person is obedience. So, what do you think knowledge is? Hold your head up high, and answer me.

THEAETETUS: Here goes, then, since you're both telling me to answer. No doubt you'll correct any mistakes I make.

SOCRATES: Yes, if we can.

THEAETETUS: Well, I think that the subjects Theodorus teaches – geometry and so on (you listed them just now) – are kinds of knowledge; and let us not forget cobbling and the *d* other humbler crafts. All of these together constitute knowledge, and each individually is a kind of knowledge.

SOCRATES: You are over-generous, my friend. I asked for one, and you are offering many; I asked for something simple, and you respond with complexity.

THEAETETUS: What do you mean, Socrates?

SOCRATES: I'm probably talking nonsense, but I'll tell you what's on my mind. When you speak of cobblery, don't you just mean the knowledge of making shoes?

THEAETETUS: Yes.

SOCRATES: What about carpentry? The knowledge of *e* making wooden objects?

THEAETETUS: Again, yes.

SOCRATES: So in both cases you are pinpointing what each craft is knowledge *of*?

THEAETETUS: Yes.

SOCRATES: But the question, Theaetetus, was not 'What are the objects of knowledge?', nor 'How many branches of knowledge are there?' We didn't ask the question because we wanted a catalogue, but because we wanted to know what knowledge is. Am I talking nonsense?

THEAETETUS: No, you're quite right.

147a   SOCRATES: Look at it this way too. Suppose we were asked about something familiar and commonplace – suppose the question was 'What is clay?' Wouldn't it be ridiculous of us to answer that there's clay for making pots, clay for making terracotta and clay for making bricks?

THEAETETUS: I suppose so.

SOCRATES: I mean, in the first place, it would be ridiculous to suppose that our answer gave the questioner any understanding of what clay is when we use the term, whether *b* we add 'for making statuettes' or mention any other craft. Or do you think that any term can be meaningful without knowledge of what it stands for?

THEAETETUS: No, of course it can't.

SOCRATES: So the phrase 'knowledge of shoes' is meaningless, unless you know what knowledge is.

THEAETETUS: Yes.

SOCRATES: So anyone who doesn't know what knowledge is[1] cannot understand cobblery or any other craft.

THEAETETUS: You're right.

SOCRATES: So it is absurd to give the name of any craft as an answer to the question what knowledge is. For that is *c* knowledge of something, and doesn't answer the question.

THEAETETUS: I suppose you're right.

SOCRATES: In the second place, all this rigmarole gets us nowhere and is quite unnecessary, because, I think, an ordinary, short answer *must* be available. For example, in the case of the question about clay, the ordinary, simple reply is that clay is earth mixed up with liquid; there's no need to say what the clay is used for.

THEAETETUS: It seems easy now, Socrates, when you put it like that. But, you know, it looks as though you're asking a similar question to one which occurred to me and your

1. The phrase translated 'know what knowledge is' here and just before is literally 'know knowledge'; the next phrase translated 'know what knowledge is' is a literal translation, however. See p. 212.

namesake, Socrates here, when we were talking together a *d* short while ago.

SOCRATES: What was that, Theaetetus?

THEAETETUS: Theodorus here was using diagrams to explain to us something about irrational square roots.[1] He showed[2] that the sides of squares whose areas are three square feet[3] or five square feet are incommensurable with one foot, and he went through the sides of every such square up to seventeen square feet, where he happened to break off.[4] Now, since there are evidently an infinite number of irrational square roots, what occurred to us was to try to gather them all under a single heading.   *e*

SOCRATES: And did you find a way of doing this?

THEAETETUS: I think we did; see what you think.

SOCRATES: Go on.

THEAETETUS: We distinguished two classes into which all numbers fall. Any number which can be the product of multiplying some number by itself, we called 'square and equal-sided',[5] on the analogy of a geometrical square.

SOCRATES: Good.

THEAETETUS: But as for the intermediate numbers – three, five and any number which cannot be the product of 148*a* multiplying some number by itself – which are always the

1. This is what the Greek *dunamis* must mean in this passage, but in itself it is a far more flexible term, meaning literally 'ability', and capable of bearing a number of mathematical meanings. Mathematical terminology was not yet fixed. In what follows it will be helpful to remember that mathematics in Plato's time was still intrinsically bound up with geometry.

2. Retaining ἀποφαίνων with the manuscripts.

3. The irrationality of $\sqrt{2}$ had long been established.

4. Or 'he somehow got tied up', or 'he broke off for some particular [mathematical] reason'. A great deal of ancient and modern controversy has arisen about this ambiguous sentence, but precisely because it is ambiguous, it cannot afford us knowledge of why Theodorus stopped where he did.

5. One of Theaetetus' two terms is redundant. This and other slight awkwardnesses in his account have been taken to suggest that he is being portrayed as a schoolboy rather than a master mathematician. See also p. 24 n. 3.

product of multiplying either a greater number by a smaller one or vice versa, and which, in geometrical terms, form figures with unequal sides, we called such numbers 'oblong', on the analogy of a geometrical oblong.

SOCRATES: Excellent. Then what happened?

THEAETETUS: We defined as 'rational lengths' all those lines which form the sides of a square whose area is one of our 'equal-sided' numbers; and we defined all those lines which form the sides of a square whose area is one of
b our 'oblong' numbers as 'irrational roots', since they are not commensurable with the former lines in length (though their squares are commensurable with the former lines).[1] A similar distinction can be made for solid figures too.[2]

SOCRATES: Nobody could have done better, my boys. I really don't think that Theodorus is going to be liable to the charge of perjury.[3]

THEAETETUS: Well, but I think you're looking for the same sort of answer to your question about knowledge, Socrates, as we came up with for rational and irrational roots – and I don't think I can do it. So Theodorus turns out to be mistaken after all!

c   SOCRATES: Hang on. Suppose it was your running ability he was praising, and he said that he had met no young man better at running; and suppose that you were then beaten in a race by a champion in his prime. Do you think that his praise would have been any the less correct?

THEAETETUS: No.

1. By definition, any integer is commensurable with any other integer, since commensurability is the ability to be measured by the same unit (see Theodorus' reference to one foot in 147d).

2. An analogous general formula could be found for rational and irrational cube roots. For a modern expression of Theaetetus' formula, see pp. 138–9.

3. See 145c. It is not immediately clear whether Socrates is praising an original discovery or a successful schoolboy exercise. Burnyeat [65] suggests a middle way: Theaetetus' work is not that much of a discovery mathematically, but it is important to the philosophical method of the dialogue (see p. 139).

SOCRATES: Well, do you think that getting clear about knowledge is really a 'minor issue', as I called it just now?[1] Don't you think that it is altogether one of the highest achievements?

THEAETETUS: Yes, I do – one of the very highest.

SOCRATES: Don't worry about yourself, then. Just assume that Theodorus knows what he is talking about, and do your *d* absolute best to express your thoughts, especially about what knowledge in fact is.

THEAETETUS: If doing my best is all it takes, Socrates, we'll get results.

SOCRATES: All right, then. You showed the way well just now, so take your answer about irrational roots as a model. What you must try to do is give a single account of the many branches of knowledge, in the same way that you gathered together the plurality of irrational roots under a single concept.

THEAETETUS: But I think you should know, Socrates, that *e* this is not the first time I've tackled this problem; I've heard about your questions at second hand. But all I've been left with are two convictions: that anything I come up with is unsatisfactory, and that I can't find anyone else giving the sort of account you're asking for – and yet, for all that, the question hasn't stopped niggling me.

SOCRATES: This isn't lack of fertility, Theaetetus. You're pregnant, and these are your labour-pains.

THEAETETUS: I don't know about that, Socrates. I'm just telling you my experiences.

SOCRATES: Don't be so serious! Haven't you heard that 149*a* my mother Phainarete[2] was a good, sturdy midwife?

THEAETETUS: Yes, somebody did tell me once.

SOCRATES: And have you heard that I practise the same profession?

THEAETETUS: No, never.

SOCRATES: But it's true, you know: I do have this skill. It's

1. 145d.

2. Phainarete is also mentioned at *First Alcibiades* 131e. His father was Sophroniscus, a sculptor.

a secret, though, my friend, so don't tell on me. Because people don't know, it isn't part of my reputation, which is only as an eccentric and someone who confuses people. I imagine you've heard that?

b THEAETETUS: Yes.

SOCRATES: Do I need to tell you the reason for my reputation?

THEAETETUS: Yes, please.

SOCRATES: If you consider midwifery as a whole, you'll soon see what I'm getting at. I mean, you are aware, of course, that no woman practises midwifery while she is still of an age to get pregnant and give birth herself. It's only those who are past child-bearing.

THEAETETUS: Yes.

SOCRATES: This is thought to be due to Artemis, who is childless, but is in charge of childbirth. She wanted to reward women who are like her, but barren women weren't the
c recipients of her gift of midwifery, because human nature is too weak to become skilled in matters of which it has no experience. Instead, therefore, she gave the job to those whom age prevents from giving birth.

THEAETETUS: That's plausible.

SOCRATES: And isn't it also plausible – isn't it necessary, in fact, that midwives are better than others at recognizing whether or not women are pregnant?

THEAETETUS: Yes.

SOCRATES: And that's not the end of their abilities: their
d chants and the drugs they administer can induce labour and relieve the pains, as they see fit; can bring a difficult birth to a successful conclusion; and can bring on a miscarriage,[1] if that is what seems best.

THEAETETUS: True.

SOCRATES: And have you also noticed that they know all there is to know about pairing types of women and men to produce the best children – in other words, that they are the most skilful match-makers?

THEAETETUS: No, I wasn't aware of that at all.

---

1. Reading νηδύν with Adam [6].

SOCRATES: Well, let me tell you, they pride themselves more on this than on cutting the umbilical cord. Look at it *e* this way: do you think that the matching of shoots and seeds to soils is the province of the *same* skill as the cultivation and harvesting of crops, or of a different one?

THEAETETUS: No, the same one.

SOCRATES: What about the case of women? Are the analogous skills different?

THEAETETUS: That's not likely.

SOCRATES: No. But the improper and unskilled pairing of *150a* couples, which is called pimping, means that midwives, who want to preserve their reputation, steer clear of matchmaking, in case this latter activity leads them to incur the charge of the former. But in fact only proper midwives are qualified to make successful matches.

THEAETETUS: Apparently.

SOCRATES: So you can see how important midwifery is, but it still falls short of *my* business. For women cannot produce offspring which are sometimes true, but sometimes illu- *b* sory, with the difference hard to discern. I mean, if that were the case, the finest and most crucial task that midwives could perform would be distinguishing the true from the false. Don't you agree?

THEAETETUS: Yes.

SOCRATES: Well, my midwifery has all the standard features, except that I practise it on men instead of women, and supervise the labour of their minds, not their bodies. And the most important aspect of *my* skill is the ability to apply *c* every conceivable test to see whether the young man's mental offspring is illusory and false or viable and true. But I have *this* feature in common with midwives – I myself am barren of wisdom.[1] The criticism that's often made of me – that it's lack of wisdom that makes me ask others questions, but say nothing positive myself – is perfectly true. Why do I behave like this? Because the god[2] compels me to attend to the labours of

1. See above all Vlastos [74] on Socrates' disavowal of knowledge.

2. The male equivalent to Artemis (149b) – probably Apollo, Artemis' brother, to whom Socrates attributed his philosophical mission (see *Apology*).

others, but prohibits me from having any offspring myself. I myself, therefore, am quite devoid of wisdom; my mind has *d* never produced any idea that could be called clever. But as for those who associate with me – well, although at first some of them give the impression of being pretty stupid, yet later, as the association continues, all of those to whom the god vouchsafes it improve marvellously, as is evident to themselves as well as to others. And they make this progress, clearly, not because they ever learn anything from me; the many fine ideas and offspring that they produce come from within themselves. But the god and I are responsible for the delivery.

e　There is clear evidence of this. Often in the past people have not been aware of the part I play; they have discounted me, and thought that they themselves were responsible for the delivery. Either of their own accord, or under the influence of others, they left me sooner than they ought to. Then, because they kept bad company, they proceeded to have only miscarriages, and they spoiled all the offspring I had delivered with wrong upbringing. They placed more weight on counterfeits and illusions than on the truth. Eventually, they gained a reputation for stupidity, and thought themselves 151*a* stupid too. Aristides the son of Lysimachus was one of these people,[1] but there were plenty of others. If they come back, begging and doing goodness knows what for my company, sometimes the supernatural sign that I get[2] does not allow me to let them be with me, but in some cases it does, and these are the ones who make progress again.

　　There's another experience which those who associate with me have in common with pregnant women: they suffer labour-pains. In fact, they are racked night and day with a far greater distress than women undergo; and the

---

1. Aristides figures in the genuine Platonic dialogue *Laches* and in the possibly spurious *Theages*, where the same story of his leaving Socrates is repeated.

2. On Socrates' *daimonion*, see *Apology* 31c–d, *Phaedrus* 242b–c and Riddell [70].

arousal and relief of this pain is the province of my expertise. *b*

So it is with them, Theaetetus. As for people who strike me as not yet being pregnant and therefore as having no need of me, this is where my skills as a kindly match-maker come into play. Though I say so myself, I'm pretty good at guessing whose company would be beneficial for them. I have handed lots of them over to Prodicus' care, and plenty to other wise and remarkable men as well.[1]

Now, why have I gone on at such length about all this to *you?* Because I suspect, as do you yourself,[2] that you are in pain, and that this is due to pregnancy. So let me take on *c* your case: remember, I'm a midwife's son and practise the art myself. When I ask a question, set about answering it to the best of your ability. And if, on examination, I find that some thought of yours is illusory and untrue, and if I then draw it out of you and discard it, don't rant and rave at me, as a first-time mother might if her baby was involved. In the past, my friend, when I've removed some piece of nonsense of theirs, people have often worked themselves up into such a state that they've been ready literally to bite me! They don't believe that I'm acting out of goodwill; it doesn't even cross their minds that no god bears ill-will towards men, and that I am *d* not motivated by ill-will either. I do what I do because it is my moral duty not to connive at falsehood and cover up truth.

So let's start again from the beginning, Theaetetus: try to define knowledge. Don't ever say that it's beyond your ability. If God is willing, and if you find the courage, the ability will follow.

THEAETETUS: Well, Socrates, it would be disgraceful for anyone, faced with the sort of encouragement you are giving, not to try his hardest to express his thoughts. So . . . I think *e* that someone *knows* something when he *perceives* it; my

1. Prodicus of Ceos was one of the most eminent sophists of the late fifth century, famous especially for his pioneering work on distinguishing near synonyms, which is parodied by Plato in *Protagoras* (337a–c, 340a–b, 358a–e).

2. 148e.

current impression, at any rate, is that knowledge and perception[1] are the same.

SOCRATES: Well done, boy! That is the way to speak up.
An excellent answer! Now then, we must investigate it together, to see whether it is in fact viable or still-born.[2] Perception, you claim, is knowledge. Yes?

THEAETETUS: Yes.

SOCRATES: Whether or not you are aware of it, however,
this statement of yours about knowledge is a substantial one;
152a it's what Protagoras used to say as well, though he used
different words to say the same thing. I mean, he says somewhere that 'Man is the measure of all things – of the things
that are, that they are; of the things that are not, that they
are not.' No doubt you've read this?[3]

THEAETETUS: Yes, often.

SOCRATES: And doesn't he mean by this that 'Each and
every event is for me as it appears to me, and is for you as it
appears for you' – you and I being 'man'?

THEAETETUS: That's what he says.[4]

b   SOCRATES: Now, he's a clever person, and unlikely to be
talking nonsense; so let's follow in his footsteps. Isn't it possible that, when the *same* wind is blowing, one of us might

1. *Aisthesis*: see pp. 143–4.

2. The word recurs at 157d, 161a and 210b. It means literally a 'wind-
egg'. The Greeks believed that a bird's egg which failed to hatch was the result
of impregnation by the wind. It is also applied to chickens' eggs which are
hatched without prior impregnation, which may be significant in the light of
Socrates' common sexual metaphor for philosophy (see pp. 140–41).

3. The bibliography (section E) mentions only a small sample of the
many discussions of this, the most famous dictum of the most famous sophist,
Protagoras of Abdera (*c.* 490–420). The verb 'to be' will quite frequently be
used in ways which are unfamiliar in English, but have to be translated
literally to preserve the sense of what is going on in the Greek (see p. 146).

4. It is not, in fact, immediately clear from the Greek whether this second
quote is an actual quotation of Protagoras, or an interpretation of the first
quote; but the similarity of the words at *Cratylus* 386a, again immediately
following the 'Man is the measure' fragment, suggests that Plato is actually
quoting.

feel chilly, while the other doesn't? Or one might feel slightly
chilly, the other really rather cold?

THEAETETUS: Certainly.

SOCRATES: So when that happens, are we to describe the
wind *per se* as cold or not cold? Or should we follow Protagoras
and say that it is cold for the one who feels cold, but not for
the one who doesn't?

THEAETETUS: That seems reasonable.

SOCRATES: And that is how the wind appears to each
of us?

THEAETETUS: Yes.

SOCRATES: Now, the phrase 'It appears to me' is the same
as 'I perceive', isn't it?

THEAETETUS: It is.

SOCRATES: So appearance is the same as being perceived, *c*
in the case of warmth and so on. I mean, as each person
perceives events to be, so they also are, I suppose, for each
person.

THEAETETUS: That sounds reasonable.

SOCRATES: Perception, therefore, is always of something
that is, and it is infallible, which suggests that it is knowledge.[1]

THEAETETUS: So it seems.

SOCRATES: Well, by heaven, there's a question here. Was
Protagoras' wisdom *all*-inclusive? I mean, did he treat us, the
masses, to these riddles, but speak the truth to his students in
secret?

THEAETETUS: What are you getting at, Socrates?   *d*

SOCRATES: I will tell you – and this is certainly a substantial theory. I mean the view that nothing is a single, non-

1. The Greek of this sentence is difficult and ambiguous. It looks at first
sight as though it means '. . . and, *qua* knowledge, it is infallible'. But this
makes a nonsense of the preceding argument, which requires that the identity
of perception and knowledge is a conclusion, not a premiss (see especially
White [17]). My translation relies on the parallel construction of Aristotle,
Physics 203b 7–8: 'Besides, it [the infinite] does not admit of coming-to-be or
ceasing-to-be, which suggests that it is a kind of principle' (translated by
E. Hussey). The two marks of knowledge cited here will naturally play an
important part in *Theaetetus*.

relative identity, and that you cannot correctly identify anything or describe what it is like. If you call something big, it
will also turn out to be small, and if you call something
heavy, it will also turn out to be light, and so on for everything, on the grounds that nothing is single and you cannot
say what it is or what it is like. In fact, everything which we
describe as 'being' is actually in the process of being generated[1] as a result of movement and change and mutual mixture. We are wrong to describe things in that way, because
e nothing ever *is*, but is continually *being generated.* The whole
succession of past sages (with the exception of Parmenides)
can be seen to agree on this point – I'm thinking of Protagoras,
Heraclitus and Empedocles – and so can Epicharmus and
Homer, the foremost composers of their types of poetry,
comedy and tragedy respectively. When Homer speaks of
'Oceanus, whence gods are generated, and mother Tethys',
he is saying that everything is the offspring of flux and
change. Don't you think that that's his meaning?[2]

THEAETETUS: I do.

1. It is not easy to find a stable translation of this key term in the flux
theory! 'Coming to be' is the most literal, but is awkward in most contexts,
so 'becoming' and 'generation' have also been used. But the reader should
be aware that they all translate the same Greek words (*gignesthai* and
cognates).

2. Plato and his peers were not historians of philosophy in our sense of
the phrase: philosophers holding fairly different ideas could be lumped together; philosophers could be lumped together with mythologers and poets;
and so on. Thus Protagoras earns his place in this list solely because of the
present Protagorean context (any later attributions of a flux theory to Protagoras are undoubtedly dependent on *Theaetetus*); Heraclitus of Ephesus
(*c.* 540–475) in fact stressed not only flux, but order within flux; Empedocles
of Acragas in Sicily (*c.* 495–435) subscribed to the common Presocratic
notion that things are a mixture of opposites; Epicharmus of Sicily (*floruit*
c. 500) was a comic playwright, lines of whose plays were popularly taken
out of context as philosophical maxims: his Fragment 2 claims that everything is in flux; Homeric studies in Plato's time included the interpretation of
his works as allegories: both Oceanus and Tethys are sea-deities, so Homer is
brought into a list of fluxists (see also *Cratylus* 402b on the same line,
Iliad 14.201, 302). On Parmenides of Elea in south Italy (*c.* 515–445), see
180d–e.

SOCRATES: What chance has any view which opposes 153a
such a mighty host, with a leader of Homer's stature, of
appearing sensible?

THEAETETUS: Not a lot, Socrates.

SOCRATES: You're quite right, Theaetetus. And there's
further compelling evidence for this theory. The process of
generation – that is, apparent being – is a result of change;
but destruction – that is, not being – is a result of inactivity. I
mean, heat and fire, which generate and nourish everything
else, are themselves generated by movement and friction.
These are changes, and they are the origin of fire, aren't
they?

THEAETETUS: They are.   b

SOCRATES: Moreover, movement and friction give rise to
living creatures as well.[1]

THEAETETUS: Of course.

SOCRATES: And a healthy physical condition is spoiled by
inactivity and inertia, but, on the whole, is preserved by exercise and change, isn't it?

THEAETETUS: Yes.

SOCRATES: And is it not by means of lessons and practice
– that is, by means of change – that the mind acquires information and that its healthy condition is preserved and
improved? But inactivity – lack of practice and learning –
leads the mind not only to learn nothing, but even to forget c
what it has learned.

THEAETETUS: Certainly.

SOCRATES: So change is good for mind and body, and lack
of change the opposite?

THEAETETUS: Apparently.

SOCRATES: Need I go on? What about torpid weather,
stagnant water and all the other instances where inactivity
causes rot and ruin, and preservation requires different

1. That is, in the sexual act. The previous illustration of fire sounds like a
Presocratic notion, possibly stemming from Heraclitus himself, for whom fire
was a kind of prime matter. The physical illustrations that follow could have
been drawn from medical theory of the late fifth century, which was often
influenced by Heraclitus.

conditions? Do I have to crown it all by pressing into service [1]
Homer's 'golden cord' and arguing that he uses this image
d for nothing other than the sun, because he wants to demonstrate that the existence and preservation of everything
divine and human depends on the cyclical motion of the sun
and the heavenly bodies, and that if they were bound down
and static, everything would be destroyed and 'what's up
would end up down', as they say? [2]

THEAETETUS: No, I think you are obviously right,
Socrates.

SOCRATES: Well then, my friend, here is a hypothesis:
take vision first. The colour white is nothing distinct in itself
either outside your eyes or in your eyes – in fact, you may not
e locate it anywhere. If you did, it would have a position and it
would be stable – in other words, it would not be undergoing
a process of generation.

THEAETETUS: What do you mean, exactly?

SOCRATES: If we follow the theory we mentioned just now,
and assume that nothing is a single, non-relative entity, then
we will find that black, white and so on are generated by the
eyes meeting the movement for which they are adapted, and
154*a* that what we call a colour is neither the thing which does the
meeting, nor the thing which is met, but something generated
in between, which is peculiar to the individual perceiver. At
least, I imagine that you wouldn't maintain that a dog or any
other animal perceives colours in the same way that you do,
would you?

THEAETETUS: No, I certainly wouldn't.

SOCRATES: What about another human being? Are his or
her perceptions similar to yours? Is this what you would
maintain, or would you much prefer to say that not even you
yourself perceive things in the same way, because you never
remain in a similar state?

1. Reading ἀναγκάζω πρόβιβάζων with manuscript B and Stobaeus.

2. This is a desperate interpretation of the beginning of *Iliad* 8. Plato
may be referring obliquely in the final words of this paragraph to the
famous Fragment 60 of Heraclitus, 'The road up and down is one and the
same.'

THEAETETUS: I prefer the latter view to the former.

SOCRATES: Now, if the objects we measure ourselves *b*
against[1] or touch were large or white or warm, then they
would never have become different (as they do), just because
a different person meets with them, unless they themselves
are changing. And on the other hand, if the perceiver, who
does the measuring or touching, were each of these things,[2]
then again, he or she would not become different just because
some other object comes along or because something happens
to an object, unless something was happening to him or her.
But everyday speech, my friend, carelessly uses words which,
from the Protagorean viewpoint and others which approximate to it, are extraordinarily absurd.

THEAETETUS: What do you mean? What's absurd in
everyday speech?

SOCRATES: Here's a small example, which will help you *c*
to see what I mean in general. Suppose we have six knuckle-
bones. If we put them next to four knuckle-bones, then we
say that they are *more* than four – one and a half times more,
in fact. But if we put them next to twelve knuckle-bones, we
say that they are *fewer* – in fact, half as many. And that's the
only way our language allows us to put it, isn't it?

THEAETETUS: Yes.

SOCRATES: Well, suppose Protagoras or someone asks,
'Theaetetus, can anything become greater or more without
being increased?' What will your answer be?

THEAETETUS: If I was thinking about just *this* question,
Socrates, I would answer 'No'. But if I was thinking about the *d*
last question you asked, I would answer 'Yes', in case I contradicted myself.[3]

1. '"Measuring ourselves against" is Protagorean for perceiving of any
kind' (Burnyeat [85], p. 79).

2. That is, white, warm, etc. Plato is denying (see 153d) that the perceived quality resides in the sense-organ or the perceiver as a whole. For a
similar denial, see *Charmides* 168d–e. On the appeal of this 'window' model
to philosophers ancient and modern, see Burnyeat [85].

3. Because he answered 'Yes' to it before.

SOCRATES: An excellent answer, by God! My friend, you are inspired! The trouble, apparently, is that if you answer 'Yes', we get the Euripidean situation of the tongue being safe from refutation, but the heart not being safe from refutation.[1]

THEAETETUS: True.

SOCRATES: Well, if you and I were clever savants and the examination of the contents of our hearts were a thing of the past, then we'd be in the happy position of having nothing *e* left to do now except put each other to the test; we'd make a contest out of it, as sophists do, and meet, with great clashing of argument on argument.[2] But as it is, since we're amateurs, our first concern will be to compare our thoughts, to see what they are and whether they are consistent or quite the opposite.

THEAETETUS: Yes, that's certainly *my* concern.

SOCRATES: Mine too. Since this is so, shall we peaceably take up the investigation? There's plenty of time: we don't *155a* need to be impatient. What we're really looking at is ourselves, to see what these phantoms are which lurk inside us. And the first of these, on examination, we will formulate, I think, as that nothing can ever become greater or smaller, in bulk or in number, as long as it is equal to itself. Right?

THEAETETUS: Yes.

SOCRATES: And the second is that something to which nothing is added and from which nothing is taken away neither increases nor decreases, but remains equal.

THEAETETUS: Exactly.

b   SOCRATES: And isn't there also a third, that it is impossible for something later to be which once was not, without

1. Plato refers to Euripides, *Hippolytus* 612: 'My tongue swore the oath, but my heart did not' – a line that soon became notorious and grist to the mill of those who quoted Euripidean lines out of context to paint him as immoral.

2. The sophists used to meet for public eristic debates, whose purpose was for one sophist to defeat the other who, for the sake of argument, adopted the opposite view. Plato prefers continued Socratic inquiry and honest statements of beliefs.

having come to be and without the process of becoming?[1]

THEAETETUS: I think so.

SOCRATES: So we're agreed on these three points, but, I believe, they fight with one another in our minds, when we think about the case of the knuckle-bones. Or here's another example: we say that I, an old man, without growing or shrinking, am now taller than you, who are young, but later on, within a year, we say that I am smaller, although my size hasn't decreased at all, and it's just that you have grown. The trouble is that this implies that I am later what I once *c* was not, despite not having undergone any coming-to-be. I mean, nothing can happen without coming-to-be, and unless I lose some of my size, I can't come to be smaller. Now, if we accept these examples, thousands upon thousands of other similar cases crowd in. You see what I mean, don't you, Theaetetus? I get the impression that you've come across these problems before.

THEAETETUS: Yes, I most certainly have, Socrates, and they arouse my curiosity no end. Sometimes I get really dizzy from considering them.

SOCRATES: It looks as though Theodorus' sketch of your *d* character was accurate, my friend. I mean, this feeling – a sense of wonder – is perfectly proper to a philosopher: philosophy has no other foundation, in fact. Whoever said that Iris was the offspring of Thaumas was no mean genealogist.[2] But I wonder whether or not you can now see why it follows from the theory we are attributing to Protagoras that these things are so?

THEAETETUS: No, I don't think I can yet.

SOCRATES: So would I be right in thinking that you will be grateful for my help in uncovering from its hiding-place

1. Reading ἀλλὰ ὕστερον with Stephanus. The fact that Proclus had to defend the reading ὕστερον ἀλλά shows that it is objectionable Greek.

2. Hesiod, *Theogony* 265–6: Thaumas ('Wonder') and Electra ('Shining') are the parents of Iris. But Hesiod is referring to Iris in her original form as the rainbow – a 'shining wonder'. Plato is referring to some allegorical extension of Iris' Homeric function as messenger of the gods: Iris becomes philosophy, the link between gods and men (see, for example, 176a–177a).

the truth concealed in the mind of a famous man – or, I
e should say, of famous men?[1]

THEAETETUS: Of course I will be grateful, very much so.

SOCRATES: Take a careful look around, then, to make sure
that none of the uninitiated are listening in on our conversation. The uninitiated are those whose sole criterion of existence is what they can get a good grip on with their hands,
and who refuse to accept that causes and effects and anything
invisible have any place in reality.[2]

THEAETETUS: These are hard, obstinate people you are
156*a* speaking of, Socrates.

SOCRATES: Yes, my boy, they are very uncouth indeed.
There's far greater sophistication among the others, whose
mysteries I am about to reveal to you. Their starting-point –
the one on which all that we were just saying depends too –
is that the universe is change and that there is nothing but
change. There are two kinds of change, which may be distinguished not by their frequency of occurrence (for both
manifest in an infinite number of ways), but by their powers:
one is active, the other passive. The intercourse and friction
of these two with each other give rise to an infinite number of
b offspring, which are always born as twins: there is the perceived thing and there is the perception, which always
emerges and is born along with the perceived thing.[3]

---

1. 'Protagoras – or, I should say, Homer, Heraclitus, etc.' (152e).

2. We need not assume that any particular philosophers are being
referred to as the 'uninitiated': what Plato says applies to anyone who believes that philosophy is idle speculation (compare *Sophist* 246a–b). However, the 'sophisticated' theory that follows is explicitly Heraclitean. While
probably a construct of Plato himself (see pp. 159–63), it may well be based
on the radical Heracliteanism of Cratylus of Athens, a contemporary of
Socrates, who apparently preferred pointing to speaking, on the grounds
that flux is so extreme that a quicker method than speech is required for
indicating things (Aristotle, *Metaphysics* 1010a 7–15).

3. I have translated *aistheton* in this passage as 'perceived thing', though
it could mean 'perceptible thing' (as at 202b). However, to say that the
things (which turn out to be qualities) are perceptible implies that they are
objectively there to be perceived, while to say that they are perceived implies

Anyway, examples of perception have various names: cases of seeing, hearing, smelling, sensations of heat and cold – yes, and what are called pleasure, pain, desire and fear; and there are infinite numbers of others which have no name, though very many have got names. Then there are the perceived things: all sorts of colours for all sorts of cases of seeing; a *c* similar variety of sounds for cases of hearing; and so on and so forth, every perceived thing being compatible with a perception.[1] So, Theaetetus, do you realize the significance of this tale in relation to what was said earlier?

THEAETETUS: Not really, Socrates.

SOCRATES: Well, let's see if we can tie it all together. You see, the implication is that although *ex hypothesi* all these things are changing, yet their change may be either fast or slow. Now, anything whose change is slow changes in the same place and in relation to something close by; that is how it produces offspring,[2] and the offspring produced in this *d* way are quicker, because they shift position and the kind of change they naturally undergo is this motion.[3]

So, for instance, consider an eye and something which is close to the eye and compatible with it, as they engender whiteness and the perception which is naturally adapted to whiteness, which are the unique offspring of the eye and the other object in just this relation. At this precise moment, the seeing is set in motion from the eyes and the whiteness is set *e* in motion from the object which is the colour-generating half of the pair (both these offspring arise between the eye and the object); the eye becomes filled with sight, and sees at this time, and becomes not sight but a seeing eye; and the object which is the colour-generating half of the pair becomes filled

---

that they arise in relation to the perceiver at the time of perception, which is in accord with the theory which follows.

1. You cannot see a smell; compatibility was also mentioned at 153e, and see especially 184e–185a.

2. By coming into relation with something close by. On 'change in the same place', see 181c–d.

3. That is, change of position.

with whiteness and, again, becomes not whiteness but white. The object which happens to be coloured by this colour could be a piece of wood or a stone or anything at all.

We should assume that the same account holds good for all other cases. We must suppose (and this is repetition by now) that nothing is hard or warm or whatever in its own right, but that all things, in all their variety, are generated during their intercourse with one another, as a result of change. In fact, we should suppose that it is impossible to take even their active and passive components singly and form, as they say, a stable notion of their existence. I mean, the active one is nothing without the passive one, and vice versa; and what is active in one relation turns out to be passive in another.[1]

The upshot of all this is what we started off saying: that nothing *is* in its own right, but is always being generated in some relation. The verb 'to be' should be deleted from all contexts, despite the fact that habit and ignorance often force us to employ it, and did so even in our recent discussion. But, the experts are telling us, we shouldn't, nor should we connive at 'it' or 'his' or 'mine' or 'this' or 'that' or any other term which suggests stability.[2] We should instead adapt our speech to the way things are, and describe them as undergoing generation, production, destruction and alteration. In fact, they say, speech which suggests stability is easily refuted. And this is how we should talk, not just where the constituents of things are concerned, but also about conglomerations of many constituents, such as the conglomerates which are called 'a man', 'a stone', and each creature and entity of any type.[3]

1. The relativism of object and eye includes the possibility that an eye could be looked at by someone else (i.e. be the active object) or do the looking (i.e. be the passive half).

2. It is left unclear how an out-and-out fluxist is to communicate at all: this is deliberate and is taken up at 183a–b as part of a *reductio ad absurdum* of flux.

3. Each event is actually an aggregate of many perceptions, each

Well, Theaetetus, do these ideas please you? Would they make a satisfying meal for you?

THEAETETUS: I don't know, Socrates. In fact, I can't even tell whether you're voicing your own opinions or just trying me out.

SOCRATES: You are not bearing in mind, my friend, that *I* have no knowledge; I cannot claim any such ideas as my own – no, I am barren as far as they are concerned. But I am acting as your midwife, and that is why I am chanting and serving up morsels of wisdom for you to taste. This will go on *d* until I have played my part in bringing your very own notion out into the world.[1] Once that stage is over, I will examine the idea to see whether it turns out to be viable or still-born. So don't be downhearted and don't let your strength desert you; be a good, courageous fellow, and tell me whatever occurs to you in relation to my questions.

THEAETETUS: Ask away, then.

SOCRATES: Once again, try to tell me if you're happy with the idea that nothing *is*, but that things are continually *becoming* good, fine and all the things we went through a short while ago.[2]

THEAETETUS: Well, on hearing your account of this view, *I* think it is remarkably reasonable and ought to be accepted just as you have expounded it.

SOCRATES: All right, but the account isn't complete yet. *e* We still have to cover dreams and illness (especially mental

---

entity a bundle of qualities; strictly, on the flux theory, there is no such thing as a stone, and a person is merely a bundle of disparate perceptions (see the Trojan Horse image of 184d).

1. Notice the implication that Theaetetus' definition of knowledge as perception does not fully count as his opinion. He must be able not only to state a definition, but also to grasp its implications: then his offspring is born (160d). This is slightly different from the practice of earlier Socratic dialogues, where the definitions are immediately subjected to testing, or the implications are part of the testing.

2. Until now we have largely been offered sensible qualities as objects of perception (except for the mention of fear, etc. at 156b), but goodness and fineness are scarcely sensible qualities. See p. 144.

illness) and all the states which are said to involve mis-
hearing or mis-seeing or mis-perception generally. As you are
no doubt aware, the consensus is that the theory we have
just gone through is disproved by all these instances, because
158a they surely involve false perceptions; it is by no means the
case that what appears to each individual is true – in fact, it is
claimed, quite the opposite is the case: *none* of these appearances is true.[1]

THEAETETUS: You're quite right, Socrates.

SOCRATES: Well then, my boy, how could one defend the
thesis that perception is knowledge and that what appears to
an individual also is for that person?

THEAETETUS: I hesitate to admit that I have nothing to
say, Socrates, because your criticism of me on that score is
b still fresh.[2] But I really can't argue that insanity and dreams
do not involve false beliefs, when madmen imagine that they
are gods, and dreamers that they have wings and are flying
in their sleep.

SOCRATES: Well, there *is* an argument you're overlooking
which is relevant, particularly to sleeping and waking.

THEAETETUS: Which one?

SOCRATES: The one which is implicit in the question,
which I imagine you've often heard, what evidence could be
brought if we were asked at this very moment whether we
are asleep and are dreaming all our thoughts, or whether we
c are awake and talking to each other in a conscious state.

THEAETETUS: Yes, Socrates, it is difficult to know what
might constitute evidence. I mean, the two states correspond
as if exact counterparts. And it's not just that the discussion
we've been having could equally well have been an illusion
in a dream; when one has the experience of dreaming that
one is describing a dream, the similarity between the two
states is extraordinary.

SOCRATES: So you see that it is not difficult to find an

1. 'Is true': literally, just 'is' (see p. 146); but 158e, where the adjective
'true' is actually written, warrants the translation here.

2. See 148c–d, 151d and 157d.

argument, when even the question whether one is awake or asleep is controversial. And we have not yet mentioned the *d* fact that the time we spend asleep is equal to the time we spend awake, and in each state our minds are convinced of the truth of their impressions at the time, with the result that we spend an equal time affirming, with similar conviction, that both the two sets of impressions are real.

THEAETETUS: Absolutely.

SOCRATES: And isn't the same argument relevant to illness and insanity, except that the time isn't equal?

THEAETETUS: Right.

SOCRATES: Well, is the truth determined by length or brevity of time?

THEAETETUS: That would be absurd on many counts.   *e*

SOCRATES: And do you have any other means of clearly distinguishing the truth and falsity of impressions?

THEAETETUS: No, I don't think I do.

SOCRATES: Now, I will tell you what might be said on this issue by those who have determined that a person's impressions at any time are true for that person. I imagine them asking, 'If two things are completely different, Theaetetus, then it is quite impossible for them to have the same powers, isn't it? And don't make the mistake of thinking that we mean that in some respects they are the same, while different in others; no, we are talking about *absolute* difference.'[1]

THEAETETUS: Yes, it is impossible for them to share any 159*a* powers[2] or anything else, when they are altogether different.

SOCRATES: And aren't you bound to concede that they are also dissimilar?

THEAETETUS: I think so.

SOCRATES: So if anything happens to be growing similar

1. Aristotle records a similar argument from Democritus of Abdera (*floruit c.* 430), which includes both relativism and absolute change (*De Generatione et Corruptione* 315b).

2. This talk of 'powers' is shorthand: to say that *a* has different powers from *b* is to say that *a* cannot do or be anything that *b* can do or be, and vice versa.

or dissimilar to anything (whether to itself or to something else), we will say that what is growing similar is becoming identical, and what is growing dissimilar is becoming different, won't we?

THEAETETUS: We have no choice.

SOCRATES: Now, didn't we say earlier that there are infinitely many active things and infinitely many passive things?[1]

THEAETETUS: Yes.

SOCRATES: And moreover that the offspring of their various combinations are not the same, but different?

b　THEAETETUS: Certainly.

SOCRATES: So let's now apply the same argument to you and me and so on. Take 'Socrates healthy' and 'Socrates ill': shall we say that the one is similar or dissimilar to the other?

THEAETETUS: Do you mean to compare Socrates ill, taken as a whole, with Socrates healthy, taken as a whole?[2]

SOCRATES: You understand me perfectly: that's exactly what I mean.

THEAETETUS: I suppose I would say that they are dissimilar.

SOCRATES: And different, therefore, *qua* dissimilar?

THEAETETUS: Necessarily.

c　SOCRATES: What about 'Socrates asleep', or qualified in all the other ways we mentioned a short while ago? Will you make the same move?

THEAETETUS: Yes.

SOCRATES: Therefore, any of the things whose nature is to be active[3] will treat me as a different person, depending on whether it finds a healthy Socrates or an ill Socrates. Right?

THEAETETUS: Of course.

SOCRATES: Furthermore, I, who am acted upon, and it,

1. See 156a.

2. 'As a whole' – that is, as consisting of constituent parts, which are always changing (see 157b–c).

3. An object such as wine: see 156a ff.

which acts, will produce different offspring in either case, won't we?

THEAETETUS: Yes.

SOCRATES: Now, when the healthy I drinks wine, doesn't it appear pleasant and sweet to me?

THEAETETUS: Yes.

SOCRATES: That is because, in terms of our earlier conclusions, the active and the passive agents produce sweetness *d* and perception, both of which are simultaneously in motion. The perception, from the passive half, makes the tongue perceive; and the sweetness, from the wine, is in motion around the wine,[1] and makes it both be and appear sweet to a healthy tongue.

THEAETETUS: Yes, that's a fair recapitulation of our conclusions.

SOCRATES: But when the wine finds me ill, then the first point to notice is that, in actual fact, it does not find the same person, does it? I mean, it's a dissimilar person it comes across.

THEAETETUS: Yes.

SOCRATES: So this pair – the wine and that sort of Socrates *e* – produce different offspring. The perception of sourness is generated and set in motion around the tongue, and sourness is generated and set in motion around the wine. The wine becomes not sourness but sour; and I become not perception but a perceiver.

THEAETETUS: Exactly.

SOCRATES: Now, if I am this sort of perceiver, I cannot become a different sort. For each perceived thing has its special perception; and each different perception makes the perceiver a different sort of perceiver, a different perceiver. Equally, that particular thing which acts on me cannot, I *160a* suppose, by coming across a different person, become qualified in the same way, with the identical offspring. I mean, it will be of a different kind and with different offspring from a different relationship.

---

1. For 'around', see 'between' (154a, 156e).

THEAETETUS: That is so.

SOCRATES: Moreover, I will not be like that to myself, and it will not be like that to itself.

THEAETETUS: No.

SOCRATES: And whenever I become a perceiver, I necessarily become a perceiver of something: I mean, per-
b ception of nothing is impossible. Equally, whenever it becomes sweet, sour or whatever, it necessarily becomes so to someone: I mean, it cannot become sweet to no one.

THEAETETUS: Absolutely.

SOCRATES: The only possible conclusion, then, I think, is that whether you say that the object and I *are* or *are becoming*, this is relative to each other. Our being is necessarily linked to something, so if it is not linked to anything extraneous, nor to our respective selves, then it must be linked to each other. From this it follows that if 'being' is predicated of anything, the suffix 'to someone' or 'of something' or 'in some relation' should be added;[1] and the same goes for 'becoming'. But the theory we've expounded suggests that we
c should not admit, in our own or in others' speech, the idea that anything is or comes to be in isolation.

THEAETETUS: Absolutely, Socrates.

SOCRATES: Now, when the object that acts on me is for me and no one else, don't I also perceive it, while no one else does?[2]

THEAETETUS: Of course.

SOCRATES: Therefore, since each perception is peculiar to my being, my perception is true for me and, as Protagoras says, I am the judge of the things that are for me, that they are, and of the things that are not, that they are not.

THEAETETUS: So it seems.

d SOCRATES: If, therefore, my reckoning of what is (or is

1. A point Plato would have done well to observe consistently himself: see pp. 175–6.

2. Notice here how 'the object that acts on me' is identified with what is perceived, although strictly this is not the object itself, but some quality. But, as we have seen, external objects are merely bundles of qualities (157b–c), so Plato's relaxed language is not too reprehensible.

coming to be) is infallible and incorrigible, then what I perceive is inevitably what I know, isn't it?

THEAETETUS: Inevitably.

SOCRATES: Your idea that knowledge is perception was excellent, then. All the theories have come to the same thing – the view of Homer, Heraclitus and all that lot, that all things are changing as if they were streams, the view of the sage Protagoras that man is the measure of all things, *and* the view of Theaetetus that, given these premisses, knowledge *e* proves to be perception. Well, Theaetetus, what do you think? Shall we say that this is the new-born baby, so to speak, which you have given birth to and I have delivered?[1]

THEAETETUS: We must, Socrates.

SOCRATES: So here, apparently, is the *je ne sais quoi* we've brought into the world, after a fairly difficult labour. Following a birth, the next stage is the *amphidromia*:[2] we must literally make a complete tour of the theory, to make sure that, if the product is not worth bringing up – if it is still-born and no true birth – we are well aware of it. I hope you don't *161a* think that, come what may, your child should be kept and not done away with. Will you stand by and watch it being tested, without behaving like a first-time mother and getting angry if it is taken away from you?

THEODORUS: Theaetetus will put up with that, Socrates; he's never ill-tempered. But please tell us: what's wrong with the theory now?

SOCRATES: How keen you are on discussions, Theodorus! I like the way you see me as a sort of repository of ideas, so that I can pick one out, just like that, to claim that the theory's wrong. You're overlooking what's been happen- *b* ing: none of the ideas come from me, but always from whoever is talking with me.[3] My knowledge is limited to a

1. See p. 41, n. 1.

2. Literally, 'running around'. Shortly after a child's birth, the midwife would run around the hearth, carrying the child, as a purification prior to it being named and accepted into the family.

3. This is more true of the Socrates of the early dialogues than of *Theaetetus*.

reasonable understanding of ideas which I get from others, the clever ones. So, in this instance too, I won't try to say anything for myself, but I will try to get Theaetetus' viewpoint.

THEODORUS: You're quite right, Socrates. Go on, then.

SOCRATES: Well, Theodorus, do you know what I find puzzling in your friend Protagoras?

c   THEODORUS: What?

SOCRATES: I'm perfectly happy with the general theory, that what appears to each person is for that person; but the beginning of the argument puzzles me. Why didn't he start *The Truth* off by saying, 'Pig is the measure of all things', or 'Baboon', or any sentient creature, however outlandish? That would have been a magnificently haughty beginning, showing that although we regard his wisdom as remarkable and

d   almost divine, yet he is in fact no better off intellectually than a tadpole, let alone another human being. What else can we think, Theodorus? If a person's impressions, gained by perception, are true for that person; if no one else is a better judge of another person's experiences, in the sense of deciding authoritatively which are true and which false; if, in other words, as we have repeatedly said, each person alone makes up his mind about his own impressions, and all of them are correct and true; if all this is so, my friend, how on earth are we to distinguish Protagoras, whose cleverness was

e   such that he thought he was justified in teaching others for vast fees, and ourselves, who are less gifted and had to go and be his students? I mean, each of us is the measure of his own cleverness – or aren't we bound to think that Protagoras said this *ad captandum vulgus*?[1] As for my own case, I refrain from mentioning how ridiculous my skill as a midwife appears; indeed, I think the whole business of dialectic does too. I mean, if each person's impressions and opinions are true, then investigating them and trying to test each other cannot fail to be long-winded, tedious nonsense, can it? That is, if

162a Protagoras' *The Truth* is true and he wasn't using the sanc-

---

1. Either in order to make a startling statement, or to flatter people.

tuary of the written word to make oracular pronouncements which he didn't really mean.

THEODORUS: Protagoras was a friend of mine, Socrates, as you remarked just now, so I wouldn't like him to be refuted as a result of what I might concede to you. On the other hand, I don't want to oppose you either, if I find myself believing what you say. So go back to Theaetetus, who seemed to be the perfect foil for you just now.

SOCRATES: Suppose you went to Sparta, Theodorus, and *b* visited the wrestling-schools there. Would you think it right to watch others – some of them not much to look at – exercising naked, without stripping off yourself and taking your turn at displaying your physique?

THEODORUS: Of course, if I had a choice in the matter and could persuade them.[1] It would be no different from me prevailing upon all of you now, as I think I shall, to let me watch, without dragging this stiff old body to the gymnasium, while you take on a younger, more supple opponent.

SOCRATES: Well, Theodorus, if that's pleasing to you, then it's not displeasing to me, as the saying goes. So here I go, *c* back to clever Theaetetus. Tell me first, Theaetetus, what you think about what we were just discussing: doesn't it surprise you suddenly to find yourself, on this way of thinking, the intellectual equal of any human being, or even any god? Or do you think the Protagorean measure applies any the less to gods than to human beings?[2]

THEAETETUS: No, I most certainly don't. And, to answer your question, yes, I am very surprised, because when we were discussing the meaning of the idea that what appears to each person also is for that person, I found the theory excel- *d* lent; but now it has undergone an abrupt reversal.

SOCRATES: That's a symptom of youth, dear boy: young

1. In combination with 169a–b, we have evidence for the Spartan prohibition on bystanders in a gymnasium. Nakedness was the norm in all Greek gymnasia. Notice how Socrates turns the image to ironic effect and implies his own inferior argumentative abilities.

2. At *Laws* 716c Plato adds that, in his view, God, not man, is the measure of all things.

people drink rhetoric in and are won over by it. What I'm getting at is that Protagoras or his representative will have a reply to what I was saying: 'Gentlemen, young and old, you are behaving like armchair orators. You bring in the gods,

e when I do not allow the question of their existence or non-existence to enter my speech or writing;[1] you speak only what the masses might like to hear, making out that it is awful for anyone not to be intellectually superior to an animal; logical proof plays no part in what you say, but you rely on probability. Imagine how utterly worthless Theodorus or any geometer would be if he were prepared to rely on probability to do geometry.'[2] So, Theaetetus, you and Theodorus had better consider whether plausibility and likelihood are accept-

163*a* able to you as modes of argument on such important issues.[3]

THEAETETUS: No, that wouldn't be right, Socrates. I'm sure you would agree with us on that.

SOCRATES: So you and Theodorus are saying, apparently, that we must find some other means of investigation.

THEAETETUS: Yes, something quite different.

SOCRATES: Well, here's a way we could see whether or not knowledge and perception are identical. I mean, that's the question which the whole of our discussion has been aiming towards, and for the sake of which we stirred up this plethora of strange ideas, isn't it?

THEAETETUS: Absolutely.

b SOCRATES: Well, are we going to say that everything we perceive by hearing or seeing we also simultaneously know? Can we really say either that, before we understand a foreign

1. In a famous sentence (Fragment 4), Protagoras said: 'I am unable to have knowledge about the existence or non-existence of the gods, or what they are like; the obscurity of the subject and the shortness of human life provide many obstacles to such knowledge.'

2. Probability was, and still is, an accepted mode of argument in rhetoric. Ironically, Protagoras himself was a master orator, and his relativism excludes the kind of objective validity he is here portrayed as requiring. For Protagoras on geometry, see pp. 193–4.

3. Burnet's Greek text ends Protagoras' response here, rather than at the sentence before.

language, we do not hear it when it is spoken, or that we both hear it and know what is being said? Again, suppose we were illiterates looking at some writing: are we to maintain either that we do not see it, or that we know it if we see it?

THEAETETUS: We will say that we know precisely those aspects which are visible or audible. In other words, we will say that we see and know the shape and colour of the writing, and hear and know the high and low pitch of the language. *c* But we will say that we neither perceive, by sight or hearing, nor know the aspects of either subject which are the province, respectively, of schooling or linguistic education.

SOCRATES: Brilliant, Theaetetus. It wouldn't be right to impede your progress by taking issue with you on this.[1] But there's another problem looming, and we'd better see how to fend it off.

THEAETETUS: What is it?

SOCRATES: I'll tell you. Suppose we were asked: 'If an *d* item of information has become known at some time, and is lodged securely in the memory of a person, is it possible for that person not to know this item, when he recalls it, at the very moment when he recalls it?' I seem to be making heavy weather of asking whether a person can be ignorant of an item of information when he is remembering it.

THEAETETUS: Impossible, Socrates. The suggestion is monstrous.

SOCRATES: Am I talking nonsense, then? Let's see. Don't you say that seeing is perceiving and that sight is perception?

THEAETETUS: Yes.

SOCRATES: So according to the view which you expressed *e* recently, someone who has seen something has come to have knowledge of whatever he saw. Is that right?

THEAETETUS: Yes.

1. Theaetetus is open to the criticism that he is implicitly restricting knowledge to mere sensation of, say, shapes and colours, with no recognition of what it is that has those shapes and colours, and even no ability to formulate what the shapes and colours are; this is liable to the argument of 184b–186e.

SOCRATES: Well, you acknowledge the existence of *memory*, don't you?

THEAETETUS: Yes.

SOCRATES: Does one remember something or nothing?

THEAETETUS: Something, of course.

SOCRATES: Something learned, something perceived – that sort of thing?

THEAETETUS: Of course.

SOCRATES: And sometimes something known?

THEAETETUS: Yes.

SOCRATES: Even when one's eyes are closed? Or does that make one forget?

THEAETETUS: No, Socrates. What a strange thing to say!

164a SOCRATES: But that's what we have to say, if we are going to keep the theory safe and sound. Otherwise it's all over for it.

THEAETETUS: Yes, I have a very strong suspicion that you're right, but I don't quite see why; so tell me, please.

SOCRATES: All right. The idea is that someone who sees something knows what he is seeing, because seeing – that is, perception – and knowledge were taken to be identical.

THEAETETUS: Certainly.

SOCRATES: But consider someone who once saw something and came to have knowledge of what he saw: isn't it the case that, with his eyes closed, he remembers it without seeing it?

THEAETETUS: Yes.

b SOCRATES: But if 'He sees' is the same as 'He knows', then 'He doesn't see' is the same as 'He doesn't know'.

THEAETETUS: True.

SOCRATES: So we find that someone can lack knowledge of what he has come to know, when he remembers it without seeing it. And that's the result we described as monstrous.

THEAETETUS: You're perfectly right.

SOCRATES: So the theory that knowledge and perception are identical apparently entails something impossible.

THEAETETUS: Apparently.

SOCRATES: They are *not* identical, then.

THEAETETUS: Probably not.

SOCRATES: So what could knowledge be? We must start *c*
again from the beginning, it seems ... But hang on, Theaetetus. What on earth are we thinking of?

THEAETETUS: What are you getting at?

SOCRATES: We seem to be leaping away from the theory
and crowing before we've actually won – like an ill-bred
fighting cock.

THEAETETUS: How so?

SOCRATES: It looks as though we are resting on our laurels
when our conclusion is concerned with mere verbal consistency and that's the only kind of advantage we have gained.
We claim that our goal is wisdom, not victory, yet we are
unwittingly behaving no differently from those awful casuists. *d*

THEAETETUS: I don't yet see what you mean.

SOCRATES: Well, I'll try to explain what's on my mind.
The question was whether someone who is remembering
something he was once acquainted with can fail to know it.
We pointed out that seeing something, and then closing one's
eyes, is remembering without seeing, from which the impossibility followed, that one is simultaneously remembering,
but not knowing. And that is how the Protagorean story
(which is yours too), that knowledge and perception are
identical, ended.

THEAETETUS: Apparently.   *e*

SOCRATES: But I don't think it would end there, my friend,
if the father of the original story were alive; he would have
plenty to say in its defence. As it is, we've been trampling it
into the mud when it's an orphan. In fact, not even the
people to whom Protagoras entrusted its care – Theodorus
here is one of them – are prepared to come to its assistance.[1]
So, in the interests of justice, we will have to do so ourselves,
it seems.

THEODORUS: It's really Callias the son of Hipponicus,[2]

1. Notice that Plato is talking about the 'joint' thesis: he says that Protagoras is the author of Theaetetus' definition. If that is so, and since the
trustees are not helping, Theaetetus is perhaps being treated as he was in
real life (see 144d).

2. A wealthy patron of the sophists; his house is the setting for *Protagoras*.

165a Socrates, not I, who is the trustee of his estate: some of us soon found we preferred geometry to abstract thought.[1] Still, we will be grateful to you if you come to his assistance.

SOCRATES: All right, Theodorus; here's my assistance, such as it is. The point is that our acceptance or rejection of ideas is normally based on a casual attitude towards language, which might lead to even stranger conclusions than the ones we've just reached. Shall I explain how to you or to Theaetetus?[2]

THEODORUS: To both of us at once, please, but let the
b younger one do the answering, because he will lose less face if he slips up.

SOCRATES: Well, here's the strangest question of all, which might be phrased as follows: 'Is it possible for someone who knows something not to know what he knows?'

THEODORUS: What shall we reply, Theaetetus?

THEAETETUS: That it's impossible, I suppose.

SOCRATES: No, but it's not, on the view that seeing is knowing. I mean, suppose you've been cornered by someone who's not going to be put off, and he covers up one of your eyes with his hands, and asks whether you can see his coat with the covered eye. How will you cope with this inescapable
c question?[3]

THEAETETUS: I will say that I can't see it with the one eye, but can with the other.

SOCRATES: So you are simultaneously seeing and not seeing the same thing?

THEAETETUS: Yes, but only in the way I said.

SOCRATES: Then he'll say: 'That's not the question I put

1. See the report of Aristotle cited on pp. 193–4: in other words, Theodorus has really betrayed his master's teaching.

2. Reading this sentence as a question. I suspect it is merely a misprint in Burnet's text not to do so.

3. The sophists in *Euthydemus* too are fond of asking 'How will you cope with . . . ?' (287b) and describe their questions as 'inescapable' (276e), so perhaps Plato is echoing common sophistic ploys.

to you. I didn't ask *how* you can be ignorant of what you know, but *if* that is possible. As it is, you are obviously seeing what you can't see; and the fact is that, according to you, seeing is knowing and not seeing is not knowing. I leave it to you to draw the conclusion from these premisses.'

THEAETETUS: Well, the conclusion is that my hypothesis *d* is contradicted.

SOCRATES: But that probably wouldn't be the end of your ordeal, my friend. Further questions of the same kind would follow: whether knowledge can be both clear and hazy; whether knowledge is restricted to objects which are near by; whether the same thing can be known strongly and weakly; and so on and so forth.[1] There are innumerable questions which a logical commando, whose argumentative skill is for hire,[2] might trap you with, once you've proposed that knowledge and perception are identical. He would launch an assault on hearing, smell and so on; he wouldn't stop refuting you until you were so dazzled by his world-famous wisdom *e* that you had been ensnared by him. Then, once he'd got you under his thumb, once you were his prisoner – only then would he release you, for a mutually agreed ransom.[3]

So you're probably wondering how Protagoras will defend himself against these assaults. We'd better try to put it into words, hadn't we?

THEAETETUS: Certainly.

SOCRATES: Well, there are all the points we've already raised in his defence, but I imagine that he will find a far superior approach to ours. He'll carry the fight to close *166a*

1. Precisely what arguments Plato is adumbrating is unclear; see p. 167.

2. The sophists taught for money.

3. As we learn from *Protagoras* 328b–c, Protagoras used to charge his pupils either a fixed fee or whatever the pupil thought the teaching had been worth – a singular example of Protagoras following his own dictum and treating his pupils' impressions as authoritative! Notice the irony of describing these 'logical commandos' in ways which are reminiscent of Protagoras, but as opponents of Protagoras' relativism: again we find that Protagoras defeats himself (see 161c–e, 171a–c).

quarters, and say: 'What a fine fellow Socrates is! He gets a child frightened by the question whether it is possible for the same person to remember and simultaneously be ignorant of the same thing; so, because he can't see what's coming next, the frightened child says "No", and Socrates makes out that *I* have been made a fool of in the argument. This is sheer laziness, Socrates. The truth of the matter is that, when you're asking questions to investigate one of my propositions, there are two possibilities: if your interlocutor replies as *I* would reply, and is caught in an error, then I am refuted; but if his

b reply is different from what mine would be, then he alone is refuted.

'What I'm getting at is this. In the first place, do you expect anyone to agree that the present memory of a past experience is in any sense a similar experience to the past one which is no longer being experienced? That's not so at all. Or again, do you expect anyone to object to the possibility of the same person knowing and not knowing the same thing? Or, even if there is some hesitation about this last point, do you expect anyone to admit that someone who is changing is the same person as he was before the process of change began? No one would even admit that here *is* a *person* at all, rather than *people* – an infinite number of people being generated, given

c this process of change. You see how you make it necessary to guard against each other's verbal traps?

'No, my dear fellow,' he will say. 'You must behave more generously than that. Tackle what I actually say, if you can.[1] What you should be trying to prove is either that perceptions are not being generated as private experiences, or, even if they are, that it still doesn't follow that what appears privately to someone comes to be (or, if we must use the term, is) for that person to whom it appears.

'When you talk about pigs and baboons, you're not only behaving like a pig yourself, but you are also inducing your audience to behave likewise towards my writings, and that's

1. This is not evidence that Plato is going to be historically accurate: for instance, he ascribes the flux theory to Protagoras, which is not historically accurate. But he is claiming that he will be fair to Protagoras.

a despicable thing to do. I claim that the truth is as I have *d*
written: each of us is the measure of the things that are and
are not. However, there is a great deal of inequality among
people, precisely because there is so much variety in the things
that are and appear to different people. In other words, so far
from denying the existence of expertise and clever people, I
actually define wisdom as the ability to make good things
appear and be for someone instead of bad things.

'Now, let me remind you not to go for what I say on the
basis merely of how I express it; I will try to make my meaning
even clearer to you. Remember, for instance, what was said *e*
earlier, that food appears and is unpleasant for someone who's
ill, but appears and is the opposite for someone who's well.[1]
Now, there's no call for the unfeasible idea that either of
these two people is *wiser*: that is, we shouldn't classify the *167a*
sick person as ignorant because he thinks as he does, nor the
healthy person as clever because he thinks differently. What
we're after is a change from one state to the other, because
one state is *better* than the other.

'It's the same in education too: what we're after is change
from one state to the better one. The only difference is that a
doctor uses medicines to bring about the change, while a
sophist uses words. But it is *never* the case that a change is
effected from earlier false belief to later true belief: it is impossible to believe something which is not the case[2] – one
can only believe what one is experiencing, and this is always
true. What is possible, however, in my opinion, is that
someone who is in an unsound mental state and whose beliefs *b*
are cognate with it can be made to think differently.[3] Now,
these different impressions are naively called "true", but what
I am saying is that although they are *better* than the others,
they are not more true at all.

1. See 159b–e.

2. Literally just 'is not', which here must mean 'is not the case' or 'is not
true' (see p. 146).

3. The text is corrupt: I read αὐτῆς with the manuscripts, and omit
χρηστή.

'I certainly do not equate wise people with frogs, my dear Socrates.[1] On the contrary, I claim that each sphere of operation has its wise practitioners: there are doctors for bodies,
c farmers for plants (for I maintain that farmers can replace unsound perceptions in sickly plants with sound, healthy perceptions and affections[2]); and I claim that politicians who are wise and good at their job substitute sound for unsound ethical notions in their communities. It is true that whatever seems ethically fine to each community also is ethical[3] for it, for as long as that rule is in force, but a wise person changes each unsound notion they have, and makes sound notions be and appear for them. By the same token, a sophist, since he is capable of guiding his pupils in the same
d way, is wise and deserves to be paid a lot by his pupils.

'So you see that some people are wiser than others, *and* that no one has false beliefs; and since this latter point shores up the idea that man is the measure, then, whether or not you like it, you must live with being a measure. Now, if you are in a position to go right back to square one and dispute this idea, then do so. You can oppose my speech with one of your own, if you want to set out your objections like that; or if you prefer to use questions, then use questions: even this method is perfectly acceptable – indeed, anyone with any sense ought to make a special point of cultivating it. But
e whatever you do, don't use questions as a means of being unfair. It is highly absurd for someone who professes a concern with virtue constantly to argue unfairly. Unfairness, in this instance, is not distinguishing eristic from dialectical discussions: the former involve as many tricks and traps as possible, but the latter involve being serious and correcting
168a the interlocutor's mistakes and errors only when they are his own fault or the result of past conditioning. If you do this, then those who join in your discussions will blame themselves, not you, for their muddles and confusion; *you* will be

1. See 161d.

2. Reading καὶ πάθας with Richards [14].

3. Literally just 'is for it', but here we are meant to supply the predicate.

popular and sought after, while *they* will hate themselves and will take refuge from themselves in philosophy, to find a way to change and escape from their former selves. But if you do what most people do – that is, the opposite to what I've been recommending – then you'll get the opposite results: instead of turning your companions into philosophers, they will hate *b* the pursuit when they get older.

'So I suggest you do what I said before: conduct a proper inquiry into the meaning of our assertions that everything is changing and that each individual's and community's impressions also are for that individual or community – and by a proper inquiry, I mean sitting down together in a spirit of goodwill, not with hostile and aggressive intentions. This will provide a foundation for considering whether or not knowledge and perception are identical, whereas your former approach was based merely on habitual use of words and expressions; and these are the means by which most people *c* confuse one another in all sorts of ways, because they can be manipulated at will.'

There you are, Theodorus; there's my contribution towards your friend's defence. It's limited, but it's the best I can do from my limited abilities. If he were alive, he'd have defended his own ideas far more impressively.

THEODORUS: You're joking, Socrates. Your defence was extremely spirited.

SOCRATES: Thank you, my friend. Now, Protagoras was telling us off for engaging a child in conversation: he said that we were using the lad's fear to score points against his *d* theory. He described such tactics as trivial and showed us, by contrast, how he treats the 'measure of everything' principle with proper regard; in other words, he told us to take his doctrine seriously. I imagine you noticed all this in his speech, didn't you?

THEODORUS: Of course I did.

SOCRATES: So do you want to do as he says?

THEODORUS: Very much.

SOCRATES: Well, look around you – all children except for you. So, if we are to do as he says, it's up to you and me to *e* treat his doctrine seriously, as we ask each other questions and answer them. Then at least we'll not be liable to the charge of turning the inquiry about his doctrine into amusement for boys.

THEODORUS: But listen: there aren't many greybeards who could follow the inquiry as well as Theaetetus.

SOCRATES: Except for you, Theodorus. It's not right for you to think that I should do all the work of defending your 169a dead friend, while you do nothing. So come with me a little way, my friend, just until we are in a position to know whether it's you who are necessarily the measure where geometrical figures are concerned, or whether everyone is just as self-sufficient as you as regards astronomy and all the other subjects in which you have the reputation of being special.

THEODORUS: It's difficult not to get drawn into the discussion, Socrates, when I'm sitting right next to you! It was wishful thinking when I said just now[1] that you would allow me not to strip off and would spare me the kind of pressure the Spartans exert – except I see you as Sciron rather b than a Spartan. No, it's more like Antaeus: that's the part you're playing. I mean, the Spartans give one the choice of leaving or stripping off, but you don't let anyone who comes near you go until you have forced him to strip off and wrestle with you in an argument.[2]

SOCRATES: That's an excellent image for what's wrong

1. 162b.

2. Sciron and Antaeus were legendary characters with some unpleasant traits. Sciron not only robbed unwary travellers, but then compelled them to wash his feet; while they were doing so, he kicked them down a cliff into the sea. Theseus eventually kicked him down the same cliff. Antaeus was a giant who compelled travellers to wrestle with him, but he was invincible as long as he remained in contact with his mother, the earth. He killed his opponents and built a house out of their skulls. Heracles lifted him off the ground and crushed him in mid-air. Both were thorough in dealing with passers-by, so why is Socrates more like Antaeus? Because wrestling is a more suitable image for arguing, but perhaps also because he is sitting in the gymnasium, his equivalent of Antaeus' mother earth (see p. 136).

with me, Theodorus, except for one point: I've got more tenacity than Sciron and Antaeus! Countless times in the past I've met a Theseus or a Heracles whose strength lay in arguing, and I've been well and truly battered by them; but that hasn't made me give up. Desire for this sort of exercise *c* has that tremendous a hold on me! So please don't say no: join the company of those who have gone a round with me. It'll do both of us good!

THEODORUS: All right, I won't resist any more; I am yours to command. There's absolutely no escaping the fate you spin of being cross-examined. But I am only available for as long as it takes to reach the point you have proposed.

SOCRATES: That'll do. Now, the thing to watch out carefully for is that we don't unwittingly carry on the discussion at a childish level and lay ourselves open again to criticism on that score.   *d*

THEODORUS: All right, I'll do my best to watch out for that.

SOCRATES: So let's begin by getting to grips again with the point which was raised before. That is, we must see whether or not we were right to be dissatisfied and to object to the idea that each person is self-sufficient with respect to intelligence, bearing in mind that Protagoras admitted that some people are special in the question of what is better and worse, and that these are the people he called wise. Isn't that so?

THEODORUS: Yes.

SOCRATES: Now, if he were here to make that admission in person, there would be no need to reopen the issue and *e* make sure about it. But as it is, it is we who have made the concession on his behalf, when we were trying to help him out; so it might be suggested that we didn't have the authority to make it for him.[1] That is why it is better to establish it

1. Since 'authority' is virtually a Protagorean key word for each person's impressions being true for that person, then there is irony here: who would claim that Socrates isn't authoritative in this instance? After all, it seemed to him that the concession was reasonable. One could say that this type of irony runs throughout the discussion of Protagoras.

with a clear and thorough discussion. You see, a great deal hinges on whether or not what he conceded is correct.

THEODORUS: You're right.

SOCRATES: So the most economical way to consider it is 170a purely by means of Protagoras' own argument.

THEODORUS: How?

SOCRATES: Like this: he says, as you know, that what appears to each person also is for the person who has that impression, doesn't he?

THEODORUS: He does.

SOCRATES: Well, Protagoras, we too are voicing 'man's' impression – or rather, the impression all men have – when we say that everyone thinks himself wiser than others in some respects, but thinks others wiser than himself in other respects. When life is threatened by war, illness or storm, then people treat their leaders in each sphere as if they were gods: they regard them as potential saviours, when the only b respect in which they are different is that they have knowledge. The whole world is full of people looking for teachers and leaders for themselves and for other creatures, to guide their actions; and then there are those who think themselves capable of teaching and leading. Faced with all this, what else can we say but that people do think wisdom and ignorance are human features?

THEODORUS: Nothing else.

SOCRATES: And don't they regard wisdom as true thought, and ignorance as false belief?

c THEODORUS: Of course.

SOCRATES: What are we to make of your theory, then, Protagoras? What should we claim: that people's opinions are always true, or that they are sometimes true, but sometimes false? Whichever of the two propositions we affirm, the result is that people's beliefs are not always true, but are both true and false.[1] I mean, can you tell me, Theodorus, if you

1. The uninteresting one of these alternatives (that if it is admitted that there are false beliefs, then there are false beliefs) is not pursued in what follows. The rest of the argument is an exploration of the other alternative.

or any Protagorean would be prepared to deny that people ever regard other people as ignorant and as having false beliefs?

THEODORUS: No, that would be implausible, Socrates.[1]

SOCRATES: And yet this denial is what the idea that man *d* is the measure is inevitably committed to.

THEODORUS: How?

SOCRATES: Suppose you make up your mind about something on your own, and then later tell me this belief of yours; and let us suppose, as Protagoras' theory states, that your opinion is true for you. But is it then impossible for the rest of us to form opinions about your opinion? And is the opinion that we form always that your belief is true? Or is it rather the case that for each of your beliefs there are thousands of opposing beliefs and thousands of people who insist that you're wrong and that your opinion is false?

THEODORUS: Good heavens, yes, Socrates – 'thick thou- *e* sands', as Homer says,[2] causing me all the bother that is humanly possible.

SOCRATES: Well then, perhaps we ought to say that your belief is true for you, but false for all these thousands of people. What do you think?

THEODORUS: It looks as though the argument leaves us no choice.

SOCRATES: What does all this entail for Protagoras? Isn't it necessarily the case that if he *didn't* believe in man being the measure, and if the common run of mankind didn't either (as in fact it doesn't), then this book of his, *The Truth*, would be true[3] for no one. He *did* believe it, however, but most *171a*

The paragraph is sometimes read as a separate argument; but it is so curtailed, and needs so much expansion to be read as an argument in its own right, that it seems better to take it as part of the run-up to the main argument.

1. Theodorus is less hard-boiled than the sophists in *Euthydemus*.

2. *Odyssey* 16.121, of the suitors wooing Penelope in Odysseus' absence.

3. Literally just 'would be for no one': the veridical use of 'to be' is intended (see p. 146).

people don't share this belief. The first notable consequence of this[1] is that the idea is more false than true, in proportion to the extent that the unbelievers outnumber the believers.

THEODORUS: That necessarily follows from the premiss that its truth and falsity are dependent upon individual impressions.

SOCRATES: And there's a second consequence, which is exquisite.[2] In saying that everyone believes what is the case, he is conceding the truth of beliefs which oppose his own; in other words, he is conceding the truth of the opinion that he is wrong.

THEODORUS: Yes.

b   SOCRATES: Now, in acknowledging the truth of the opinion that he is wrong, wouldn't he be admitting that his own opinion is false?

THEODORUS: Necessarily.

SOCRATES: But the others are convinced of their own correctness, aren't they?

THEODORUS: Yes.

SOCRATES: And Protagoras' written statements again commit him to admitting the truth of this conviction.

THEODORUS: Apparently.

SOCRATES: Therefore, from all sides, Protagoras' doctrine entails that it is arguable – or rather, that he will admit ... when he concedes that statements contrary to his own are
c   true, then even Protagoras himself will concede that no dog and no ordinary person is a measure of anything at all, unless he understands it. Yes?

THEODORUS: Yes.

SOCRATES: So, faced with universal dissension, *The Truth* of Protagoras fails to be true for absolutely everyone, himself included.

1. That is, for Protagoras. This is supposed to be self-refutation, not objective argument. Plato never held that the majority opinion was necessarily correct.

2. What follows is a version of the famous recoil argument which Democritus used against Protagoras (according to Sextus, *Against the Mathematicians* 7.389).

THEODORUS: We're running my friend too hard, Socrates.

SOCRATES: But have we left the truth behind? That's the important question, my friend, and it's not clear that we have. Now, since he's older, he's likely to be wiser than us, I suppose; and if he were suddenly to pop his head up from the *d* ground, then in all probability he would expose my argument for a lot of nonsense, confound you for agreeing to it, and in no time at all he'd pop back down again and be off.[1] But the way I see it is that we are what we are, that's the only material we've got to work with, and we always have to speak our minds. So, at the moment, shouldn't we say that everyone would concede at least that people differ from one another in degrees of wisdom and ignorance?[2]

THEODORUS: *I* think that's right.

SOCRATES: And should we also say that the theory is at its strongest in the position we sketched in our defence of *e* Protagoras, that most things (things that are warm, dry, sweet – everything of this type) are as they seem to each person; but that health and sickness constitute a prime area where, if difference is to be admitted at all by the theory, it is not the case that the females of the species,[3] or children, or animals for that matter, are self-sufficient at prescribing and effecting cures for themselves, and that here, if anywhere, some people are superior to others?

1. There have been several suggestions, often delightful, as to the source of this image. Given the recurring image of Protagoras as leader of a secret cult (152d, etc.) and even as an oracle (162a), I think it is worth remembering that the head of the mystic hero Orpheus is occasionally portrayed as appearing from the underworld to make pronouncements. Does the suggestion that Protagoras could still defend himself imply that Plato was aware of the flaw in the argument (see pp. 174–6)? Perhaps not, since Protagoras doesn't seem to stop for much discussion. So the image is probably just a piece of comic irony. Notice too the irony in suggesting that Protagoras, who holds that all beliefs are true, would find a way to prove Socrates' argument false! On this, compare *Euthydemus* 286c ff.

2. 'Everyone' in this sentence now includes Protagoras. Plato will now argue that he has proved that Protagoras must modify his position.

3. Plato generally shares the common Greek view that women are second-class humans, though he occasionally allows greater equality.

THEODORUS: I think that is right.

172*a* SOCRATES: And in the public sphere too, we should say that the kinds of behaviour which each community forms an opinion about and sanctions also really are, or are not, morally, legally and religiously acceptable for it, and that in these areas no individual or community is any wiser than another. But when it is a matter of establishing what is or is not advantageous for a community, then here, if anywhere, the theory will again concede that some advice is better than other advice and that one community's decisions may differ from another's in respect of truth, and should never go so far as to claim that whatever a community thinks is *b* advantageous for it and establishes as such will certainly *be* advantageous as well. The people who hold the theory should make this concession despite the fact that in the *other* area – that is, matters of ethical and religious propriety – they are prepared to maintain that there is no objective existence, but that society's beliefs become true at the moment the decision is taken, and remain true for as long as they are in force. Those who aren't strict adherents to the Protagorean line also regard wisdom more or less as we have been saying.[1] But this, Theodorus, brings us face to face with an argument which will make even what we've been discussing *c* seem relatively trivial.

THEODORUS: Well, we've got time, haven't we, Socrates?[2]

SOCRATES: Obviously. And you know, my friend, this isn't the first time, not by a long chalk, that it's occurred to me that those who spend a lot of time doing philosophy are likely to make fools of themselves when they speak in a law-court.

1. Reading ὅσοι γε δή with the manuscripts. I take the 'incomplete Protagoreans' here simply to be ordinary people.

2. There is an ill-defined thread of the relationship between time and philosophy running through the dialogue. Apart from this section, see 143a–b, 150e, 154e, 180b, 187d and 201b. Perhaps the dramatic setting of the dialogue, with Socrates shortly to go to trial (210d), explains this thread: philosophy takes time, i.e. Socrates is bound to be at a loss in court (see also e.g. *Gorgias* 521c–522e).

THEODORUS: What do you mean?

SOCRATES: If you compare those who have spent their lives hanging around lawcourts and places like that with those who have been trained in philosophical pursuits, it's like comparing the upbringing of slaves with that of free men. *d*

THEODORUS: Why?

SOCRATES: Because the latter always have what you mentioned – time. They carry on their conversation unhurriedly, in peace and quiet. This is the third change of direction *our* discussion has undergone,[1] and philosophers are equally ready to change direction, if a topic crops up which is more attractive than the one to hand, as is the case with us. The duration of the discussion doesn't bother them; it could be long or short. Their only concern is to reach the truth.

A speaker in a lawcourt, however, is different: his allotted time is slipping away and forcing him to hurry his speech.[2] *e* Nor can he talk about whatever strikes his fancy: he's got an adversary standing over him, wielding necessity in the form of a document stating what the issues of the case are, which is read out to ensure that the speaker confines himself to these issues. It's always one slave telling tales about another to their master, who sits there dispensing judgement.[3] What's at stake is never anything unrelated to the speaker's own person; in fact, life itself is often the reward for the fastest runner. As a result of all this, they have become tense and *173a* neurotic. They know how to speak flatteringly to their master and how to behave to get into his good books, but their minds are narrow and crooked. They became slaves when

1. Plato could be thinking of (1) Theaetetus' first stab at defining knowledge, (2) all that followed from the definition of knowledge as perception and (3) now this; or of (1) the first criticisms of Protagoras, (2) the recoil argument and (3) now this.

2. Literally 'the flowing water urges him on ...': several categories of speech in Athenian lawcourts were timed by a water-clock.

3. The master is the Athenian people; any citizen over thirty could sit on a jury, which usually numbered well into the hundreds.

they were young, and slavery prohibits growth, integrity and freedom, makes devious deeds inevitable, and puts minds that are still impressionable through extremes of danger and fear, which cannot be dealt with honestly and truthfully. So in no time at all they turn to deceit and repaying wrong with further
b wrong; they become warped and stunted in many ways. In the end, when they become adults, they are left with minds which are incapable of a single wholesome thought. They have become highly skilled and intelligent – or so they think.[1]

That's what this lot are like, Theodorus. Now, would you like us to describe the members of *our* ensemble,[2] or shall we get straight back to our discussion? Do you think, if we carry on, that we'd be overdoing it and abusing the freedom we mentioned a short while ago to change direction?

THEODORUS: No, Socrates, let's have the description. I
c mean, you were quite right to say that it is not we, the members of this ensemble, who are at the beck and call of arguments. On the contrary, the arguments are *ours* – our servants, as it were, each waiting for our decision before it is completed. We are not dramatists, with judge and audience set over us to criticize and control us.[3]

SOCRATES: So, since that's apparently what you want, let's describe the consummate philosopher – I mean, why should one bother with second-rate practitioners?[4] The first point to notice about the consummate philosopher is that,
d man or boy, he's never known the way to the agora, let alone whereabouts in it the lawcourts are, or the council-house, or

1. Compare *Republic* 519a ff.

2. The word is literally 'chorus', and leads to Theodorus' theatrical analogy. See also the 'harmony of discussion' of 176a.

3. In the Athenian theatre of the time, plays were written as one-off performances, to be entered into a contest. Those that were chosen for performance were judged and graded; the official judges relied heavily on audience reaction.

4. Thus Plato licenses the exaggerations which follow; on second-rate philosophers, see *Euthydemus* 304d–307c, *Republic* 489d–497a.

any other official building for public meetings.[1] He doesn't
see or hear laws or statutes, either at the stage of discussion
or when they've been written down. As for political clubs
eager for office,[2] as for gatherings, receptions and parties
complete with dancing-girls – it doesn't occur to him even in
his dreams to get involved. Is such-and-such a citizen of good
or bad birth? Has so-and-so inherited some defect or other
from his male or female forebears? Our philosopher is less
aware of these matters than he is of how many drops there
are in the proverbial ocean. In fact, he doesn't even know *e*
that he doesn't know all these things. I mean, he is detached
from them not because he is after a reputation, but the truth
is that only his body has taken up residence in the city and
can be found here, while his mind disdains all these matters,
seeing them as petty and worthless, and wings its way
everywhere, as Pindar says, 'from beneath the earth to above
the heavens'[3] – the plane surfaces of the earth being the
province of geometry, the heavens of astronomy; his mind is
constantly exploring the general nature of every entity as a *174a*
whole, but no local object becomes its perch.

THEODORUS: What do you mean, Socrates?

SOCRATES: The story about Thales is a good illustration,
Theodorus:[4] how he was looking upwards in the course of
his astronomical investigations, and fell into a pothole, and a
Thracian serving-girl with a nice sense of humour teased him

1. Plato softens this at *Philebus* 62a–d: even philosophers can be practical.
Gorgias 484c–485e is worth comparing with this passage's description of the
philosopher: Plato has Callicles lay into Socrates, in terms very similar to
those we find here, for philosophical unworldliness. Here, then, Plato inverts
Callicles' censure into praise.

2. These clubs were a regular feature of Athenian political life and were
the nearest thing they had to pressure-groups.

3. No extant poem of Pindar's contains this fragment (Fragment 292 in
Christ's edition).

4. Thales of Miletus (*floruit c.* 590) was one of the Seven Wise Men of
Greece, and an archetypal philosopher, attributed with many theoretical and
practical ideas. Very little is known about him, though he seems to have
occupied a hinterland between philosophy and mythology.

for being concerned with knowing about what was up in the sky and not noticing what was right in front of him at his feet. Anyone who spends time in philosophical pursuits is

b liable to the same teasing. You see, it really is the case that he doesn't notice his next-door neighbour: it's not just that he doesn't notice what his neighbour is up to; he almost isn't aware whether his neighbour is a human being or some other creature. But what is it to be a human being? What behaviour or experiences are proper to just this type of being and differentiate it from all others? These questions interest him, and he looks into them painstakingly. Now do you see what I mean, Theodorus, or not?

THEODORUS: Yes, and you're right.

SOCRATES: All this bears out what I was saying at the

c beginning about such a person at a social or public gathering. When he is compelled, in a lawcourt or anywhere else, to speak about things that are right in front of his feet or in his direct line of vision, he becomes a source of amusement, not just to Thracian girls, but to the general public. His impracticality pitches him into potholes and a whole pack of problems,[1] and he is terribly gauche, which earns him the reputation of stupidity. When it comes to defaming people,[2] he has nothing specific to say to anyone's discredit; he doesn't know anyone's bad points, because it's never been a subject that's interested him. So he doesn't know what to do, and

d looks foolish. And when it comes to panegyrics and extolling others, he cannot disguise his laughter, which is genuine, not affected, but makes him seem an imbecile. You see, when he hears a tyrant or a king being eulogized, to his mind it's a herdsman being congratulated for a high yield, and rulers are just like keepers of pigs, sheep or cattle, except that the creature they farm and milk is more intractable and treacherous than other animals; and to his mind a ruler is bound to become just as uncivilized and coarse as a herdsman, because

1. The alliteration is Plato's: notice, in general, how he is using rhetorical flourishes to denigrate rhetoric!

2. This was an expected part of Greek rhetorical practice.

he has no time for culture, and the fortifications which he's *e*
erected around himself are no different from a mountain
corral. And when he's told that so-and-so, with a thousand
acres or more, has got a fantastic amount of land, the quantity
strikes him as trifling, accustomed as he is to considering the
whole earth. And when people sing in praise of lineage, saying
that such-and-such a member of the upper classes can point
to seven generations of wealthy ancestors, he considers the
eulogy to be thoroughly short-sighted and due to the uneducated inability ever to see things as a whole or to work 175*a*
out that everyone has countless thousands of ancestors and
forebears, among whom there have been rich men and
beggars, kings and slaves – thousands of each for each of us,
and any of them could have been a foreigner or a Greek.[1]
But when he is faced with people giving themselves airs about
a list of twenty-five ancestors traced back to Heracles the
son of Amphitryon,[2] their narrow-mindedness seems extraordinary to him: God knows what the twenty-fifth back from
Amphitryon was like, and the fiftieth back from that one. *b*
This inability to free the mind of stupid vanity and to think
rationally amuses him. Anyway, in these and all similar cases,
the philosopher is mocked by the general public, sometimes
for apparently being arrogant, sometimes for not noticing
what's at his feet and for finding particular situations confusing.

THEODORUS: You have hit the nail on the head, Socrates.
SOCRATES: Yes, but what about when the philosopher
hoists up a non-philosopher, my friend?[3] Suppose he finds
someone prepared to drop considerations of who's wronging *c*
whom how in favour of investigating what right and wrong
are in themselves and how they differ from each other and
from everything else, or to put aside saying, 'The king of

1. The Greeks usually considered themselves to be superior to all other
races.

2. The Greeks did not at this time distinguish sharply between history,
on the one hand, and legend, myth and prehistory, on the other.

3. Compare *Republic* 515e ff.

Persia is happy',[1] and 'Because of his money', in favour of investigating what kingship is, and what human happiness and misery are, and how, given human nature, the one can be gained and the other avoided. When the time comes for

d that narrow-minded, litigious neurotic to explain his views on all these matters, then the tables are turned: then the height at which he's suspended and the view from up in the air make him feel dizzy, because he's not used to them; he's troubled and confused, he talks gibberish.[2] And this is amusing, but not to Thracian girls or any other ill-bred person (for they are not there to see him); it's amusing to all those whose upbringing was the opposite of slavish.

So there are the two types, Theodorus. There's the one you

e call the philosopher, whose upbringing has been genuinely free and unhurried, and who can't be blamed for looking simple and being useless when he is confronted with menial tasks – if, for instance, he doesn't know how to make the bed or sweeten a sauce or a flattering speech. Then there's the other one, who can do all these things keenly and quickly, but who doesn't know how to strike up an elegant and free-spirited song[3] – no, nor how to play his part in the harmony

176a of discussion and properly celebrate the life of gods and happy men.[4]

THEODORUS: I find what you're saying very convincing, Socrates. If only everyone could hear you; then there'd be more peace and less evil in the world.

SOCRATES: The elimination of evil is impossible, Theodorus: there must always be some force ranged against good.[5] But it is equally impossible for evil to be stationed in

1. Omitting εἰ with several manuscripts. The question whether the king of Persia is happy seems to have been a common debating topic of the time.

2. Reading βαρβαρίζων with the manuscripts.

3. Reading ἐλευθέρως with the manuscripts.

4. The harmony of philosophy is a common image in Plato: see especially *Laches* 188d. The word translated 'happy' (*eudaimon*) is really untranslatable: in philosophical contexts it stands for the ideal human state.

5. Compare *Lysis* 220c–d.

heaven; its territory is necessarily mortal nature – it patrols this earthly realm. That is why one should try to escape as quickly as possible from here to there.[1] The escape-route *b* is assimilation to God, in so far as this is possible, and this assimilation is the combination of wisdom with moral respect for God and man.[2]

But, my dear friend, it is uphill work convincing people that the reason invariably put forward for the obligation to escape from iniquity and pursue virtue – that is, to gain a reputation as a good person rather than a bad one – is *not* a valid reason for fulfilling this obligation. That's just an old wives' tale (as they say), as far as I can see; but we can express the truth as follows. It is utterly and completely impossible for God to be immoral and not to be the acme of *c* morality; and the only way any of us, for our part, can approximate to God is to become as moral as possible. Whether a person is truly clever, or is nothing and less than a man, depends on this. To recognize this is true wisdom and virtue; not to recognize it is proof of ignorance and evil. Everything else that passes for cleverness and wisdom arises either in struggling for political power (in which case it is tawdry), or in practising some craft (in which case it is mechanical). So it is far, far preferable not to use the word 'clever' to describe *d* the lack of scruple which leads people to behave immorally in their words or deeds. The criticism is a source of pride for such people; to their way of thinking, they are not being called irrelevant, useless burdens on the earth, but are being attributed the features which make for political survival. So it's up to us to tell them the truth: they are exactly the sort of people they think they are not, and all the more so for not thinking it. And the reason is that they are ignorant of the penalty for immorality, which is the last thing one should be

1. Plato's language suggests that he saw the battle against evil as continuous, rather than one which can ultimately be won. On the issue of evil in Plato, see Guthrie [30], pp. 92–100.

2. The idea that assimilation to God is man's religious goal is constant in Plato. Wisdom is the goal of philosophy (*philosophia*, 'love of wisdom').

ignorant of. The penalty is not corporal or capital punishment, as they think, which they can sometimes avoid; no, the

e penalty for immorality is inescapable.[1]

THEODORUS: What penalty do you mean?

SOCRATES: There are two real and unshakeable archetypes, my friend, one of blessed divinity, the other of godless misery.[2] But they fail to see that this is so, and their inanity and utter stupidity blind them to the fact that their immoral

177*a* actions cause them to be assimilated to the one and to become dissimilar to the other. The penalty they pay for this is that their mode of existence resembles the archetype they are close to. But suppose we were to tell them that if they don't get rid of this 'cleverness' of theirs, then when they die they will not be received into that realm which is untainted by evil, but will remain for ever in this world, living lives after their own likeness, as evil people surrounded by evil.[3] If we tell them this, it will sound to them exactly as though people who are clever and unhindered by scruples are being spoken to by fools.

THEODORUS: Yes, you're quite right, Socrates.

b SOCRATES: I know, my friend, believe me. Still, there is one thing I've seen happen. When one of them has to join in a *private* discussion about the things he denigrates, if he is man enough to keep at it for a long time and not run away like a coward, then an extraordinary thing happens, my friend: he ends up being dissatisfied with what he's saying, his famous rhetoric dries up, and he's reduced to a childish state!

---

1. On punishment after death, see the myths of *Phaedo*, *Gorgias* and *Republic*.

2. Compare Empedocles, Fragment 132: 'Blessed is he who has attained the wealth of godlike mind; wretched is he whose thinking of the gods is murky.'

3. That is, not only will they be bound to the cycle of reincarnation, whereas philosophers break free, but also they will be reincarnated as evil people. Compare *Phaedrus* 248c–249d, *Phaedo* 83d–84b and *Timaeus* 42a–d, 90e–92c.

Anyway, all this is actually a digression, so let's leave it there; otherwise our original argument will be submerged as more and more issues keep streaming in. I think we should *c* go back to where we were before. What do you think?

THEODORUS: Well, *I* rather enjoy listening to this kind of talk, Socrates: it's easier to follow at my age. But we'll return to the argument again, if you like.

SOCRATES: Well, we were considering the theory that reality is in motion, and that what appears to each person also is for that person;[1] and we'd reached the point of saying that those who hold this theory are prepared to insist on it in most cases, and above all where ethics is concerned. They say that this is the prime instance and that whatever a com- *d* munity believes to be ethical and establishes as such also *is* ethical for the community which establishes it, as long as the rule remains in force. But where a community is deciding what is good for it, we were saying that no one is foolhardy enough to continue to maintain that, here too, whatever a community thinks is beneficial for it and establishes as such also is beneficial for it, for as long as it remains in force – unless he's talking about the mere word 'beneficial' remaining in use, but that would surely make a mockery of the theory, wouldn't it?

THEODORUS: Certainly.

SOCRATES: So one shouldn't just talk about the word, but *e* should consider the actual thing to which the word refers.

THEODORUS: Yes.

SOCRATES: Whatever word is used, it is benefit that a community aims for in establishing rules; that is, all the rules it establishes are meant to be as beneficial as possible for itself, and the achievement of this is limited only by what it believes to be beneficial and what it is able to establish. Don't you think that's the goal of rule-making?

THEODORUS: Yes, precisely.   178*a*

SOCRATES: And does each community always succeed, or does it often fail as well?

1. Notice once again the joint thesis of Protagoreanism and flux combined.

THEODORUS: *I* think it fails as well.

SOCRATES: Now, the same point would be set on an even firmer foundation if it was approached by considering the general class of things to which benefit in fact belongs; the class as a whole, I think you will agree, has to do with the future. I mean, rules are made to be beneficial in time to come – for which the correct term is 'the future'.

b   THEODORUS: Certainly.

SOCRATES: All right, then. Let's ask Protagoras (or it could be anyone else who holds the same theory) the following question: 'Protagoras, you lot say that man is the measure of everything – white, heavy, light and so on and so forth – on the grounds that he has in himself the authority to decide about such things, so that when he thinks that things are as he is experiencing them, these thoughts are really true for him. Isn't that so?'

THEODORUS: Yes.

SOCRATES: 'And, Protagoras,' we'll continue, 'does he also
c have in himself the authority to decide about things that will occur in the future? Is it the case that things turn out to be for someone as he thought they would be? Take heat as an example. When some layman thinks that he will catch a fever and that this heat will occur, and someone else, who's a doctor, thinks the opposite, whose opinion are we to say that the future will conform to? Or are we to say that it will conform to *both* opinions, in the sense that he will not be feverish and hot to the doctor, but will be to himself?'

THEODORUS: That would be absurd.

SOCRATES: 'And, I think, when the question is whether
d wine will turn out sweet or dry in the future, the farmer's opinion, not the musician's, is authoritative.'

THEODORUS: Of course.

SOCRATES: 'And again, when the issue is future assonance or dissonance, a physical-education teacher's opinion is not going to be better than a musician's about what will turn out to be tuneful even to the teacher's ears.'

THEODORUS: Of course not.

SOCRATES: 'Moreover, when a meal is being prepared, the

future participant in the meal, assuming he's not a cook, is a
less authoritative judge of the prospective taste than the cook.
We're not yet making any claims about what is currently *e*
tasty to anyone, or was in the past; we're asking about what
will appear and be to people in the future. Is each person, in
himself, the best judge in these cases? Or is it rather the case,
Protagoras, that, at least as regards which arguments will be
persuasive to any of us in a lawcourt, you would be a better
judge of the future than some amateur or other?'

THEODORUS: Well, this is certainly something he used to
give particularly strong assurances about, that he was better
at it than anyone else.

SOCRATES: Good heavens, of course he did, my dear
fellow! None of his students would have paid him vast 179*a*
amounts of money if he had really[1] convinced them that
they, by themselves,[2] were as good as anyone, even seers, at
assessing the future and what impressions people would have
in the future.

THEODORUS: You're absolutely right.

SOCRATES: Now, rule-making and benefit have to do with
the future, and it is universally acknowledged that a community, when it makes rules, is bound often to fall short of its
goal of maximizing its benefit. Right?

THEODORUS: Certainly.

SOCRATES: It follows, then, that it would be perfectly
reasonable for us to tell your master that he has no choice *b*
but to go further than the concession that some people are
wiser than others, and also concede that while *these* people
are 'measures', there is nothing at all to make me, with my
ignorance, a measure, though the argument we came up
with in his defence a short while ago tried to make me one,
whether I liked it or not.[3]

THEODORUS: Yes, Socrates, I think that is the theory's
weakest point, though it also lays itself open to criticism in

1. Reading δή with Campbell [1], p. 137.

2. Reading αὐτῷ with the manuscripts.

3. See 167d.

that it makes others' beliefs authoritative, and they were shown to believe that his theory has not a shred of truth in it.

c   SOCRATES: That's by no means the only way, Theodorus, in which the theory lays itself open to the counter-argument that *not* every opinion is true.[1] But it is more difficult to argue for the possible falsity of impressions which are based on perceptions, and thus on a person's immediate experience. Perhaps I'm talking nonsense in saying that it's more difficult: it may be that these impressions are completely unassailable, and conceivably those who claim that they are clear[2] and are instances of knowledge are quite right. If that is so, then Theaetetus here was on target when he suggested that per-

d ception and knowledge are identical. So we must move in closer, as our speech in defence of Protagoras told us to;[3] we must investigate this 'reality in motion' and test it thoroughly, to see whether it is sound or flawed. But there's a major controversy raging about this issue, in which quite a few people have been involved.

THEODORUS: It certainly is a major controversy, and one which is rapidly increasing in Ionia,[4] because the Heracliteans are setting a cracking pace for the adherents of this theory.

SOCRATES: All the more reason, my dear Theodorus, for us to investigate it and to start with first principles, just as

e they advocate.

THEODORUS: You're absolutely right, Socrates, especially since, in considering these Heraclitean theories (though, as you say, they may be Homeric or may even pre-date

1. It is not clear whether Plato has any specific argument in mind or is simply stressing the counter-intuitive nature of the denial of false beliefs.

2. That is, that each person perceives what is the case (for himself) without any distortion.

3. See 166c and 168b.

4. The area of Asia Minor around Miletus and Ephesus, where Heraclitus came from.

Homer[1]), one can no more have a rational conversation with those very Ephesians who claim to be the pundits than one can with lunatics. I mean, they are certainly faithful to their texts – they are literally in motion! Their ability to stay put for a discussion or a question, or to keep still and ask and answer questions in due order, is worse than useless – though 180a even that's an exaggeration: there's not the tiniest amount of tranquillity in these people. Suppose you ask a question: they draw enigmatic phrases, as it were out of a quiver, and let fly. Suppose you ask for an explanation of these phrases: you just get hit with another weird metaphor. You'll never get anything conclusive out of any of them – but then, they themselves don't from one another either! They take a great deal of care not to allow any certainty to enter their speech or their minds. I suppose they think that certainty is fixed; and b fixedness is the arch-enemy, whose utter banishment is the object of their efforts.

SOCRATES: Perhaps your experience of them has been restricted to when they are on the warpath, not at peace; after all, you're not of their circle.[2] I dare say that when they have time on their hands they discuss such matters with those of their pupils they want to make similar to themselves.

THEODORUS: Pupils? What pupils? People like that don't become pupils of one another. They spring up automatically c here, there and wherever inspiration strikes them; and they don't recognize one another's claims to knowledge. So, as I was about to say, you'll never get an explanation from *them*, even if they're intending to give you one! It's up to us: we must treat the theory like a geometrical problem and look into it by ourselves.

SOCRATES: That sounds reasonable. Now, we've been bequeathed this problem by two sets of people, haven't we? There are those who lived a long time ago, who used poetry

1. See 152e. At *Cratylus* 402b Plato attributes flux to Orpheus, who as a legendary hero may fairly be said to pre-date Homer!

2. Notice that Theodorus, a quasi-Protagorean, is definitely not a Heraclitean, which helps to show that the 'secret doctrine' is not Protagorean; see further pp. 150–51, 189–90.

d to keep the secret from the majority of mankind, and stated that all things are engendered by Oceanus and Tethys – that is, by water in motion – and that nothing is at a standstill; then there are those in more recent times, whose superior cleverness meant that they could openly assert the theory and make their wisdom so accessible that even cobblers could understand the theory, relinquish the silly idea that although some things are continually changing, others are at rest and, having understood that everything is changing, pay due respect to their teachers. But I was in danger of forgetting the other side to the controversy, Theodorus, the assertion that

e 'It is necessary that the universe has a title such as "unchanging"',[1] and all the other propositions which people like Melissus and Parmenides maintain and which contradict the former theory – that all is one, and that this oneness is fixed within itself, having no space in which to change or move.[2]

So, my friend, how shall we deal with all these people? Our gradual advance has led us unwittingly on until we've ended up between the two camps. If we don't find a way to keep
181*a* them at bay and make good our escape, we'll have to take the consequences, just like those who play that game in the gymnasia, where if they are caught by both sides, they are pulled in opposite directions across a line. Anyway, I think we should inspect the first lot first, the ones we have already made a start on, the flowing people; if we find that they make sense, we'll help them pull us over to their side, in our attempt

1. The text of this fragment of Parmenides is uncertain, but the fact that Simplicius quotes versions of the same words makes it certain that the text is not merely a corrupt citation of Fragment 8.38. It is similar to 8.38, but the received text of that line is significantly different, especially since it has strong punctuation in the middle: it is inconceivable that Plato would quote the end of one sentence and the beginning of another, where neither makes sense on its own. Our line is probably best read, therefore, as an independent fragment of Parmenides. I have translated Burnet's text, without too much confidence; but whatever text is adopted should provide Plato with an immediately obvious contrast with a universe in flux.

2. See Parmenides, Fragment 8. Melissus of Samos (*floruit c.* 450) was an eminent Parmenidean.

to escape the others. But if we think that those whose standpoint is a standstill universe are closer to the truth, we will come over to their side and escape, in this case, from those who try to change the unchanging. If we find that *b* *neither* group has anything reasonable to say, that'll be equivalent to thinking that insignificant people like ourselves have got something to contribute, while we disparage the all-wise sages of ancient times; so we'll look pretty foolish. What do you think, Theodorus? Is there anything to be gained by advancing into such dangerous territory?

THEODORUS: It would be distinctly unsatisfying not to look into these two theories, Socrates.

SOCRATES: All right, since *you* are so keen. Now, I think an inquiry into change should start by seeing what those *c* who claim that everything is changing mean by change. What I'm getting at is this: are they talking about only one kind of change, or two kinds? *My* impression is that they're talking about two kinds, but we're in this together: it shouldn't just remain my impression. You must see what I mean as well, so that we bear the consequences together. So tell me: do you say that something is changing when it is shifting position from one place to another, or even when it remains on the same spot, but is turning around?

THEODORUS: Yes.

SOCRATES: All right; so that's one kind of change. But what about when something is in the same place, but grows *d* old, or becomes black instead of white, or hard instead of soft, or is altered in any other way? Shouldn't that be distinguished as a separate kind of change?[1]

THEODORUS: Necessarily.

SOCRATES: So here are our two kinds of change, I think: alteration and motion.[2]

THEODORUS: Yes, you're right.

---

1. It is obviously not being said that something which is altering *must* be in the same place: Plato is simply distinguishing the two types of change.

2. Compare *Republic* 380e, *Parmenides* 138b, *Cratylus* 439e. Aristotle adds generation/destruction and growth/diminution.

SOCRATES: Armed with this distinction, we are now ready to talk to those who claim that everything is changing, and ask: 'Is your claim that everything is changing in *both* ways? *e* Is everything both moving and altering, or are some things changing in both ways, while others are changing in only one of these two ways?'

THEODORUS: To tell the truth, I'm not sure what to reply; but I suppose they would say both ways.

SOCRATES: Well, if they don't, my friend, they will find that things are both changing and at rest, and that the proposition that everything is at rest will be just as correct as that everything is changing.

THEODORUS: You're quite right.

SOCRATES: So since things must be changing, and since 182*a* lack of change cannot be a property of anything, then everything is always undergoing every kind of change.

THEODORUS: Necessarily.

SOCRATES: There's another aspect of the theory to consider. We attributed to them the view that heat, whiteness, etc., are engendered somewhat as follows:[1] each of them is in motion, along with perception, between the active and the passive agents; the passive half consequently becomes[2] not perception but percipient, and the active half becomes not quality but qualified in some way. Isn't this the view we attributed to them? Now, perhaps this word 'quality' strikes you as strange.[3] Perhaps you don't understand the abstract *b* term, so I'll just talk about particular cases. You see, the active half doesn't become heat or whiteness, but hot or white, and so on. I'm sure you remember what we said before, that nothing – not even the active and passive agents – is a single, non-relative entity, but that perceptions and perceived things are the offspring of the intercourse between the active and passive halves with each other, which then

1. See 156a–157c.

2. Reading ἐπιγίγνεσθαι.

3. Presumably Plato has just coined the Greek word *poiotes*, 'of-such-a-kind-ness'.

become, respectively, qualified in some way and percipient.

THEODORUS: Of course I remember.

SOCRATES: Anyway, it doesn't matter whether this or *c* something else is the meaning of the theory. Let's just concentrate on the purpose of our discussion and ask: 'According to you, everything is changing and flowing. Right?'

THEODORUS: Yes.

SOCRATES: 'Now, is everything undergoing both of the changes we distinguished? Is everything both moving and altering?'

THEODORUS: They must be; otherwise they're not completely changing.

SOCRATES: If things were only moving, but not altering, we would be able to describe the qualities of the moving things as they flow, wouldn't we?

THEODORUS: Yes.

SOCRATES: But since it isn't even the case that something *d* in flux *remains* flowing white – since it changes and there turns out to be flux even of the whiteness, and to be change to another colour (otherwise one could pinpoint it as stable in this respect), then is it ever possible to name the colour of anything, with any hope of being correct?

THEODORUS: Impossible, Socrates, and equally impossible for anything like that, given that, since it is flowing, it is slipping away even while one is speaking.

SOCRATES: And what shall we say about perception – about seeing and hearing, for example? Is it ever stably just that seeing and just that hearing?   *e*

THEODORUS: No, it can't be, if everything is changing.

SOCRATES: So if everything is changing in all respects, we shouldn't talk of seeing something rather than not seeing it, and any other perception is no more perception than not perception.

THEODORUS: No.

SOCRATES: Now, according to Theaetetus and me, it's perception which is knowledge.

THEODORUS: True.

SOCRATES: Therefore, when we were asked to define

knowledge, our answer named something which is no more knowledge than not knowledge.

183a   THEODORUS: So it seems.

SOCRATES: What brilliant support we could end up providing for our answer! We went all out to show that everything is changing, in order to prove that answer of ours to be correct, but what we've proved, apparently, is that every answer to any question is equally correct! It is just as correct for people to say 'It is like this' as 'It is not like this' – or rather, 'It becomes like this' and 'It doesn't become like this', to avoid expressions which bring people to a standstill!

THEODORUS: You're right.

SOCRATES: Not quite, Theodorus. I said 'like this' and 'not like this'. But one shouldn't use the phrase 'like this', because

b anything 'like this' has stopped changing; and the same goes for 'not like this', because that isn't change either.[1] No, those who hold this theory need to set up another language, since at present they don't have expressions which fit the theory, except 'not like this either': this would be particularly suitable for them, provided they go on and on saying it.[2]

THEODORUS: Yes, that's the most appropriate locution for them.

SOCRATES: So we have broken free of your friend, Theodorus. We do not yet find ourselves in a position to agree

c with him that *every* person is the measure of all things, but only wise people. And we will not accept that the idea that everything is changing entails the identity of perception and knowledge – unless Theaetetus here has some new argument to produce.[3]

THEODORUS: I'm delighted to hear you say that, Socrates, because our arrangement was that when we'd reached a conclusion on this matter – that is, when the discussion of

1. Compare *Cratylus* 439e. Plato rejects 'not like this' in case it is taken to imply 'but like that'.

2. Retaining δ'οὕτως with the manuscripts and punctuating with a colon after οὐδ' οὕτως (see Hackforth [32]).

3. Retaining τι with the manuscripts.

Protagoras' theory was over – I too ought to be set free of answering your questions.

THEAETETUS: Not yet, Theodorus, not until you and Socrates have done what you proposed just now, and dis- *d* cussed the alternative view, that the universe is at rest.

THEODORUS: What's this, Theaetetus? Are you, at your age, trying to lead your elders astray by suggesting that they fail to comply with their agreements? No, you had better make yourself ready to continue the argument with Socrates.

THEAETETUS: If that's what he wants. But I'd much prefer to listen to something on the topic I mentioned.

THEODORUS: Giving Socrates the opportunity for discussion is like giving cavalry the opportunity to fight on level ground! Go on, ask a question: he'll give you something to listen to.

SOCRATES: Actually, Theodorus, I don't think I will do as Theaetetus suggests, at least not on that specific topic.[1]   *e*

THEODORUS: Why not?

SOCRATES: My respect for Melissus and the other proponents of the view that the universe is one being and at rest makes me want to avoid a shoddy inquiry into their theory; and there is one being above all that I respect – Parmenides. To my eyes, Parmenides is, in the words of Homer, 'worthy of esteem and awe'.[2] You see, I met him once,[3] when I was quite young and he was quite old, and I was impressed by a certain depth[4] in him that struck me as altogether noble. So 184*a* I am afraid of us not understanding what he said and failing even more to grasp the intentions underlying what he said. But my greatest fear is that if we give way to these gate-crashing topics, we will never get around to looking into the

---

1. The discussion is reserved for *Sophist*. Note the coming pun on 'one being'.

2. *Iliad* 3.172, of a father by a daughter-in-law.

3. See *Parmenides*.

4. The word may also imply 'still waters' – that is, as opposed to the frenzy of the Heracliteans at 179e–180b.

question which was the original impetus for our discussion, namely what knowledge is. This is particularly true in the case of the topic we are touching on at the moment, which is so vast that just glancing at it wouldn't do it justice, but a satisfactory treatment would take time and would consign the inquiry about knowledge to oblivion. We must avoid both of these courses. Instead we should utilize my skill as a
b midwife to deliver Theaetetus of the ideas about knowledge which constitute his pregnancy.[1]

THEODORUS: All right. If you want, that's what we'll do.

SOCRATES: Well then, Theaetetus, here's another aspect of the issue for you to consider. Your suggestion was that *perception* is knowledge, wasn't it?

THEAETETUS: Yes.

SOCRATES: If you were asked, 'With what do people see white and black objects, and with what do they hear high and low pitch?', you would reply, 'With eyes and ears', I suppose.

THEAETETUS: I would.

c   SOCRATES: It is usually good manners not to be fussy about words and phrases – that is, not to scrutinize them closely; in fact, pedantry is more likely to be discourteous. Sometimes, however, it is necessary, and now is one of those times: I must take exception to a degree of incorrectness in your reply. I mean, would it be more correct to say that eyes are what we see *with*, or what we see *by means of*? And that ears are what we hear *with*, or what we hear *by means of*?

THEAETETUS: I think we perceive things by means of them rather than with them, Socrates.

d   SOCRATES: Yes, it would be peculiar, my boy, if each of us were like a Trojan Horse, with a whole bunch of senses sitting inside us, rather than that all these perceptions converge on

---

1. Strictly, Theaetetus gave birth at 160e and Socrates is now testing the offspring in the *amphidromia*. But Socrates is already looking ahead to Theaetetus' next idea, since the equation of perception and knowledge has all but been demolished. Given the mutual entailments of Theaetetus' definition, relativism and flux, the demolishment of relativism and flux deals with the definition as well.

to a single identity (mind, or whatever one ought to call it), *with* which we perceive whatever there is to be perceived *by means of* its organs, the senses.[1]

THEAETETUS: Yes, I prefer this idea to the other one.

SOCRATES: Now, the reason I'm being precise about this is to see if it is the same faculty in ourselves with which we hit upon white and black objects by means of the eyes, and *e* other kinds of things by means of the other sense-organs. If you were asked about this, would you be able to refer all of this to the body? Presumably it's better for me not to butt in, but for you to speak for yourself by answering these questions. So tell me: do you attribute to the body, or to something else, each of the organs by means of which you perceive things that are hot, hard, light and sweet?

THEAETETUS: To the body.

SOCRATES: And are you also prepared to agree that the things you perceive by means of one faculty cannot be per- 185*a* ceived by means of another – for example, that objects of hearing cannot be objects of seeing, and vice versa?

THEAETETUS: Of course I agree.

SOCRATES: It follows, then, that if something occurs to you about both of them together, it cannot be perception, by means of one or the other of the sense-organs, which would encompass both together.

THEAETETUS: No.

SOCRATES: Take a sound and a colour, and let me ask you first whether *this* occurs to you about both of them, that they both are?

THEAETETUS: Yes.

SOCRATES: And also that each of them is different from the other, but the same as itself?

THEAETETUS: Of course. *b*

SOCRATES: And that together they are two, but that each of them is single?

THEAETETUS: Yes, that too.

1. The Greek is literally 'by means of its organs [or instruments], as it were', which suggests that this is the first occurrence of the term 'sense-organs'.

SOCRATES: And are you able to ask yourself whether they are similar or dissimilar to each other?[1]

THEAETETUS: I suppose so.

SOCRATES: Now since you cannot grasp their common ground by means of hearing or seeing, by means of *what* do all these shared features occur to you? Here is another piece of relevant evidence: if it were feasible to ask whether or not they were both brackish, no doubt you'd be able to tell me
c what you would investigate with, which obviously wouldn't be sight or hearing, but something else.

THEAETETUS: Of course: the faculty that operates by means of the tongue.

SOCRATES: Right. Now, by means of *what* does the faculty operate which reveals to you the common ground shared by all objects (including the ones we've mentioned), which you refer to when you say 'is', 'is not' and talk about the other features which came up in the recent questions? What organs will you assign to all these features? By means of what organs does the perceiving part of us perceive them?

THEAETETUS: You mean being and not being, similarity and dissimilarity, identity and difference, oneness and any
d other number that may be relevant to these objects; and you're obviously not excluding 'even', 'odd' and other mathematical concepts. And your question is by means of which physical faculty we perceive these things with the mind.[2]

SOCRATES: That is exactly my question, Theaetetus. You have caught my drift exceedingly well.

THEAETETUS: But I honestly can't come up with an answer, Socrates, except to say that I think it is fundamentally wrong to look for a special organ for these things, analogous

1. The question sounds peculiar, but I suppose it does make sense to say that a colour isn't like a sound. The first premiss of this argument, that each sense has its own special objects, is common, but not altogether unassailable. What about shape, which is an object of both sight and touch?

2. Notice the shift from the formulation that the mind 'perceives' *that* a colour and sound 'are', to the mind directly perceiving the being of a colour and a sound: see p. 212 on the grammar of Greek epistemological terms.

to the special organs for the other objects; it seems to me that in every case the mind investigates the common features by *e* means of itself.

SOCRATES: Theodorus said you weren't good-looking, Theaetetus – [1] he was wrong! If an argument looks good, the arguer is good-looking, and a fine person as well. To cap it all, you have done me a good turn: your opinion that while the mind investigates some things by means of the physical faculties, it investigates other things by itself, has saved me from a rather long discussion, since I already held this opinion, but I wanted you to as well.

THEAETETUS: Well, I do.   186*a*

SOCRATES: In which category do you put being, which is the prime feature everything has?

THEAETETUS: *I* put it in the class of things which the mind gets at by itself.

SOCRATES: And the same goes for similarity, dissimilarity, identity and difference?

THEAETETUS: Yes.

SOCRATES: What about fineness and despicability, goodness and badness?

THEAETETUS: I think these too are prime examples of things whose being the mind investigates in relation to each other, by using past and present actions to calculate, within itself, about future behaviour.[2]   *b*

SOCRATES: Hang on. Doesn't the mind perceive the hardness of something hard by means of touch, and likewise the softness of something soft?[3]

THEAETETUS: Yes.

SOCRATES: But when it comes to their being (that is, that they both are) and their mutual opposition and, again, the being of their opposition, the mind by itself has the job of

1. At 143e.

2. See 178a ff.

3. Notice how, having refuted relativism and flux, Plato can speak as if objects may be objectively hard, rather than that their hardness comes to be in relation to a perceiver at a particular instant.

reaching a decision by reviewing them and comparing them with each other.

THEAETETUS: Certainly.

SOCRATES: So there are some things – all those experi-
c ences which reach the mind by means of the body – which people and animals are naturally capable of perceiving from birth; calculating about the being and benefit of these things, however, only comes (if at all) laboriously, by means of a long, arduous process of education. Is that right?

THEAETETUS: Absolutely.

SOCRATES: Well, is it possible for someone who can't apprehend being to apprehend truth?

THEAETETUS: No.

SOCRATES: And if the truth of something is not apprehended,[1] there can't ever be knowledge of that thing, can there?

d   THEAETETUS: Of course not, Socrates.

SOCRATES: Therefore knowledge is not located in immediate experience, but in reasoning about it, since the latter, apparently, but not the former, makes it possible to grasp being and truth.

THEAETETUS: Clearly.

SOCRATES: Now, can you call these two faculties by the same name, when they are so different?

THEAETETUS: No, that would certainly be wrong.

SOCRATES: Well, what name do you give to the former – to seeing, hearing, smelling, feeling cold, feeling warm . . .?

e   THEAETETUS: Perceiving. What else could I call it?

SOCRATES: You call the whole lot perception, then?

THEAETETUS: I have to.[2]

SOCRATES: That is, something which, we agreed, plays no part in grasping truth, since it doesn't even grasp being.

THEAETETUS: That's right.

SOCRATES: And therefore has nothing to do with knowledge either.

---

1. Reading ἀτυχής, ἤ with Westerink [16], after Proclus.

2. Theaetetus seems to be acknowledging the restriction in this section of the term 'perception' to non-cognitive sensation.

THEAETETUS: No.

SOCRATES: It follows, then, Theaetetus, that perception and knowledge cannot ever be identical.

THEAETETUS: Evidently not, Socrates. It is perfectly clear now that knowledge is different from perception.

SOCRATES: But the reason we embarked on this discussion 187a was not to find what knowledge is *not*, but what it *is*. Still, we have got somewhere: we've completely given up looking for knowledge in perception. Instead we'll look for it in whatever one calls that function of the mind when it is involved with things by itself.

THEAETETUS: That's called thinking, Socrates, I suppose.

SOCRATES: You're right, my friend. Now, erase from your mind everything that's gone before, and start all over again, b to see if things are a bit clearer now that we've got this far. Tell me once again what knowledge is.

THEAETETUS: Well, I can't say that it's thinking as a whole, since the beliefs that are formed can be false. But perhaps true belief is knowledge: I'll try this answer. If, as the argument progresses, it turns out to be wrong and we find ourselves in the same position that we did just now, then we'll try another idea.

SOCRATES: That's the spirit, Theaetetus: it's much better to speak up like that, rather than being afraid to answer, as you were at first.[1] If we carry on like this, then one of two things will happen: either we will find what we're after, or we c will be less inclined to think we know what we do not know in the slightest – and even this is a handsome reward. Anyway, let's look at what you're saying. There are two kinds of belief, one true, the other false, and you're defining knowledge as true belief. Right?

THEAETETUS: Yes. I mean, that's my impression at the moment.

SOCRATES: Well, I wonder if it's worth resuscitating something about belief that came up before.[2]

1. 148b, 148e.

2. See 167a–b for the Protagorean denial of false belief. At the time Socrates countered by pointing to the matter of fact that false belief happens;

THEAETETUS: What?

d   SOCRATES: This is by no means the first time that the problem has been a source of considerable puzzlement for me, when I think about it on my own or talk about it with others, because I am unable to say what this experience is and how it occurs to people.

THEAETETUS: What experience?

SOCRATES: Believing something false. Even now I'm in two minds again: I'm wondering whether we ought to drop the issue, or investigate it, but with a different approach to the one we took a short while ago.

THEAETETUS: Of course we should investigate it, Socrates, if we think there's the remotest need to do so. I mean, you and Theodorus were quite right when you were talking recently about having time and said that there's no urgency in discussions like ours.[1]

e   SOCRATES: You're right; thanks for the reminder. I mean, it is probably relevant for us to retrace our steps, because it is better to deal thoroughly with a little than unsatisfactorily with a lot.

THEAETETUS: Of course.

SOCRATES: Now then, what are we actually saying? Is our claim that false belief is possible in any given instance, so that one of us may believe something false, while the other believes something true, because this is the way things are?

THEAETETUS: Yes, that's what we're saying.

188*a*   SOCRATES: Now, isn't it the case, for each and every item, that it is either known or not known? I'm not taking the intermediary states of learning and forgetting into consideration at the moment, since they are irrelevant to the argument.

THEAETETUS: In that case, Socrates, the only remaining

---

but now he will be concerned with the philosophical problem of how to account for false belief – this is the 'different approach' mentioned in 187d.

1. See 172c–d.

possibilities are either knowing or not knowing something.[1]

SOCRATES: Well, doesn't this make it inevitable that belief is either about something known or about something not known?

THEAETETUS: Yes.

SOCRATES: And it is impossible for something known to be unknown, or for something unknown to be known.   *b*

THEAETETUS: Of course.

SOCRATES: Is false belief, then, mistaking something known for something else which is also known, which would mean that both things are simultaneously known and not known?

THEAETETUS: No, that's impossible, Socrates.

SOCRATES: Well then, is false belief mistaking something not known for something else which is also not known? An example of this would be someone who doesn't know either Theaetetus or Socrates being able to conceive the notion that Socrates is Theaetetus or that Theaetetus is Socrates.

THEAETETUS: Impossible.   *c*

SOCRATES: Well, it can't be mistaking something known for something not known, or something not known for something known.

THEAETETUS: That would be extraordinary.

SOCRATES: So how is false belief possible? I mean, on the assumption that everything is either known or unknown, we have given all the circumstances in which belief can arise, and it turns out to be impossible for there to be false belief in these circumstances.

THEAETETUS: You're perfectly right.

SOCRATES: So perhaps we ought to conduct the inquiry not on the basis of what is known and unknown, but on the *d* basis of what is and is not.

THEAETETUS: What do you mean?

SOCRATES: It may simply be that believing what is not

---

1. In *Meno* Plato resolved this dichotomy by taking latent knowledge into consideration; in the Aviary model of 197a ff. he will do the same, but in quite a different mood (see p. 245).

about something is inevitably false belief, whatever else the
mind is doing.

THEAETETUS: That sounds plausible, Socrates.

SOCRATES: So suppose we are challenged with the question, 'Is what you have said possible for anyone? Can any
person believe what is not, either about anything in particular
or in any absolute sense?' What will our reply be? I suppose
we'll retort, 'Yes, it is possible, when someone thinks and

e what he thinks is not true.'

THEAETETUS: Yes.

SOCRATES: Now, is this sort of thing possible elsewhere?

THEAETETUS: What sort of thing?

SOCRATES: Can sight be of something, but be sight of
nothing?[1]

THEAETETUS: Impossible.

SOCRATES: In fact, if there is sight of any one thing, then
there is sight of one of the things that are. Or do you think
that any one thing can be among the things that are not?

THEAETETUS: No, I don't.

SOCRATES: So any one thing that is seen is something
which is.

THEAETETUS: Obviously.

189a SOCRATES: And any one thing that is heard is also something which is.

THEAETETUS: Yes.

SOCRATES: And any one thing which is touched is also
something which is, *qua* being one thing.

THEAETETUS: Again, yes.

SOCRATES: But isn't the object of any belief some one
thing?

THEAETETUS: Necessarily.

SOCRATES: And if it is some one thing, then isn't the object
of belief something which is?

THEAETETUS: Yes, agreed.

---

1. The argument that follows is bound to be stilted in English. It draws
on the fact that the Greek for 'nothing' (*ouden*) is literally just a negated
form of the word for 'one thing'.

SOCRATES: Therefore, if the object of a belief is what is not, the object of this belief is nothing.

THEAETETUS: Evidently.

SOCRATES: But if there is no object to a belief, then that is not belief at all.

THEAETETUS: That seems obvious.

SOCRATES: Therefore, it is not possible to believe what is *b* not, either about anything which is or in any absolute sense.

THEAETETUS: Evidently not.

SOCRATES: It follows that false belief is different from believing what is not.

THEAETETUS: So it seems.

SOCRATES: This method of inquiry, therefore, has been just as unsuccessful in showing how there can be false belief as the one we adopted just before it.

THEAETETUS: Yes, quite so.

SOCRATES: But perhaps what we term false belief happens as follows.

THEAETETUS: How?

SOCRATES: We describe false belief as a sort of cross-believing,[1] when the mind exchanges something that is for *c* something else that is, and one is claimed to be the other. On this analysis, the object of belief is always something that is; it's just that one thing has become the object of belief instead of the other. This missing of the target might fairly be called false belief.

THEAETETUS: Now I think you've hit the nail on the head. When someone thinks 'ugly' instead of 'beautiful' (or vice versa), that is truly false belief.

SOCRATES: You obviously have a low opinion of me, Theaetetus, and don't think you need be cautious.

THEAETETUS: Whatever makes you say that?

SOCRATES: I think you think that I won't take you up on your phrase 'truly false' and ask if anything can be 'slowly *d* fast' or 'light in a heavy way', or if, in general, anything which has an opposite can occur in the opposite way to itself,

1. Plato coins a word to cater for the special type of mistake of taking one specified thing to be another specified thing.

having abandoned its own nature for the nature of its opposite.[1] Anyway, I don't want your bravado to be wasted, so I'll drop the issue. But the idea that false belief is cross-belief seems all right to you, you say?

THEAETETUS: Yes.

SOCRATES: So, in your opinion, it is possible for the mind to take something as something else and not as itself.

THEAETETUS: Of course it's possible.

e   SOCRATES: Now, when the mind operates like this, isn't it bound to be thinking either of both items or of one of the two items?[2]

THEAETETUS: Yes.

SOCRATES: I mean, either both at once or one after the other.

THEAETETUS: You're quite right.

SOCRATES: And do you describe thinking as I do?

THEAETETUS: How is that?

SOCRATES: As a discussion which the mind has with itself about whatever it is investigating.[3] Now, I'm not making this assertion as an expert: it's just that the image I get of thinking is that the mind is simply carrying on a conversation:
190a it asks itself questions and answers them, saying yes or no. And when it reaches a conclusion (which may take quite a ⌐

1. This is only a joke, of course: it also occurs at *Republic* 382a–b; and at *Philebus* 23a–b Plato talks of 'causing pleasure pain' in a similar jocular fashion.

2. This is a puzzling statement: if two things are being confused, how could one be thinking of only one of them? I take it that it is explained by 'either both at once *or one after the other*': the latter phrase qualifies the idea that one may be thinking of only one of the two things. In order to make this clearer (so that it is Socrates who adds the qualification), I restore the attributions of these lines which the majority of manuscripts have. Burnet's text, following other manuscripts, gives all of 'Yes . . . one after the other' to Theaetetus, then all of 'You're quite right . . . as I do' to Socrates.

3. Compare *Philebus* 38c–39c, *Sophist* 263e–264a. This notion is a starting-point of modern epistemology: 'A piece of factual knowledge must be either a statement or as complex or capable of becoming as complex as a statement' (Pears [46], p. 9).

long time or may involve a sudden leap), stops being divided and starts to affirm something consistently, we call this its belief. So I call belief a statement, but one which is not made aloud and to someone else, but in silence to oneself. What about you?

THEAETETUS: So do I.

SOCRATES: So when someone believes that one thing is something else, he is apparently also saying to himself that one thing is something else.

THEAETETUS: Of course. *b*

SOCRATES: Try to remember, then, if you have ever said to yourself that what is beautiful is definitely ugly, or what is immoral is moral. In short, see if you have ever attempted to convince yourself that one thing is definitely something else. Isn't exactly the opposite true, in fact, that you have never, even in sleep, defiantly told yourself that what is odd is, without a doubt, even, or anything else like that?

THEAETETUS: You're right.

SOCRATES: And you're not alone in this. Do you think *c* that anyone, sane or insane, seriously says to himself and tries against the odds to convince himself that what is a cow is a horse and that what is two is one?

THEAETETUS: No, I certainly don't.

SOCRATES: So, on the assumption that believing is making an internal statement, no one whose mind has a grasp on both of two things, and who therefore makes statements – that is, has beliefs – about both, could state and believe that what is different is different. Now it is your turn not to take me up on the way I've used the word 'different':[1] what I mean is that no one believes that what is ugly is beautiful, and so on. *d*

THEAETETUS: All right, Socrates, I'll let it pass. I agree with you.

SOCRATES: It follows that it is impossible for someone who has beliefs about two things to believe that one of them is the other.

1. Socrates light-heartedly suggests that the phrase 'what is different is different' is as obscure as the oxymoron of 189d. I read τὸ ῥῆμα ἐν μέρει περὶ τοῦ ἑτέρου with Jackson [12], following Archer-Hind [7].

THEAETETUS: So it seems.

SOCRATES: Moreover, someone who has formed a belief about only one of them, not the other, will never believe that one thing is the other.

THEAETETUS: You're right, since that would involve him also having a grasp of something he doesn't have a belief about.

SOCRATES: Therefore, cross-believing cannot be the result either of having beliefs about two things, or of having a belief
e   about only one of two things. So the definition of false belief as cross-belief is rubbish. I mean, this approach is clearly just as unsuccessful as the ones we tried before at showing how there can be false belief.

THEAETETUS: It seems so.

SOCRATES: But if we don't find how there can be false belief, Theaetetus, we will be forced to make all sorts of strange admissions.[1]

THEAETETUS: What?

SOCRATES: I won't tell you until I've tried every possible approach: I mean, I can see no integrity in us being forced to make the admissions I'm thinking of just because we are still
191a finding things difficult. If we escape and achieve our goal, that will be the time, when we're beyond the reach of ridicule, to talk about how *others* are burdened with these admissions. But if we remain thoroughly entangled in difficulties, I suppose that, in humility and disgust,[2] we'll submit to the topic and let it trample us and do whatever it likes with us. Anyway, I may have found a way for our inquiry to continue: see what you think.

THEAETETUS: Go on.

SOCRATES: I am going to maintain that we were wrong to

1. Including, perhaps, a return to Protagoras' position.

2. The word is literally 'being sea-sick'. There are verbal echoes of Sophocles, *Ajax* 1142–9, which contains a story about a braggart on land whom sea-sickness soon cut down to size, to the scorn of those he himself had scorned on land. Doing philosophy is also likened to the risks of seafaring at *Philebus* 29b, *Laches* 194b, *Euthydemus* 293a and *Republic* 457b (see 472a).

have agreed that error cannot occur by something unknown being thought to be something known.[1] There is a way in *b* which this is possible.

THEAETETUS: Are you thinking about what I had an inkling of when we were describing the experience before? It occurred to me then that sometimes I, who know Socrates, can see a stranger from a distance and think that he is Socrates, whom I know. I mean, this situation fits what you're saying.

SOCRATES: And the reason we ignored it was because it made us not know things we know, even though we know them. Right?

THEAETETUS: Yes.

SOCRATES: That's because we didn't find the right way to put it. There's an alternative description, which may prove *c* helpful. But even if it proves a hindrance, we're in such straits that we've got to assess every argument by looking at it from all angles. So see if my alternative makes any sense. Is it possible for something previously unknown later to be learned?

THEAETETUS: Certainly.

SOCRATES: And more and more things can be learned?

THEAETETUS: Of course.

SOCRATES: So, for the sake of argument, imagine that our minds contain a wax block, which may vary in size, cleanliness and consistency in different individuals, but in some *d* people is just right.

THEAETETUS: I can imagine that.

SOCRATES: And let us say that it is a gift of Memory, the mother of the Muses,[2] and that whenever we want to remember something we've seen or heard or conceived on our own, we subject the block to the perception or the idea and

---

1. See 188c; at 191e Plato adds that they were also wrong to have made the same agreement about two known things (188b).

2. This is a traditional genealogy, occurring at Hesiod, *Theogony* 52–4 and often elsewhere; it stems from the fact that the first poets were oral poets, requiring excellent memories.

stamp the impression into it, as if we were making marks with signet-rings. We remember and know anything imprinted, as long as the impression remains in the block; but we forget and do not know anything which is erased or

e cannot be imprinted.

THEAETETUS: All right, let's make this assumption.

SOCRATES: Well, consider a person who has knowledge in this way, and suppose he is also reflecting about something he is seeing or hearing. What about the following analysis of how he might form a false belief?

THEAETETUS: What?

SOCRATES: Sometimes by confusing two separate things which he knows; sometimes by confusing something he doesn't know with something he does. These are situations we earlier declared to be impossible, but we were wrong.

THEAETETUS: And what do you say now?

192*a*   SOCRATES: It is important to start by sifting out certain cases.[1] [1] If *a* is known (that is, the mind retains its impression in the memory), but is not being perceived, it cannot be confused with *b*, which is also known (that is, retained) and also not being perceived. [2] If *a* is known, it cannot be confused with *b*, which is not known (that is, of which there is no impression). [3] If *a* is not known, it cannot be confused with *b*, which is also not known. [4] If *a* is not known, it cannot be confused with *b*, which is known. [5] If *a* is being perceived, it cannot be confused with *b*, which is also being perceived. [6] If *a* is being perceived, it cannot be confused with *b*, which is not being perceived. [7] If *a* is not being perceived, it cannot be confused with *b*, which is also not

b being perceived. [8] If *a* is not being perceived, it cannot be confused with *b*, which is being perceived. [9] Moreover, if *a* is known and is being perceived (that is, if the memory-mark is retained and matched up to the perception), it cannot be confused with *b*, which is also known and also being perceived (that is, whose mark is also retained and is matched up to the perception). This is even more impossible than the earlier

---

1. I have inserted numerals into the text for ease of reference.

cases, if it were realistic to talk of degrees of impossibility. [10] If *a* is known and is being perceived (that is, if the impression in the memory is correctly lined up), it cannot be confused with *b*, which is known. [11] If *a* is known and is being perceived (that is, if the memory-impression is as stated before), it cannot be confused with *b*, which is being perceived. *c* [12] If *a* is not known and is not being perceived, it cannot be confused with *b*, which is also not known and not being perceived. [13] If *a* is not known and is not being perceived, it cannot be confused with *b*, which is not known. [14] If *a* is not known and is not being perceived, it cannot be confused with *b*, which is not being perceived.

In all these cases, impossibility is too weak a description for the chances of false belief occurring. But there are some cases left, where, if anywhere, false belief arises.

THEAETETUS: Which are they? If you tell me, they might help me to understand a bit better; at the moment, I'm lost.

SOCRATES: [15] If *a* is known, it can be confused with *b*, which is known and is being perceived. [16] If *a* is known, it can be confused with *b*, which is not known, but is being perceived. [17] If *a* is known and is being perceived,[1] it can be confused with *b*, which is also known and also being *d* perceived.

THEAETETUS: Now I'm even more confused than before.

SOCRATES: Well, I'll rephrase them for you. I know Theodorus (that is, I have a memory within myself of what he is like), and I know Theaetetus in the same way. Sometimes I see them (or touch, or hear, or perceive them in some other way), sometimes I don't. But sometimes, although I am not perceiving either of you, I none the less remember you both and know you in myself. Right?

THEAETETUS: Certainly.   *e*

SOCRATES: So here's the first point I want you to be clear about, that both possibilities exist: something known may or may not be currently perceived.

THEAETETUS: True.

1. Reading *d* with Ast.

SOCRATES: And does the same obtain also for what is not known, that it may well not even be currently perceived, or it may *only* be currently perceived?

THEAETETUS: Yes, that is so too.

SOCRATES: See if you follow better now, then. If Socrates
193*a* knows Theodorus and Theaetetus, but is not currently seeing them or perceiving them in any other way, he could never form the belief within himself that Theaetetus is Theodorus. Does that make sense or not?

THEAETETUS: Yes, it's true.

SOCRATES: And this is the first of the cases I described.[1]

THEAETETUS: Yes.

SOCRATES: The second was that if I know one of you, but don't know the other, and am currently perceiving neither of you, I could never confuse the one I know with the one I don't know.

THEAETETUS: Right.

b SOCRATES: And the third was that if I know neither of you, and am currently perceiving neither of you, I cannot confuse one of the two I don't know with the other whom I also don't know. Please imagine that I've repeated the rest of the cases I enumerated before, where I will never form false beliefs about you and Theodorus, either because I know or don't know both, or because I know one but not the other; and the same goes for perception as well. Do you follow?

THEAETETUS: Yes.

SOCRATES: Well, one remaining case,[2] where false belief must arise, is when I know you and Theodorus, and retain the marks of both of you (as if you were signet-rings!) in that
c hypothetical wax block; I see you both indistinctly at a distance; I am motivated to assign each one's proper mark to the appropriate visual perception – that is, I want to recognize you, by inserting and fitting the perceptions I have of you to their memory-traces; but then I make a mistake and, just like those who put their shoes on the wrong feet, I get

1. Case [1]; cases [2] and [3] immediately follow.

2. Case [17].

things the wrong way round and apply the sight of each of you to the other's mark – or my mistake could be likened to the experience of looking in a mirror, when the flow of vision transposes left and right.[1] This is the time when cross-belief *d* – that is, false belief – occurs.

THEAETETUS: I think you're probably right, Socrates. You have given a wonderful account of what happens to belief.

SOCRATES: But that's not all: it can also occur when I know both of you, and additionally perceive one of you, but not the other – but don't have my knowledge of the one I am perceiving matched to the perception.[2] This was how I put it before, but you didn't understand me then.

THEAETETUS: No.

SOCRATES: What I was saying then[3] was that if *a* is known and is being perceived, and the knowledge of *a* is *e* matched to the perception, he will never be confused with *b*, who is also known and perceived, and the knowledge of whom is also matched to the perception. Wasn't that what I said?

THEAETETUS: Yes.

SOCRATES: But there remained the case I mentioned just now,[4] where we agree that false belief occurs – if both *a* and *b* are known, and both *a* and *b* are being seen (or perceived in *194a* some other way), but each mark[5] is not matched to its perception. It is like the shot of a bad archer, which swerves from the target and misses – and another word for such missing is 'error'.

THEAETETUS: Naturally.

SOCRATES: And when there is a current perception for

1. See *Timaeus* 46a–c.

2. Case [15].

3. Case [9], used to illustrate the difference between matching and mismatching.

4. Case [17] again; it is repeated because it can now be distinguished from [9], with which it is identical apart from the crucial point about mismatching.

5. Reading τὸ σημεῖον with manuscripts BW.

one of the marks, but not the other, and the mark of the absent perception is fitted to the current perception, then thinking is thoroughly erroneous.[1]

b To sum up: if our present view is sound, it is apparently impossible to be in error and to have false beliefs about things which are unknown and have never been perceived. It is in cases where things are both known and are being perceived that belief wheels and whirls about, and ends up true or false.[2] It is true when it brings together stamps and imprints in a perfectly straight line; it is false when it swerves and goes askew.

THEAETETUS: Well, does the view hold good, Socrates?

c SOCRATES: You'll be even more inclined to think so when you've heard what I'm about to say; I mean, it is good to have true beliefs, but bad to be in error.

THEAETETUS: Of course.

SOCRATES: And it is said that the reason for this is as follows. When a person's mental wax is deep, plentiful, smooth and worked to the right consistency,[3] then whatever enters by means of the senses and makes marks on the 'heart' (Homer's word hints at the heart's similarity to wax[4]) ... anyway, people whose wax is like that get marks imprinted

d which are clean and of sufficient depth to last a long time. In the first place, then, such people are good at learning; secondly, they have good memories; thirdly, their beliefs are true, because they don't mismatch perceptions and marks. This in turn is because their marks are clear and well spaced, so that they can quickly distribute everything from the real world (as it is called) to the proper impressions.[5] People like this are called clever, don't you think?

1. Case [15] again.

2. This is a casual summary, since it implies only case [17] of the three cases where false belief was said to be possible.

3. Reading εἰργασμένος with the manuscripts.

4. A Homeric word for 'heart', the seat of the emotions and even understanding, is ker; the Greek for 'wax' is keros. The pun is untranslatable.

5. Reading ἐπὶ τὰ αὐτῶν ἐκμαγεῖα ἕκαστα.

THEAETETUS: An extraordinarily good account.

SOCRATES: All right. But when a person has an 'unkempt *e* heart' (which was praised by the poet in his great wisdom),[1] or when it is dirty, with impurities in the wax, or when it is too moist or too hard – well, moist wax makes for good learning ability, but forgetfulness, hard wax for the opposite. Those in whom it is unkempt and rough, a gritty sort of thing, contaminated and clogged with earth and dirt, get unclear impressions. Hardness causes impressions which are unclear because they lack depth. And moistness causes impressions which are unclear too, because they collapse and 195*a* get blurred. And, as if all this weren't enough, there are impressions which are even less distinct: those which are crowded together for lack of space in a mind which is half-formed and narrow. So all these people are liable to false beliefs, because when they see or hear or think of something, they are unable to assign it quickly to its proper impression. This makes them slow-witted and, because they assign things to the wrong impressions, they invariably mis-see and mis-hear and mis-think. These are the people, then, who are said to be in error about things and to be ignorant.

THEAETETUS: Nobody could explain it better, Socrates.   *b*

SOCRATES: Are we to say, then, that there are such things as false beliefs?

THEAETETUS: Definitely.

SOCRATES: And true ones?

THEAETETUS: And true ones.

SOCRATES: So we now think we have satisfactory grounds for concluding that, beyond the shadow of a doubt, there are both these kinds of belief. Yes?

THEAETETUS: Most emphatically.

SOCRATES: There can't be many afflictions, Theaetetus, which are more awful and unpleasant then verbiage.

1. *Iliad* 2.851, 16.554. The phrase is literally 'shaggy heart', and is reckoned to be a transferred epithet from the virility of a hairy chest! This would be something for Homer to praise, but Plato takes the word to imply a dirty wax block.

THEAETETUS: Now what are you getting at?

c   SOCRATES: I'm fed up with my own stupidity and verbiage. Yes, that's the right word. What else could you call stretching arguments this way and that, because of being too dense to listen to reason, and clinging resolutely to each and every thesis?

THEAETETUS: But what in particular are you annoyed at?

SOCRATES: I'm not just annoyed; I'm afraid too, of what response I would make to the question, 'So, Socrates, you've made a discovery, have you? That false belief lies not in the relation of perceptions to one another or of thoughts to one

d   another, but in the linking of perception with thought?' I would agree, I suppose, and give myself a pat on the back for this fine discovery of ours.

THEAETETUS: *I* think this breakthrough is fine, Socrates.

SOCRATES: 'So,' he goes on, 'does your position entail that a man, whom we are only thinking of, but not seeing, could never be confused with a horse, which we are also only thinking of, and not seeing or touching or perceiving in some other way?' I imagine I'll agree.

THEAETETUS: Yes, you'd be right to do so.

e   SOCRATES: 'Well then,' he'll say, 'doesn't it follow that an eleven which is only being thought of, and nothing else, could never be confused with a twelve which is also only being thought of?' Come on, it's your turn to answer.

THEAETETUS: My answer is that sight or touch might make someone take eleven for twelve, but he could never form this mistaken belief about the contents of his mind.

SOCRATES: What about when someone considers five and

196a seven in his own mind, all by himself? I'm not talking about someone intending to investigate five people and seven other people, or anything like that; I mean five and seven themselves, which we agree are recorded on the wax block and cannot be the objects of false belief. What do you think? On any occasion when they are thought about – that is, become the subjects of internal conversation – and the question arises what their sum is, does it ever happen that one person concludes that they are eleven, another that they are twelve, or does everyone conclude that they are twelve?

THEAETETUS: Good heavens, no! Eleven is the more likely *b* answer! And the greater the number that is thought about, the greater the chance of error. I mention larger numbers because I take you to be talking about any number.

SOCRATES: You're right. And don't you think that what is happening in this situation is precisely that twelve is being confused in the wax block with eleven?

THEAETETUS: It looks that way.

SOCRATES: Doesn't this revive what we were saying at the beginning?[1] I mean, this is an experience of something known being mistaken for something else which is also known, which is what we were describing as impossible. And that was exactly the reason we found it impossible to account for false belief, because otherwise there would inevitably have been simultaneous knowledge and ignorance of the same *c* thing.

THEAETETUS: You're quite right.

SOCRATES: So we must drop our assertion that false belief is thought swerving in relation to perception, because if that were right, purely mental error would be impossible. But as things stand, either there is no such thing as false belief, or something known can be not known. Which of these alternatives do you prefer?

THEAETETUS: That's an impossible choice you're offering, Socrates.

SOCRATES: But it looks as though the argument will not *d* sanction both alternatives. We must stop at nothing, however; so what about trying a bit of skulduggery?

THEAETETUS: What?

SOCRATES: Being prepared to describe what knowing is like.

THEAETETUS: Why is this skulduggery?

SOCRATES: It has apparently slipped your mind that the whole discussion, right from the start, has been an inquiry

1. See 188b.

into knowledge, on the basis of our ignorance of what it is.

THEAETETUS: I appreciate that.

SOCRATES: Then doesn't it strike you as dishonourable for us to assert what knowing is like, when we are ignorant about knowledge? But in fact, Theaetetus, our conversation
e has been contaminated by impurities for a long time! Countless times we've said 'We know' or 'We do not know', 'We have knowledge' or 'We have no knowledge', as if we could understand each other in the slightest, as long as we remain ignorant about knowledge. And never mind the past; we're at it again at the moment! We've just used the words 'ignorant' and 'understand', as if we had a right to use them while knowledge eludes us.

THEAETETUS: But how will you carry on the conversation, Socrates, if you avoid these words?

197a SOCRATES: I'll have to use them: my character leaves me no choice, since I'm not a casuist. If one of *them* were here now, he would claim to avoid these words, and he would come down on us extremely hard for the faults I've mentioned. Anyway, we're not up to this standard, so do you want me to take that step? Shall I describe what knowing is like? I think it might be helpful.

THEAETETUS: Yes, please go ahead. We'll hardly hold it against you if you fail to avoid those words.

SOCRATES: Well, have you heard the topical description of knowing?

THEAETETUS: Probably, but I can't recall it at the moment.

b SOCRATES: They say it is the having of knowledge.[1]

THEAETETUS: That's right.

SOCRATES: Let's make a small change and describe it as the possession of knowledge.

THEAETETUS: What's the difference, in your opinion?

SOCRATES: There probably isn't any; but why don't you hear my idea and help me assess it?

1. The description occurs at *Euthydemus* 277b, in the mouth of the sophist Dionysodorus. It may well be a sophistic dictionary definition: the sophists were often concerned with the correct meaning of words.

THEAETETUS: I will, if I can.

SOCRATES: Well, I don't think possession and having are the same. For instance, if someone has bought a coat and owns it, but isn't wearing it, we say that he possesses it, but doesn't have it.

THEAETETUS: True.

SOCRATES: Do you think it is equally possible to possess, *c* but not have, knowledge as well? Think of the analogy of someone who has tracked down some wild birds (pigeons or whatever) and keeps them at home in a pigeonry he's constructed. Surely we would say that in a sense he always has them, because he possesses them, wouldn't we?

THEAETETUS: Yes.

SOCRATES: But in another sense he has none of them, except potentially. Because they are under his control in his own enclosure, he has given himself the ability to track down, get hold of and *have* any one of them he wants, and to let it go *d* again; the occasion is up to him, and he can do this as often as he likes.

THEAETETUS: True.

SOCRATES: Here we go again, then. Earlier we constructed a kind of block of wax in our minds; now let's equip each mind with an aviary for all sorts of birds, some in exclusive flocks, some in small groups, and some flying alone, here, there and everywhere among all the rest.[1]

THEAETETUS: All right. What next?   *e*

SOCRATES: We need to make the following points: that the space is empty in infants; that the birds are to be thought of as pieces of knowledge; that to acquire a bird and confine it in the enclosure is to have learned or discovered the matter with which the piece of knowledge is concerned; and that this is what knowing is.

THEAETETUS: Granted.

SOCRATES: So what words should we use for subsequently 198*a*

1. It is not clear that there is any particular significance to this: perhaps 't is that some pieces of information carry others with them by association, either exclusively (within a single topic/species of bird) or crossing boundaries between topics; others carry no such associations.

tracking down any piece of knowledge that is wanted, for getting hold of it and having it, and for letting it go again? Do you think we should use the same names as for the original acquisition, or different ones? I'll give you a lead, to help you understand my meaning better: you acknowledge the existence of arithmetic, don't you?

THEAETETUS: Yes.

SOCRATES: Take this, then, to be the tracking down of pieces of knowledge of any number, odd or even.

THEAETETUS: All right.

SOCRATES: Arithmetic, I suppose, is the skill which affords
b control over pieces of numerical knowledge, and which allows those who transmit such knowledge to others to do so.

THEAETETUS: Yes.

SOCRATES: And we call transmission 'teaching', reception 'learning', and having, through possessing in our hypothetical aviary, we call 'knowing'.

THEAETETUS: Certainly.

SOCRATES: Now pay attention to the next step. The complete mathematician has in his mind pieces of knowledge of all numbers and therefore knows every number, doesn't he?

THEAETETUS: Of course.

c   SOCRATES: So he's in a position to count, isn't he, either by counting numbers to himself, or by counting numbers of external objects?

THEAETETUS: Of course.

SOCRATES: And an accurate description of counting is investigating how much some number in fact is, isn't it?

THEAETETUS: Yes.

SOCRATES: We find, therefore, that the person who, we agreed, knows every number *investigates* what he knows – as if he didn't know them. There are logical puzzles along these lines, which I'm sure you've come across.[1]

1. See especially *Meno* 8od–e: 'A person cannot try to discover either what he knows or what he does not know: he would not seek out what he knows, for since he knows it there is no need for the inquiry; nor would he seek out what he does not know, for he does not even know what he is to look for.' Plato's answer in *Meno* is again to distinguish between potential

THEAETETUS: I have.

SOCRATES: Now, we can employ the analogy of the *d*
acquisition and tracking down of pigeons to point out that
there are two kinds of tracking: one takes place before
acquisition and as a means to acquisition; the other takes
place after acquisition, as a means to getting hold of and
having in one's grasp what one has possessed for a while.
And this explains how even things which were learned some
time ago (that is, the pieces of knowledge which have been
present for some time) can be re-learned, in the sense of
getting hold of and having the relevant piece of knowledge,
which was acquired at some earlier date, but was not immediately available to the mind. Right?

THEAETETUS: Yes.

SOCRATES: You can now see the point of my recent *e*
question as to what we should call it when a mathematician
sets out to count or a literate person to read. It looks as
though these are cases of someone knowledgeable setting out
to re-learn from himself what he already knows.

THEAETETUS: But that sounds strange, Socrates.

SOCRATES: But are we to say that he reads or counts
what he does *not* know, when *ex hypothesi* he knows every 199*a*
letter or number?

THEAETETUS: No, that doesn't make sense either.

SOCRATES: So perhaps we should say that we're not
bothered about terminology: anyone can stretch 'knowing'
and 'learning' as he fancies. We have, however, distinguished
the possession of knowledge from the having of it. We are
saying that it is impossible not to possess a possession, and
that therefore it is never the case that something known is
not known. What is possible, however, is to get hold of a false
belief about something known, because it is possible not to
have the knowledge of it and to get hold of the wrong piece of *b*
knowledge instead. Suppose someone is tracking a piece of
knowledge among those that are flitting about, and gets hold

---

and actual knowledge; but see p. 245 for the difference between *Meno* and
Theaetetus.

of the wrong one by mistake: *that* is when he thinks that eleven is twelve, because he gets hold of the knowledge of eleven instead of the knowledge of twelve, as one might get hold of a wood-pigeon instead of a regular pigeon.

THEAETETUS: Yes, this makes sense.

SOCRATES: But when he gets hold of the one he intended to get hold of, then, we will claim, he is not in error and
c believes what is true. Is this how true and false belief arise? Have we unburdened ourselves of the earlier problems? I wonder whether or not you agree with me.

THEAETETUS: I do.

SOCRATES: Yes, we have in fact shed 'not knowing something known', because it is never the case that a possession is not possessed, whether or not there is any error involved. However, I think another, more frightening issue is looming.

THEAETETUS: What?

SOCRATES: If false belief turns out to be interchanging pieces of knowledge . . .

THEAETETUS: Then what?

d SOCRATES: In the first place, it means that a person's ignorance of a piece of knowledge which he has is due, not to ignorance, but to his own knowledge! Secondly, isn't the idea, that the latter piece of knowledge is believed to be the former (and vice versa), quite ridiculous, since it means that although knowledge is present, it is possible for the mind to know nothing and be ignorant of everything? I mean, if you follow this line of reasoning, then if knowledge can make one ignorant, what's to stop ignorance making one know something, or blindness making one see?

e THEAETETUS: Perhaps, Socrates, we were wrong to restrict the birds to pieces of knowledge, and we should have included pieces of ignorance flying about in the mind as well. Then a person who is tracking birds can sometimes get hold of a piece of knowledge of something, but sometimes a piece of ignorance of the same thing. False belief would be due to the piece of ignorance, true belief to the piece of knowledge.

SOCRATES: I can't help admiring you, Theaetetus; but please think again about your suggestion. I mean, suppose you were right, that someone who gets hold of a piece of ignorance will form a false belief. That's what you're saying, isn't it?   200a

THEAETETUS: Yes.

SOCRATES: Of course, he won't *think* that his belief is false.

THEAETETUS: No.

SOCRATES: He'll think it's true, and he'll behave as if he knew what in fact he is in error about.

THEAETETUS: Agreed.

SOCRATES: So he'll think that he has tracked down and has a piece of knowledge, not a piece of ignorance.

THEAETETUS: Obviously.

SOCRATES: So we've gone through all this rigmarole only to find ourselves back at the original difficulty. Our friend, the expert in refutation, will laugh and say, 'Gentlemen, you have several choices: either both the piece of knowledge and *b* the piece of ignorance are known, in which case something known is confused with something else which is also known; or neither are known, in which case something unknown is confused with something else which is also unknown; or one of them is known, but not the other, in which case something known is confused with something unknown (or vice versa). Which choice will you take? Or will you resort to there being *further* pieces of knowledge, of the original pieces of knowledge and ignorance, which are confined in *further* ridiculous aviaries or wax blocks, and which are known by their pos- *c* sessor as long as he possesses them, even if he doesn't have them available in his mind? This is a guaranteed method of running round and round in circles, always returning to the same spot, and getting nowhere.' What will we reply to this, Theaetetus?

THEAETETUS: Help, Socrates! *I* don't know what we should say.

SOCRATES: So perhaps the argument is justified in telling us off; perhaps it is showing us that we were wrong to abandon the inquiry into knowledge and try to deal with false belief first. The fact is that a satisfactory understanding *d* of knowledge is prior to the possibility of knowing about false belief.

THEAETETUS: At the moment, Socrates, I can only agree with you.

SOCRATES: Let's start all over again, then: how is knowledge to be defined? I'm assuming that we're not ready to give up yet.

THEAETETUS: Certainly not, unless *you* are.

SOCRATES: Well then, how can we describe it with the least risk of contradicting ourselves?

e   THEAETETUS: The same as we tried before, Socrates. I'm incapable of coming up with anything else.

SOCRATES: What was that?

THEAETETUS: That true belief is knowledge. At any rate, true belief is incorrigible and always has fine and beneficial consequences.[1]

SOCRATES: Experience will be the best teacher, Theaetetus, as the river-guide said. In our case too, if we go ahead and probe this idea, we might stumble upon what we're after,
201*a* but staying still never brought anything into focus.

THEAETETUS: You're right: let's get on with the inquiry.

SOCRATES: Well, this won't take long. There's a whole area of expertise which proves that true belief isn't knowledge.

THEAETETUS: What do you mean? Which area of expertise?

SOCRATES: The one practised by those paragons of wisdom, who are called orators and lawyers. I'm sure you appreciate that these people do not teach, but use their expertise to persuade and make others believe whatever they want them to believe. Or do you think that there are teachers skilful enough to be able, in the short time allotted,[2] satis-
b factorily to teach the truth about events, when the people

---

1. Incorrigibility is, of course, a chief mark of knowledge (see 152c, 160d, 186e). The commendable consequences of true belief are presumably that it doesn't lead to error or erroneous action – but then this is false, since a true belief can be a premiss for a false conclusion.

2. See p. 67, n. 2.

they are teaching weren't there in person at the robbery or whatever crime it was?

THEAETETUS: No, I don't think that at all. I think they can only persuade.

SOCRATES: And to persuade people is to make them believe something, in your opinion?

THEAETETUS: Yes, certainly.

SOCRATES: Now, when a jury has been persuaded, fairly, of things which no one but an eyewitness could possibly know, then, in reaching a decision based on hearsay, they do so without knowledge, but get hold of true belief, given that *c* their verdict is fair because what they have been made to believe is correct.

THEAETETUS: Absolutely.

SOCRATES: But if true belief and knowledge [1] were identical, my friend, then even the best juryman in the world would never form a correct belief, but fail to have knowledge; so it looks as though they are different.

THEAETETUS: Something I'd forgotten has just come back to me, Socrates: I once heard someone suggesting that true belief accompanied by a rational account is knowledge, whereas true belief unaccompanied by a rational account is distinct *d* from knowledge; and he also said that things which are not susceptible to a rational account are not knowable – that's what he actually called them [2] – whereas things which are susceptible to a rational account are knowable.

SOCRATES: I'm glad you brought this up. But tell me on what grounds he distinguished things which are knowable from those which aren't, to see if you and I have heard the same version.

THEAETETUS: I don't know if I can unearth that, but I think I could make sense of someone else's explanation!

1. Omitting καὶ δικαστήρια with Heindorf.

2. On this translation, Theaetetus is expressing surprise at the idea that the elements are unknowable. An alternative translation – 'I quote his actual word' – suggests more strongly that Plato has a definite person in mind, rather than that he is perpetuating the whimsy of external authorship for the theory. See pp. 223 ff.

SOCRATES: Here's my dream, then, to compare with
e yours.[1] I have the impression that I too have heard a theory,
that the primary elements, as it were,[2] of which human
beings and everything else are composed, are not susceptible
to rational accounts. Each of them, taken just by itself, can
only be named, but nothing else can be said about it. You
can't say that it is, or that it is not: that would already be to
202*a* attribute being or not being to it, but nothing extra should be
assigned to it at all, if that thing itself is independently to
enter a discussion. In fact, you shouldn't even use 'itself',
'that', 'each', 'independent', 'this' or any other extra, since
these attributes run around and get applied to everything,
and are different from what they are attributed to. If it were
possible for a primary to be spoken of, if it had its own appropriate account, all these attributes should be avoided in
speaking of it. But in fact it is impossible to give a rational
b account of any of these primaries; it is only possible to name
it, since a name is all it has. However, it is different in the
case of the things that are composed of these elements: just as
the elements are woven together, so their names[3] may be
woven together to produce a spoken account, because an
account is essentially a weaving together of names. This
explains how although the elements are unaccompanied by a
rational account and are unknowable (but perceptible), yet
the complexes are knowable, accessible to a rational account,
and susceptible to true belief. So when someone gets hold of a
true belief about something, but can't give an account of it,
c his mind is not in error about it, but he doesn't *know* it: I
mean, anyone who can't give and receive an account of
something is ignorant of it. But if in addition he gets hold of a
rational account of it, everything that we have mentioned,
including being perfectly knowledgeable, becomes possible.

1. See pp. 217–18 on the use of the image of a dream.

2. 'Element' translates *stoicheion*, which also means 'letter' or 'unit of sound': see p. 218.

3. That is, the names of the elements, not the names of the things that are composed of the elements.

Is this the version you heard in your dream, or is yours different?

THEAETETUS: No, that's it exactly.

SOCRATES: Well, are you happy with it? Will you adopt the suggestion that knowledge is true belief accompanied by a rational account?

THEAETETUS: Absolutely.

SOCRATES: Theaetetus, have we now found a way to *d* grasp, on this day, something which many intelligent people have spent a long time looking for and which still eludes them, though they have grown old in the attempt?

THEAETETUS: Well, I think this theory is all right, Socrates.

SOCRATES: Yes, it may well be that the definition itself is correct. I mean, surely a rational account and true belief are prerequisites of knowledge? But there's one aspect of the theory which I'm not happy with.

THEAETETUS: What's that?

SOCRATES: Where it is apparently at its most ingenious, in the claim that the elements are unknowable, but the com- *e* plexes are knowable.

THEAETETUS: Isn't this correct?

SOCRATES: We'd better find out. We've got hostages, so to speak, for the theory, in the models it used when making this claim.

THEAETETUS: What models?

SOCRATES: Letters and syllables.[1] What else do you think the author of the theory had in mind?

THEAETETUS: Nothing else.

SOCRATES: So let's lay hands on them and force them to *203a* reveal the truth – or rather, let's interrogate ourselves, to see whether or not our literacy was gained in a way that fits in with the theory.[2] Here's the first question: can one give a rational account of syllables, but not of letters?

THEAETETUS: It seems probable.

SOCRATES: Quite; I think so too. At any rate, surely you'll

1. See p. 116, n. 2.

2. See 206a especially.

have an answer about the first syllable of 'Socrates', if someone asked, 'Tell me, Theaetetus, what is SO?'

THEAETETUS: Yes, my reply would be that it is S and O.

SOCRATES: So there's your account of the syllable, isn't it?

THEAETETUS: Yes.

b SOCRATES: All right, then: tell me also what your account of S is.

THEAETETUS: How can one say what the elements of an element are? I mean, the fact is, Socrates, that S is one of the soundless letters, but makes a noise as if the tongue were hissing. Or take B: this is both soundless and noiseless, as are most of the letters. So the idea that they are not susceptible to a rational account is excellent; even the seven most distinct letters only have sound, but no rational account at all.[1]

SOCRATES: Here's an actual firm conclusion in our inquiry into knowledge, then.

THEAETETUS: Evidently.

c SOCRATES: But have we proved that although letters are not knowable, yet syllables are?

THEAETETUS: It's *plausible*.

SOCRATES: Well, we have a choice: either we say that a syllable is both of its letters (or all its letters, if there are more than two); or we say that a syllable is some single identity which comes into being when the letters are combined. Which do you think it is?

THEAETETUS: I think we should say that it's all its letters.

SOCRATES: So see how this works in the case of the two letters, S and O. Together they are the first syllable of my name. Does anyone who knows the syllable know both the letters?

d THEAETETUS: Of course.

1. The Greeks classified letters according to how much breath is used in sounding them: thus those which use the most breath are the seven vowels (literally 'the sounded ones'); those which use the least are the mutes (our 'stops'), which are 'soundless and noiseless'; and between these are various Greek letters, which we would class as nasals, sibilants and continuants, but which Aristotle called semi-vowels, which are 'soundless, but make some noise'. See *Cratylus* 424c–d and *Philebus* 18b–c.

SOCRATES: He knows the S and the O.

THEAETETUS: Yes.

SOCRATES: Well, can he be ignorant of each of them individually, and know both while knowing neither?

THEAETETUS: No, that would be an odd and irrational thing to say, Socrates.

SOCRATES: But if each must be known for both to be known, then knowledge of the letters is a necessary prerequisite to knowledge of the syllable – and that would be the last we'd see of our fine theory!

THEAETETUS: A rather sudden departure.   *e*

SOCRATES: Because we weren't keeping a close eye on it. Perhaps the syllable should not be taken to be the letters, but a single something which arises out of the letters, has its own identity and is different from the letters.

THEAETETUS: All right. That may be more like it.

SOCRATES: Let's look into the idea; it might provide a way to put an end to our cowardly betrayal of an important and imposing theory.

THEAETETUS: Yes.

SOCRATES: Suppose what we are now saying is right, and   204*a*
a complex (of letters or anything else) is a single identity which arises out of the combination of the several elements.

THEAETETUS: All right.

SOCRATES: The complex must not have parts, then.

THEAETETUS: Why not?

SOCRATES: Because wherever there are parts, the whole is necessarily identical to the set of its parts – unless you think that the whole too is a single identity which arises out of its parts and is different from the set of its parts. Is that what you think?

THEAETETUS: Yes.

SOCRATES: Do you think that a totality and a whole are identical, or different from each other?   *b*

THEAETETUS: I don't know for certain, but your standing orders[1] are for me to volunteer answers, so I'll take the plunge and say that they are different.

1. 187b.

SOCRATES: You're right not to hold back, Theaetetus; we must see if your answer is right too.

THEAETETUS: Yes, it needs further consideration.

SOCRATES: So the thesis before us is that a whole and a totality can differ. Right?

THEAETETUS: Yes.

SOCRATES: Well now, is there a difference between a totality and a complete set? For example, when we say 'one, two, three, four, five, six', or 'two times three', or

c 'three times two', or 'three plus two plus one', are we talking about the same thing in all these cases, or different things?

THEAETETUS: The same thing.

SOCRATES: That is, six?

THEAETETUS: Precisely.

SOCRATES: So each expression refers to a set of six?

THEAETETUS: Yes.

SOCRATES: And isn't there a totality that is referred to when we refer to the set?

THEAETETUS: Necessarily.

SOCRATES: That is, six?

THEAETETUS: Precisely.

d SOCRATES: In the case of anything which consists of quantity, therefore, doesn't 'the totality' and 'the complete set' refer to the same thing?

THEAETETUS: Obviously.

SOCRATES: So what we are saying[1] is this, that the quantity of an acre and an acre are the same thing. Yes?

THEAETETUS: Yes.

SOCRATES: And likewise for the quantity of a mile.

THEAETETUS: Yes.

SOCRATES: Moreover, the quantity of an army and an army are the same thing; and this is equally true of anything else of this kind. In these cases the total quantity is the totality of each thing.

THEAETETUS: Yes.

---

1. Reading λέγομεν with some manuscripts.

SOCRATES: Is the quantity of any of these things different *e*
from its parts?

THEAETETUS: No.

SOCRATES: Now, anything which has parts consists of
parts, doesn't it?

THEAETETUS: Obviously.

SOCRATES: And we have agreed that the complete set of
parts is the totality, since the total quantity is the totality.

THEAETETUS: Yes.

SOCRATES: Now, if a whole were the same as the complete
set of parts, it would be a totality. The thesis before us, therefore, entails that a whole does not consist of parts.

THEAETETUS: Apparently not.

SOCRATES: But what can a part be a part of, if not a
whole?

THEAETETUS: A totality.

SOCRATES: You're putting up a brave defence, Theaetetus. 205*a*
But isn't something a totality precisely when there is nothing
missing?

THEAETETUS: Necessarily.

SOCRATES: And isn't a whole exactly the same thing –
something from which nothing is missing? Isn't it the case
that if something has anything missing, it is neither a whole
nor a totality? You see, the same consequence arises from the
same condition in both cases.

THEAETETUS: I now think that there is no difference
between a totality and a whole.

SOCRATES: Now, weren't we just saying[1] that wherever
there are parts, the whole – that is, the totality – is identical to
the set of its parts?

THEAETETUS: Yes.

SOCRATES: So let's return to the point I was trying to
make before: the dilemma is that either the syllable is not the *b*
same as its letters, in which case it cannot have the letters as
parts of itself, or it is the same as its letters, in which case they
are just as knowable as it. Isn't that so?

1. 204a.

THEAETETUS: Yes.

SOCRATES: And it was in order to avoid the latter consequence that we suggested that the syllable was *not* the same
as its letters, didn't we?

THEAETETUS: Yes.

SOCRATES: But if, then, *letters* are not parts of a syllable,
what else could be? Can you think what the parts of a syllable
are, if you discount the letters?

THEAETETUS: Not in the slightest, Socrates. I mean, on
the assumption that there are parts of a syllable, it is absurd
to discard the letters and look elsewhere.

c   SOCRATES: So the present argument forces us to conclude,
Theaetetus, that a syllable is a single identity which is not
divisible into parts.

THEAETETUS: It looks that way.

SOCRATES: Do you remember, my friend, that not long
ago we accepted and approved the idea that there is no
rational account of the primary constituents of things, because each of them, taken just by itself, is incomposite? We
agreed that one should not say of any of them that it 'is' or
that it is 'this', on the grounds that these predicates are different from it and are not intrinsic to it; and we agreed that this
is the reason why each of them is not susceptible to a rational
account and is unknowable.

THEAETETUS: I remember.

d   SOCRATES: In other words, the reason is that[1] each of
them is single in form and indivisible into parts, isn't it? At
any rate, I can see no other reason.

THEAETETUS: There obviously isn't any other reason.

SOCRATES: Therefore, if a complex or a syllable has no
parts and is a single identity, hasn't it turned out to be the
same kind of thing as an element or a letter?

THEAETETUS: Absolutely.

SOCRATES: There are two possibilities, then. If a syllable is
a whole and is the same as its constituent letters (however
many there may be), then, since we found that a complete set

1. Reading τό with Bonitz.

of parts is the same as a whole, a syllable and its letters are equally knowable and expressible in a rational account.

THEAETETUS: Certainly. *e*

SOCRATES: If, on the other hand, a syllable is single and indivisible, then it is just as inexpressible in a rational account and as unknowable as a letter, and for the same reason.

THEAETETUS: I can only agree.

SOCRATES: It follows that we should not accept the view that whereas a syllable or complex is knowable and expressible in an account, a letter or element is not.

THEAETETUS: No, we shouldn't, if we find the argument convincing.

SOCRATES: In fact, wouldn't your personal experience 206*a* of becoming literate incline you more to the opposite view?

THEAETETUS: What do you mean?

SOCRATES: I mean that all the time you were learning, you were doing nothing else but trying to distinguish the shape and sound of each letter just by itself, so as not to be confused by its applications in speech and writing.

THEAETETUS: You're perfectly right.

SOCRATES: And when you were a pupil at the music teacher's, wasn't the goal to be able to follow each sound and *b* say which note it was – notes, as no one would dispute, being the elements of music?

THEAETETUS: Precisely.

SOCRATES: Therefore, if it is legitimate to draw inferences from the elements and complexes with which we are personally familiar to other cases, we will claim that elements can be known far more clearly, and that a perfect grasp of any subject depends far more on knowing elements than on knowing complexes; and if anyone says that a complex is by its nature knowable, while an element is not, we will not take him seriously, whether or not he means to be serious.

THEAETETUS: Definitely.

SOCRATES: I think this is a thesis whose truth we could *c* find other ways to demonstrate. But let us not be distracted by them into ignoring the matter before us, which is the meaning of the notion that a rational account added to true belief yields knowledge in the full sense of the word.

THEAETETUS: Yes, we must look into this.

SOCRATES: All right, what do we understand by 'rational account'? There seem to me to be three possibilities.

THEAETETUS: What are they?

d   SOCRATES: The first would be to express one's thought in words and phrases by means of speech – forming an image of one's belief in this oral emission, as if in a mirror or a pond. Don't you think that this is a rational account?

THEAETETUS: I do. At any rate, we say that someone doing this is speaking or giving an account.

SOCRATES: But on the other hand, this is something everyone can do; some do it faster than others, but anyone who's not been deaf and dumb from birth can express what he thinks about anything. So this would obviously mean that
e   every correct belief is accompanied by a 'rational account', and we would be left with no way to distinguish mere correct belief from knowledge.

THEAETETUS: True.

SOCRATES: Well, we shouldn't just summarily condemn as nonsense the assertion that knowledge is to be defined in the way we are currently considering. We probably haven't yet found what the assertion means; perhaps it's referring to the ability to reply to a question about what something is by
207a means of the elements of that thing.

THEAETETUS: Please could you give me an example, Socrates.

SOCRATES: I'm thinking of how Hesiod, for instance, says about a wagon, 'There are one hundred timbers to a wagon.'[1] Now, I couldn't say what they are, and I don't suppose you could either; we'd be happy, if someone asked us what a wagon is, to be able to reply, 'Wheels, axle, chassis, rails, yoke.'

THEAETETUS: Quite.

1. *Works and Days* 456.

SOCRATES: But he'd probably think that we're making fools of ourselves. I mean, our belief is correct and we've given an account, but suppose the question had been *b* what your name is, and we'd answered by going through its *syllables*: it'd be foolish to fancy ourselves literate and to think that we knew and had given an expert account of the name 'Theaetetus'. He'd probably counter by saying that it's impossible to give a *knowledgeable* account of anything, until true belief is supported by going through its *elements* from beginning to end – as we said earlier, in fact.[1]

THEAETETUS: Yes, we did say that.

SOCRATES: Well, the same goes for the case of the wagon too: *we* have only correct belief, but someone who is also able to explain what it is by going through those hundred parts has got hold of a rational account, as well as having true *c* belief; instead of having to rely on conjectural beliefs, he has become expert and knowledgeable about what a wagon is, because he's gone through the whole from beginning to end, by means of its elements.

THEAETETUS: Does this strike you as a sound view, Socrates?

SOCRATES: Tell me if it strikes you as sound, my friend; then we can look into it. Do you approve of the idea that to go through the elements of something is to give a rational account of that thing, whereas to go through complexes or any even larger units there may be is to fail to give a rational account?
d

THEAETETUS: Yes, I certainly accept the idea.

SOCRATES: Do you do so in the belief that knowledge of something involves uncertainty either about whether some element belongs to it or to something else, or about whether its elements are this or that?

THEAETETUS: Definitely not.

SOCRATES: Have you forgotten, then, that when you were

1. 206a: in other words, this is the type of 'rational account' the dream theory assumed (see pp. 218ff.).

just starting to learn your letters, you and your fellow pupils did just that?[1]

THEAETETUS: Are you thinking of how we were uncertain
e which letters belonged to a syllable, and which syllable was the right one to put a certain letter in?

SOCRATES: Yes, that's what I mean.

THEAETETUS: Well, I most certainly have not forgotten that! And no, I don't think that people in this condition yet have knowledge.

SOCRATES: So when someone is at that stage and is writing 'Theaetetus', and thinks he ought to write THE and
208a does so, and when he next tries to write 'Theodorus', and thinks he should write TE and does so, will we say that he *knows* the first syllable of your names?

THEAETETUS: But we've just agreed that someone in that condition doesn't yet have knowledge.

SOCRATES: And is there anything to stop this person being in the same condition vis-à-vis the second, third and fourth syllables of your name?

THEAETETUS: No, nothing.

SOCRATES: But when he writes 'Theaetetus' with all the letters in their proper order, he'll have correct belief and he'll be using the method of going through it element by element, won't he?

THEAETETUS: Obviously.

b   SOCRATES: And, as we agree, he is not yet knowledgeable, but just has correct belief. Right?

THEAETETUS: Yes.

SOCRATES: He has a rational account, though, and it's accompanied by true belief. I mean, he's used the element-by-element method, and that's what we agreed constitutes a rational account.

THEAETETUS: True.

SOCRATES: It follows, my friend, that it is possible for true belief to be accompanied by a rational account and still not be entitled to the name of knowledge.

1. Reading αὐτὰ ταῦτα.

THEAETETUS: So it seems.

SOCRATES: It looks as though our wealth was illusory, then: we were just dreaming when we imagined that we held in our hands the truest possible account of knowledge. Or could it be that this unfavourable verdict is premature? The definition we've just been considering may well not do, but *c* there's still one left of the three possibilities we mentioned for the meaning of 'rational account' in the definition of knowledge as correct belief accompanied by a rational account.

THEAETETUS: Yes, there's still one left; thanks for the reminder. The first was a sort of image of thought in speech; the second, which we've just finished with, was approaching the whole by means of the elements. What is the third one?

SOCRATES: Probably the most common: being able to mention some mark which differentiates the object in question from everything else.

THEAETETUS: Can you give me an example of such an account of something?

SOCRATES: Take the sun as an example, if you like: I think *d* you'd be on safe ground with the idea that it is the brightest of the heavenly bodies which travel round the earth.

THEAETETUS: Yes.

SOCRATES: Do you see the point? It's what we were just saying: if you get hold of what uniquely differentiates something from everything else, you will arguably get a rational account of just that thing; but if the feature you get hold of is shared, your account will be concerned with however many things share this feature.

THEAETETUS: I understand. And I think that this des- *e* cription of a rational account is a good one.

SOCRATES: So when understanding some item's difference from everything else is added to correct belief about that item, it changes from being an object of belief to being an object of knowledge.

THEAETETUS: That's the idea, anyway.

SOCRATES: But now that I've got close to it, Theaetetus, I absolutely fail to understand it in the slightest – it's like getting close to a half-tone drawing.[1] As long as I stood back, I thought it was meaningful.

THEAETETUS: *Now* what are you getting at?

209a   SOCRATES: I'll tell you, if I can. Suppose I have correct beliefs about you: if in addition I get hold of the rational account specific to you, then I know you; if I don't, I have only beliefs about you.

THEAETETUS: Yes.

SOCRATES: And 'rational account' here means explaining your uniqueness.

THEAETETUS: Yes.

SOCRATES: So when I had only beliefs, I had no grasp at all in my mind of what constitutes your uniqueness. Is that it?

THEAETETUS: Apparently.

SOCRATES: I was thinking only of shared features, which aren't specific to you.

b   THEAETETUS: Necessarily.

SOCRATES: But how on earth, then, in that situation, were my beliefs about you rather than anyone else? Imagine me thinking that Theaetetus is the one who is a human being, has a nose, eyes and mouth, and so on for the rest of his anatomy. What guarantee is there that these thoughts put me in mind of Theaetetus, rather than Theodorus or the proverbial 'most unremarkable Mysian'?[2]

THEAETETUS: None.

SOCRATES: And suppose I didn't think only of someone c with eyes and nose, but of someone with bulging eyes and a snub nose: even so, is there any guarantee that I'll be thinking of you, rather than of myself or someone else with these features?

THEAETETUS: No.

SOCRATES: In fact, I think, Theaetetus will not be the object of my beliefs until his particular snubness of nose (and

1. Literally 'a shadow painting'. The technique is obscure, but the effect was obviously the same in this respect as our half-tone drawings.

2. Mysia was a country occupying north-west Asia Minor. Its inhabitants were proverbially feeble, and hence pre-eminently overlookable.

all the other features which make you what you are) has
made its mark and been recorded in my memory as different
from all the other snubnesses I have seen; and then, if I meet
you tomorrow, these features will call you to my mind and
make me have correct beliefs about you.

THEAETETUS: You're absolutely right.

SOCRATES: Therefore, correct belief too has to do with the *d*
uniqueness of anything.

THEAETETUS: Evidently.

SOCRATES: Well, is there any other way we can interpret
the idea of getting a rational account in addition to correct
belief? I mean, if it is telling us additionally to believe in what
way something is unique, that turns out to be a ridiculous
uggestion.

THEAETETUS: Why?

SOCRATES: It is suggesting that we still need correct belief
about the uniqueness of things whose uniqueness we already
have correct belief about! The proverbial turning of the *scy-*
tale [1] or pestle or whatever would be an understatement if *e*
applied to this suggestion: it would be closer to the mark to
call it blind man's advice. I mean, telling us that we require
something we already have, in order to get to know what we
believe, looks like the work of someone who's well and truly
in the dark.

THEAETETUS: So tell me if your recent question implied
that you had something to say. [2]

SOCRATES: If the suggestion that we still need a rational

1. This phrase is explicable by reference to Plutarch, *Lysander* 19. The
scytale was a baton and parchment used for carrying secret messages from
one Spartan commander to another. Two identical batons were made. One
commander would spiral a thin strip of parchment around his baton and
write a message along the length of the baton; when the parchment was
unwrapped, the message was unintelligible until wrapped around the twin
baton. Thus 'the turning of the *scytale*' refers to the useless attempt to
decipher the fragmented message by unravelling the parchment when it was
separated from its baton.

2. Reading εἰπὲ δὴ εἴ τι νυνδὴ ὡς ἐρῶν ἐπύθον. The text is corrupt,
but seems to refer to Socrates' question, 'Is there any other way . . .?' (209d).

account means that we need to *know* the unique feature, not just have beliefs about it, then, my boy, this – the finest of our definitions of knowledge – would be showing its naivety. I

210*a* mean, to know is to have got hold of knowledge, isn't it?

THEAETETUS: Yes.

SOCRATES: And this seems to entail the reply, to the question what knowledge is, that it is correct belief accompanied by knowledge of uniqueness, since that's how the definition would understand the addition of a rational account.

THEAETETUS: You're probably right.

SOCRATES: And nothing could be sillier than for us, who are engaged in an inquiry into knowledge, to say that it is correct belief accompanied by knowledge (of uniqueness or whatever). Therefore, Theaetetus, knowledge can be neither

b perception, nor true belief, nor true belief with the addition of a rational account.

THEAETETUS: Apparently not.

SOCRATES: Well, are we still pregnant? Is anything relevant to knowledge still causing us pain, my friend, or have we given birth to everything?

THEAETETUS: *I* most certainly have: thanks to you, I've put into words more than I had in me.

SOCRATES: And does our midwifery declare that everything we produced was still-born and that there was nothing worth keeping?

THEAETETUS: Absolutely.

SOCRATES: Well, Theaetetus, if you set out at a later date

c to conceive more ideas, and you succeed, the ideas with which you'll be pregnant will be better because of this inquiry of ours; and even if you don't get pregnant, you'll be easier to get on with, because you won't make a nuisance of yourself by thinking that you know what you don't know. This self-responsibility[1] is all my skill is capable of giving, nothing

1. It is tempting to remember that the final attempted definition of *sophrosyne* (here translated 'self-responsibility') in the early Socratic dialogue *Charmides* is 'knowledge of knowledge' (166e) – which is what Socrates is after in *Theaetetus*. But then it should also be remembered that this definition is rejected in *Charmides*.

more; I have none of the knowledge and skill that other people have – the important and remarkable people of our own times and times past. But God granted my mother and me our skill as midwives, she to attend women, I to attend young and honest men, and anyone who is good-looking. *d*

Anyway, now I have an appointment at the King's Porch, to face the indictment which Meletus has brought against me. But let's meet here again tomorrow morning, Theodorus.[1]

1. The dramatic setting of *Sophist* is the day after *Theaetetus*.

Essay

۶۰

At very first sight, *Theaetetus* looks like an early Socratic dialogue: the occasion of the dialogue is carefully staged, with an attention to detail which is reminiscent of the early dialogues; Socrates is the main speaker throughout; his irony (disavowal of knowledge) is a recurrent theme (e.g. 150c–d, 157c, 161b, 189e), as is his campaign against unexamined dogmas (187c, 210c); the whole discussion is prompted by Socrates asking for a definition of a term; attempted definitions are demolished one by one, so that the conclusion of the dialogue is aporetic – no satisfactory definition has been found; having Socrates meet a young Athenian aristocrat is typical, as is the preliminary banter between the two of them; and Theaetetus' first response to Socrates' question, 'What is knowledge?', is typical of other first responses to such questions in the early dialogues.

Despite this appearance, however, no scholar would today deny that *Theaetetus* is one of Plato's later compositions (written, say, *c.* 360 B.C.). The thoroughness of the arguments and stylometric considerations alone bear this out; one of the purposes of this essay will be briefly to show why the philosophy of the dialogue forces us to conclude that it is not only a late composition, but indeed belongs to a period when Plato was having doubts about some of his earlier ideas and assumptions.

If the dialogue is late, why did Plato choose to give it all the Socratic trimmings? The short answer, I believe, is that *Theaetetus* is a kind of homage to Socrates. The Socrates of the early Platonic dialogues spent his time asking awkward questions like 'What is courage?' or 'What is justice?' He was convinced that each of these questions is answerable, that such moral terms are capable of some single, simple definition – that is, that they are knowable. He was further convinced that without such knowledge we could not live a truly moral life. Thus knowledge is at the heart of his work. Plato's homage is to ask in *Theaetetus* what precisely this thing, knowledge, is. This is homage to Socrates as a philosopher, since the nest of questions about knowledge is central to all philosophy: 'What is knowledge?', 'What can we know?', 'How do we know anything?', and so on.

The idea that *Theaetetus* is a kind of homage to Socrates and his work is corroborated by the presence of the marvellous description of Socrates as a midwife (148e–151d), which we will consider in due course. But, of course, this purpose by no means exhausts the dialogue: the chief purpose is to explore the concept of knowledge, and so far we have dealt only with the trimmings. The bulk of this essay will be concerned with the philosophy of the dialogue, and with trying to get to grips with Plato's epistemology. Even if the dialogue fails in its ostensible aim to define knowledge, this is not to say that we learn nothing about Plato's epistemology.

The dialogue falls into four parts. The first part (142a–151d) is introductory; the second part (151d–186e) deals at length with Theaetetus' first attempt to define knowledge – he tentatively suggests that it is perception (*aisthesis*); the third part (187a–201c) consists largely of a so-called digression, on how false belief is possible, but arises from Theaetetus' second attempted definition, that knowledge is true belief (*alethes doxa*); the fourth part (201c–210d), leading up to the aporetic conclusion of the dialogue, is concerned with the definition of knowledge as true belief which is accompanied by the ability to give some account which justifies one's belief.

This is in a sense a paradigmatic progression of epistemological arguments. It seems obvious that our knowledge must be based ultimately on our acquaintance, by perception, with the outside world. If we refute the claim of perception to be knowledge, it is natural to turn next to consider states in which we reflect about the outside world and about relations between objects in the outside world.

The arguments of the dialogue are among the tightest in

the Platonic corpus; the philosophy is often tough. For both these reasons, *Theaetetus* requires some commentary. What follows is not intended to be a complete commentary, but may serve to point out some difficulties and areas of interest, and to stimulate the reader to delve more deeply into the dialogue. To that end also, I have appended a fairly thorough bibliography. If I seem to refer too often to the work of other scholars, this is because an introductory essay such as this one should be a guide to the secondary literature, as well as to the primary text. Since the purpose of the dialogue is epistemological, I have spent more time on those sections which inform us about Plato's epistemology. For convenience of cross-reference with the translation, I have discussed each section of the dialogue in order, rather than discussing the dialogue thematically. The following table may help to clarify both this and the architecture of the dialogue.

Topic	Translation (*pages*)	Essay (*pages*)
PART ONE: INTRODUCTION	15–29	135–41
Prologues	15–19	135–7
First approach to knowledge	19–25	137–9
Socrates as midwife	25–9	140–41
PART TWO: KNOWLEDGE AND PERCEPTION (*First definition*)	29–91	142–94
Theaetetus and Protagoras	29–31	145–8
The secret doctrine	31–48	149–59
Criticism of Protagoras	48–78	163–81
Criticism of the secret doctrine	78–85	181–3
Criticism of the first definition	85–91	184–8
PART THREE: KNOWLEDGE AND BELIEF (*Second definition*)	91–115	194–216
How is false belief possible?	91–114	195–215
Criticism of the second definition	114–15	215–16
PART FOUR: KNOWLEDGE AND JUSTIFIED TRUE BELIEF (*Third definition*)	115–30	216–39
Socrates' dream	115–17	217–25
Criticism of the dream theory	117–23	225–30
Criticism of the third definition	123–30	230–39

❧ PART ONE: INTRODUCTION (142a–151d) ❧

The conversation between Socrates, Theaetetus and Theodorus which makes up the dialogue is supposed to be read out by Euclid of Megara to Terpsion. Thus we get two prologues: one with Euclid and Terpsion, and another with Socrates and his two interlocutors.

❧ First Prologue (142a–143c) ❧

Euclid and Terpsion meet somewhere in Megara, perhaps at Euclid's house. Euclid has been with Theaetetus, who is returning wounded to Athens from a battle near Corinth. The date of this battle, and thus the dramatic date of the reading of the dialogue, is uncertain. Athens fought a major war against Sparta near Corinth in 394 B.C. and for a few years following, but Theaetetus would then have been in his early twenties. Since the implication of the prologue is that Theaetetus is dying, and since later writers credit him with a number of important mathematical discoveries, it may be doubted whether such an early date is plausible; some of Theaetetus' work was on solids, and Plato can still complain at *Republic* 528d (written *c.* 375) that the study of solids is 'in a ridiculous state'. Athens was again at war in the vicinity of Corinth in 369, and this is the more plausible date: the prologue suggests that Theaetetus is no longer young (142c). It is dramatically unsuitable for Terpsion to have waited thirty years before asking Euclid to recount the dialogue, but Plato may not have been disturbed by this factor: we will meet in the second prologue another example of such minor imprecision.

Of Euclid and Terpsion, the two characters of the first prologue, we know little. Both were with Socrates at his death in 399 (*Phaedo* 59c). Terpsion looks like a minor member of the Megarian group of Socratic followers; Euclid was the leader of the group. He had been a constant companion of Socrates for a while, despite having to travel to Athens from Megara during war years when Megarians were not allowed in Athens. After Socrates' death he established his own school of philosophy in Megara, blending Socratic ethics and dialectic with Eleatic metaphysics and dialectic. None of his work survives. Apart from his general interest in Socratic philosophy, the attack on Heracliteanism in the second part of the dialogue makes Euclid, as an Eleatic, a suitable person to introduce the dialogue (see 180c–e for the opposition between Heracliteanism and Eleaticism).

The dramatic details of the prologue are interesting. Though Plato tries to establish other dialogues as authentic records of Socratic conversations, this is the only one which is supposed to be actually read. And at 143b–c Plato, through Euclid, professes himself tired of the narrative form of writing, preferring the direct dialogue form. The narrative form is dropped (though tacitly) in the course of *Parmenides*, so this supports the idea that *Theaetetus* was written after *Parmenides* (see pp. 239–46); but since the direct dialogue form was used occasionally in earlier dialogues, this would hardly be conclusive evidence on its own, even though the narrative form never reappears in later dialogues.

❧ Second Prologue (143d–145c) ❧

The scene is a gymnasium in Athens, a typical haunt of Socrates and other philosophers: the gymnasia were popular meeting-places. Euclid's reference at 142c to Socrates' impending execution, and especially the final words of the dialogue, establish the year as 399 B.C., shortly before Socrates' trial. However, Plato is obviously not concerned to be meticulous about the dramatic date, since at 142c–143a he allows Euclid enough time to return more than once to Athens to pester Socrates for details of the conversation, which he could scarcely have done if Socrates was about to die.

Socrates is found chatting with Theodorus, who then introduces his young pupil Theaetetus to him. Theodorus of Cyrene, a philosopher and mathematician, is visiting Athens, which was the cultural centre of the Greek world, and lecturing there: it looks as though he was a professional teacher, like the sophists, who taught for money. Almost all we reliably know about Theodorus, and quite a bit of what we know about Theaetetus, may be read in our dialogue. At the beginning of 144c, and occasionally elsewhere, we hear that we are to imagine others present at the conversation; the only one named, however, is Socrates' namesake (147d), later to play a part in the dialogue *Statesman*.

We may ask ourselves why Plato chooses to have Socrates discuss knowledge with two mathematicians (this is not quite the 'documentary fallacy' of, say, asking how many children Lady Macbeth had). The answer, of course, may be that this conversation did historically take place, with just these participants, and Plato is merely recording it (albeit in terms of his own philosophy). But supposing the whole dialogue is a Platonic fiction, it is probably worth remembering that mathematics was the most exact science of the time: mathematicians, if anybody, might be supposed to have knowledge, given that knowledge involves certainty and truth.

✍ First Approach to Knowledge (145c–148d) ✍

Socrates introduces the topic of the dialogue by asking, 'What is knowledge?' Theaetetus' reply mentions many different branches of knowledge. This is a typical first response from a Socratic interlocutor, and is typically rejected by Socrates as giving only examples, and therefore begging the question and falling far short of being a definition. Socrates is looking for some single phrase which may be substituted for 'knowledge' in every occurrence of the term; which does not beg any questions or become liable to counter-examples; which explains why all instances of knowledge are what they are; and which may therefore be said to define, and even be, the thing, knowledge. This is a brief outline of a fascinating topic in Socratic philosophy, which has been much discussed: see any or preferably all of Irwin [68], pp. 37–68, Robinson [71], Chapter 5, Santas [72], Chapters 3 and 4, and Woodruff [77], pp. 136–60.

In *Theaetetus*, Plato tries to justify Socrates' rejection of examples. Is it a good justification? As already mentioned, it is because examples implicitly use the term to be defined and therefore beg the question. If carpentry is to be defined as 'knowledge of making wooden objects', then to define knowledge in terms of carpentry mentions the definiendum in the definiens. It is a constant and sensible principle in Socratic and Platonic epistemology that knowledge has to be based on knowledge (see Fine [145]): in searching for a definition of X, it is no good saying 'X is Y' if Y is unknown – that will not make X known. Offering examples in place of a definition is a version of transgressing the principle that knowledge has to be based on knowledge.

At 147b, Socrates says bluntly that 'no term can be meaningful without knowledge of what it stands for'. This is a common Socratic idea about the benefit of having a defini-tion, but has been honoured with the title 'the Socratic fallacy' (Geach [66]): surely we can use terms correctly even if we cannot define them? However, what he means, arguably, is that someone who has a definition of X has knowledge of X; he does not preclude himself or the rest of us from having beliefs about X and being able to recognize instances of it. He doesn't mean that we cannot, in an ordinary sense, know what carpentry is until we know what knowledge is; he means that we cannot have a philosophic understanding of carpentry. Thus elsewhere Socrates allows that examples of X and uncontroversial beliefs about X are useful checks on proposed definitions of X; and in our dialogue see 196d–197a, where Socrates brings up the fact that one has to be able to use terms even when one cannot define them. His claim, then, implicitly comes to the view that belief (ordinary knowledge) may be verified by knowledge in the strict sense. But he should have *explicitly* allowed for the limited usefulness of examples, and allowed that not every X is such that a list of examples is less useful for understanding X than a grasp on what is common to these examples (but the latter is a Witt-gensteinian objection). On the whole issue in *Theaetetus*, see Burnyeat [63].

Socrates first (147c) uses clay to illustrate the sort of answer he wants: clay is earth mixed up with liquid (his use of humdrum illustrations is a source of irritation to several interlocutors in the dialogues); then Theaetetus provides his own mathematical illustration of surds (147c–148b): his definition in effect is, 'For any positive integer n, $\sqrt{n}$ is irrational if and only if there is no positive integer m, such that $n = m \times m'$ (Burnyeat [65], p. 494). This is almost certainly Plato's acknowledgement of some work the historical Theaetetus carried out (though the historical Theaetetus seems to have gone further and defined *types* of irrational as well; the other main contribution attributed to him by later historians of mathematics is the theoretical construction of the five regular solids).

However, whether this was the work of the historical Theaetetus, or whether it is a fiction of Plato's for the purpose of the dialogue, need not concern us here. At any rate, Theaetetus improves on a method of Theodorus (147d). We have no indication of how Theodorus proved the incommensurability of $\sqrt{3}$, $\sqrt{5}$ ... $\sqrt{17}$ (for various suggestions, see Brown [60]; Brumbaugh [62], pp. 38–44; Heath [67], pp. 204–9, and Wasserstein [76]); but apparently he had to prove each separately, whereas Theaetetus provides a general formula. This is the importance of the mathematical example to the philosophy of our dialogue. For the independent importance of this piece of mathematics, see Brown [61], pp. 235–40; Heath [67], pp. 209–12, 216–17, and Wasserstein [76]; the work is enshrined in Euclid, *Elements* 10.9.

The example is also important in another respect. Precisely because it provides the kind of simplicity and generality that Socrates is after for the question about knowledge, it can provide the impetus for further exploration (as, historically, it perhaps did for the study of irrationals). Thus the forthcoming proposed definitions of knowledge each provide impetus for examination (Burnyeat [65]). In this context, it is worth noting that this introduction to *Theaetetus* is remarkably similar to that of *Meno*. In both dialogues the interlocutor gives a list of examples rather than a definition; in both dialogues mathematics is used as a model for definition; in both dialogues incommensurability is involved in the mathematical model; in *Meno* Socrates goes on to demonstrate how to elicit answers, and in *Theaetetus* the immediately following passage on midwifery depicts the background to such eliciting. In other words, we may say that Theaetetus' mathematical example is not only a model of simplicity and generality, but also provides impetus for midwifery in its field.

❧ Socrates as Midwife (148e–151d) ❧

In likening Socrates to a midwife, Plato provides a brilliant
image to account for Socrates' constant profession of ignorance (midwives are barren), but equally constant ability to
elicit people's ideas. The passage scarcely needs introduction:
it is best just to read and enjoy it, with one proviso. Although
the fame and fluency of the section should be appreciated,
they should not obscure the fact that the image is almost
certainly a Platonic fiction: there is no other record of Socrates
calling himself a midwife. At *Clouds* 135–7, the comic poet
Aristophanes has a student of Socrates respond to a noisy
knocking on the door by saying, 'You have precipitated the
miscarriage of a discovery.' But this should be taken to be a
spontaneous comic image: if the historical Socrates had
dubbed himself a midwife, Xenophon and other dialogues of
Plato would report it, but they do not. The image of mental
labour is of course quite natural; and it recurs in Plato at
Symposium 206c–e, *Republic* 490b and *Phaedrus* 278a–b. In
our dialogue, Plato has Socrates say that his midwifery is a
secret (149a), which no doubt indicates its fictional nature.
It is also likely that Plato extends the image: when Socrates
claims that midwives are match-makers (149d), the facts
that Theaetetus doesn't know this and that Socrates provides
a short argument for it suggest that it is an extension con-
trived for the parallel with Socrates (see 151b and *Laches*
201a, for example, for Socrates' 'match-making').

There is a vein of sexual imagery running throughout the
dialogues, sometimes in Socratic, sometimes in Platonic
contexts, but it leads in no certain direction, and the
metaphor in *Theaetetus* is partly similar to, but partly different
from, these earlier images. On the issue in general, see Vlastos
[73]. It is interesting to note, however, that when at 151b
Socrates says that he hands barren students over to the
sophists, there is not only palpable irony here, but also a
veiled compliment: the sophists receive those who are not *yet*
pregnant, the implication being that they can get people pregnant (but also that they should entrust the delivery and
testing of the offspring to Socrates). The image of sexual union

is here restricted to the sophists and their pupils; in earlier dialogues the attraction of Socrates for his young followers had played a part (see, for instance, the beginnings of *Lysis* and *Charmides*). Nevertheless, Socrates never consummated the union (see Alcibiades' speech in *Symposium*); in the metaphor, this now becomes the difference between the sophists filling minds from outside and Socrates leaving it up to the young man himself, so that the result is *self*-responsibility (210c).

It is best not to push the images too far, but to allow this passage of *Theaetetus* to stand on its own as a complete and vivid metaphor for Socrates' method of questioning and testing answers, while apparently being ignorant himself. The discussion by Burnyeat [64] could hardly be bettered.

We should finally notice that despite the parallelism of *Theaetetus* and *Meno* (p. 139), midwifery does not presuppose *Meno*'s theory of recollection (which is probably Platonic rather than Socratic), although it has been taken to do so since ancient times. The theory of recollection claims that we have the answers within us, and that Socratic questioning can elicit them. But the elicited answers are necessarily correct, whereas Socrates as a midwife may deliver 'still-born' ideas; and the possibility is present in *Theaetetus* that some people are never pregnant, and even (see 210c–d) that Theaetetus himself may never conceive again. Both the theory of recollection and the image of midwifery deal with the same area (Socratic method), but they do so independently and with different emphases.

So the first, introductory part of the dialogue ends. Socrates, as midwife, has recognized that Theaetetus is pregnant with potential knowledge of knowledge – that is, that he might be able to define knowledge. Socrates' job now is to elicit a definition (which, however, does not count as a birth until its implications have been grasped: see p. 41 n. 1). In order to do so, he has prepared the ground by stating what a proper definition should be like. The rest of the dialogue is taken up with successive attempted definitions and their implications, and with refuting these definitions.

◄ PART TWO: KNOWLEDGE AND PERCEPTION ►
(151d–186e)

Theaetetus first defines knowledge as perception. We now embark upon the philosophical meat of the dialogue, and it will help to begin by explaining my translation of the key epistemological terms.

◄ Translation of Terms ►

I have translated the Greek term *episteme* and its cognates throughout as 'knowledge', 'know', etc. This is the standard translation. Recently, however, some scholars have begun to prefer 'understanding' (see Burnyeat [130], Moline [42] and Moravcsik [43]). Their reasons for preferring 'understanding' as a translation are various. Burnyeat, for instance, points out that Plato is somewhat ambivalent about whether or not *episteme* is transmissible, and that Plato believes that some kind of justification is central to *episteme*. Since Burnyeat believes that transmissibility is essential to the concept of knowledge, but not to understanding, and that it is not essential, but secondary, to explain how or why we know what we know, whereas such justification is crucial to the concept of understanding, then he holds that 'understanding' is a less misleading translation of Plato's use of *episteme* than 'knowledge'. Moline, on the other hand, is more concerned with capturing the motivational aspect of *episteme*: it is a spur to action.

It would take us too far afield, and involve too technical a discussion, to enter fully into this controversy. It will have to be enough to state that the translation 'knowledge' seems to be adequate for our dialogue. The term *episteme* is common in all genres of literature before Plato, where it means 'knowledge': Plato would have to have signalled the fact that he was departing from standard usage. Arguably, understanding is knowledge of causes; if so, then it is still a species of knowledge (see Barnes [127]). It seems best to retain the translation 'knowledge', but enter any caveats that particular contexts might require. Such caveats are more necessary in early and

middle-period dialogues (see Gosling [26], Chapter 4) than in
Theaetetus.

The second term which claims our attention is *doxa*, and
its cognates. Here I have less readily defensible grounds for
employing the translation 'belief'. The alternative would be
'judgement'; the difference between the two is that the former
is dispositional, while the latter is episodic. That is, if I believe
that *p*, I have a general disposition or tendency; if I judge that
p, however, then that is what I am doing just at the moment.
The difficulty is that Plato sometimes uses *doxa* dispositionally
and sometimes episodically. Rather than misleading English
readers by using different translations in different contexts, it
is preferable to employ a single translation for Plato's single
term. Besides, even in English, the distinction is not hard and
fast: we use 'belief' episodically and 'judge' dispositionally, on
occasion. I settle for 'belief' rather than 'judgement' because
belief is the more common concept investigated in modern
epistemology, and because *prima facie* true belief is a better
candidate for knowledge than true judgement, because knowledge too is dispositional, for the most part. I have used 'belief'
in all important epistemological contexts, but elsewhere 'opinion' also translates *doxa*, and occasionally even 'impression'
(see below).

Finally, what about the term *aisthesis*? I have translated
this as 'perception'; some scholars prefer 'sensation'. The most
important thing is to bear in mind (see especially Hamlyn
[35]) that the single Greek term could mean either 'sensation'
or 'perception'; in other words the Greeks could not clearly
and easily distinguish between mere non-cognitive sensation,
and perception, which is cognitive and involves recognition
of what is being perceived. We will find, in fact, that Plato
is as clear as we could expect: he demolishes the claim of
aisthesis to be knowledge by considering both its cognitive
and its non-cognitive uses.

However, when the term *aisthesis* first occurs in the
dialogue, in Theaetetus' first definition of knowledge, it is

pointless to ask whether exclusively sensation or exclusively
perception is meant. Theaetetus is using an ordinary Greek
term in an ordinary broad way. It is highly to Plato's credit
that although he begins on Theaetetus' (and Protagoras')
ground and uses the term equally broadly, he does go some
way towards separating out the threads. This kind of reflection on ambiguities present in one's own language is often
extremely difficult. I use the translation 'perception', because
it is less narrow than 'sensation'. Plato does not talk solely
about sensation, so nor should we. 'Perception' is the closest
we can get in English to the initial vagueness of *aisthesis*: the
dictionary definitions of both terms range from sensation to
mental understanding.

One of the consequences of the vagueness of *aisthesis* for
our dialogue is that it enables us to see the continuity of
Plato's argument. He begins on equally vague grounds, using
sensible qualities as paradigmatic cases of what *aisthesis* is
concerned with (e.g. 152b–c, 154b, 156d, etc.; it is not, of
course, clear whether these sensible qualities are what we
might call mere sense-data, or also involve some interpretation), but also introducing non-sensible qualities (157d) and
faculties which are clearly not mere sensation: pleasure, pain,
desire, fear, memory, dreams and opinions all occur in the
course of the discussion, and all are legitimate entries (*pace*
many commentators who accuse Plato of unfairness). To take
the most extreme example, that of opinions, the equation of
aisthesis with appearing (*phainesthai* or *dokein*) warrants this,
since *doxa* (opinion, belief, judgement) is simply the noun
from *dokein* (hence *doxa* has occasionally been translated
'impression'). But he seems to be worried by this vagueness,
and I argue in the appropriate places (especially p. 181)
that he steadily attacks the whole range of *aisthesis*, before
finally trying to restrict the term to mere sensation, non-
cognitive apprehension of sensible qualities (184b–186e).
Then, having made this restriction, in the immediately ensuing part of the dialogue, he turns to *doxa*, having narrowed
that down, properly, to what the mind does.

ᐊᔇ Theaetetus and Protagoras (151d–152c) ᵉᕋ

Theaetetus' first proper attempt to define knowledge is that it is perception. All the discussion up to 186e stems from this definition. The length at which Plato treats it tells us immediately that our dialogue is a late composition, because he would previously have dismissed the idea out of hand (see p. 240), and that Plato is undertaking a serious, not cursory, philosophical examination of the issue.

His way of tackling the issue is roundabout. He reserves a head-on approach for later, and initially assimilates the identification of knowledge and perception with, first, Protagorean relativism and, second, the Heraclitean doctrine that all things are in flux. At first sight, these three theses seem far from identical, and Plato's strategy is therefore both bold and odd; but we may take it as a sign of thoroughness: Plato is setting Theaetetus' definition on its strongest foundation, and in attempting to refute Protagoras and Heraclitus, he is attempting to block off all avenues to the idea that perception is knowledge, before finally dealing with the idea itself.

The question how much of what Plato attributes to Protagoras in our dialogue is reliable information about the historical Protagoras is treated later (pp. 188–94). Here we need only follow the course of the argument.

The discussion starts with a couple of judicious quotes from Protagoras' modestly titled book *The Truth*, which between them establish that things are as they appear for each individual. This is illustrated in an example of the same wind appearing to be more or less cold to different people. The formula 'Things are as they appear to each individual' is reasonably identified with 'Things are as each individual perceives them to be.' The conclusion is that perception, *qua* relative, has the two crucial marks of knowledge: its objects *are* (for the individual) and it is infallible.

Strictly speaking, it should be noticed, the deduction that perception is infallible – that is, infallibly correct – is invalid (Gosling [26], pp. 145–6). The argument establishes only the relativity of perceptions, that each individual is the authority on what he thinks is the case; it does not establish that each individual is correct about what is the case. Protagoras may even be committed to the idea that knowledge is feeling certain (on which see Ayer [19], pp. 14–26); more likely, he thought that relativism guaranteed correctness: he ignores the possibility of distorted perceptions by making perception entirely relative to the perceiver (see 157e–160c, and Burnyeat [85]).

The sentence 'The objects of perception are (for the individual) and perception is infallible' uses a locution which in English is bound to sound strange: 'Its objects are.' 'Are what?' the English reader wants to ask, but he or she would be only partially correct. The verb 'to be' (*einai*) is ambiguous. It is ambiguous in English, but it is even more ambiguous in Greek. Consider, for instance, the proposition which occurs in the concluding part of the dialogue, 'A whole is its parts.' In English, as in Greek, the 'is' here could mean 'is identical to' or 'is composed of'.

The situation in Greek is even worse. There are three chief usages of the verb *einai* which should be borne in mind constantly. There is the normal predicative or copulative use, in which the verb joins a predicate to a subject: 'The sky is blue.' There is an existential use, which in English is naturally translated 'exist', and is perhaps preserved in English only in sentences like 'God is'. Finally, there is the veridical use, in which 'is' means 'is the case' or 'is true'. (I have tracked some of the vagueness of *einai* in footnotes to the text.) As a consequence of this ambiguity, the verb 'to be' caused immense difficulties for Greek philosophers, and we come across one or two of these difficulties in *Theaetetus*.

To return to Protagoras. According to the three senses of *einai* outlined in the previous paragraph, the statement that 'Its objects are' could mean either that they are whatever the individual perceives them to be (cold, warm, etc.), or that they exist for the individual, or that they are true for the individual. It would be foolish to decide uncompromisingly that Protagoras (or Plato's Protagoras) meant only one of these, to the exclusion of the others. In this section of the dialogue the predicative use is uppermost, whereas in 157e–160c, for example, which is also supposed to be Protagorean, the veridical use is uppermost. At 167a the veridical use is followed shortly, at 167c, by the predicative.

There is a further ambiguity in the idea that 'Things are as each individual perceives them to be.' It has a weak and a strong version: the weak version is, 'The wind is cold for me if I perceive it as cold'; the strong version is, 'The wind is cold for me if and only if I perceive it as cold.' The latter version, but not the former, may mean that perception is the *only* means I have for getting at what is the case.

The thrust of this section is twofold. First, Plato argues that Theaetetus' definition implies Protagoras' doctrine, which it does: if perception is knowledge, then things are as each individual perceives them to be. But second, at the beginning of 152a, Plato claims that the two theses are identical, which means that the reverse implication, from Protagorean doctrine to Theaetetus' definition, should also obtain. This is obviously less likely: if things are as each individual perceives them to be, it follows that perception shares features with knowledge, but it does not follow that perception *is* knowledge.

However, if we adopt the stronger version of the Protagorean doctrine, then Plato may be making Protagoras' case as strong as possible. If *only* perception is knowledge, then not only is all perception knowledge, but all knowledge is perception. The charitable interpretation of what Plato is up to in this section has him saddling Protagoras with this stronger version. This is the charitable interpretation, because it means that not only does Theaetetus' definition entail Protagorean doctrine, but also Protagorean doctrine entails Theaetetus' definition. Thus Plato would be right to call the two theses identical and continually to discuss Protagorean doctrine in the course of discussing Theaetetus' definition. Without this identity, the whole discussion of Protagoras, which occupies so much of the dialogue, is little more than a red herring.

Note, in passing, that the fact that Plato uses sensible

phenomena such as a cold wind to illustrate the point about
aisthesis does not mean that *aisthesis* is exclusively sensation (see pp. 143–4). It obviously includes sensation, but that
is the only conclusion it is legitimate to draw. His use of
sensible phenomena to illustrate the concept may be no more
than a use of the most accessible examples.

It is important to see, right from this early stage of the
dialogue, just how interesting and important Protagoras'
position is, and therefore how valuable is Plato's development
and criticism of it in what follows. Otherwise the length of
Plato's discussion might seem to be unnecessary hot air. The
basis of Protagoras' position is the fact of conflicting appearances: the wind seems cold to one person and warm to another. Now, it is not just that the fact of conflicting appearances has given rise to elegant, fascinating and important
philosophical theories from Protagoras, through Plato's
middle period, to Scepticism, the British Empiricists and even
up to Bertrand Russell and beyond; it is also that all of us,
every day, come across conflicting appearances. It is this
everyday situation that Protagoras is addressing, not any
tradition of philosophical argument. And if what I perceive
conflicts with what you perceive, what are we to do? There
are often no external, objective criteria which might allow
one of us to claim that the other is wrong. So it is often sheer
stubbornness or arrogance to claim that I am right and you
are wrong, and few of us take this course: if we want to avoid
scepticism and withholding judgement about the wind's qualities altogether, we prefer implicitly to adopt the relativist position that both perceivers are correct, in their own ways. What
Protagoras apparently did, and what Plato does, probably
more fully, in *Theaetetus*, is to develop the implications of this
ordinary, everyday situation, and thus to prompt us to think
about it. Is everything private and are we locked into our
own private worlds? What is it to claim that both perceivers
are correct in their own ways? What kind of world would
allow them both to be correct? This latter question is the one
Plato turns to next.

⊷ The Secret Doctrine (152c–160e) ⊶

Plato next attributes to Protagoras a secret doctrine (indicating, no doubt, that the historical Protagoras said nothing explicit to this effect), which is a version of the theory of the constant flux of things, which Plato regularly attributes to Heraclitus. The secret doctrine is stated (152d–e), backed up (153a–d), and applied in a preliminary way to perception (153d–154b), so that certain puzzles can be stated (154b–155c); finally, the secret doctrine of perception is more fully stated (155e–157c), an objection is disposed of (157e–160d), and Theaetetus' definition, Protagoras' relativism and the secret (Heraclitean) doctrine are all declared to be identical (160d–e).

The secret doctrine of flux is initially stated to be that every attribute of things is relative: you cannot securely describe something as big, because in another relation it will appear small (152d). This is immediately said to entail that we should not use the word 'be' at all: 'become' is more accurate. 'X is big' is to be rewritten as 'X is becoming big' or 'X is in the process of being generated as big' (152d–e). According to the logical thinking of the time, 'is' implies stability (see especially the end of *Republic* 5); so faced with the apparent impermanence of things, some philosophers preferred to use 'becomes', which reflects this instability. Plato himself subscribed to this view in his earlier writings: on the implication of his rejection of the view later in *Theaetetus*, see pp. 242–3.

Next (153a–d) we get a series of generalizations to establish that change and flux generate things; finally, it is pointed out that, on the theory, sensible qualities such as colour are involved in the process of generation. Since they are not stably what they are, but are relative, they may be said also to be relative to an individual perceiver. What Smith perceives as white is not exactly the same as what Jones perceives as white; if it was, whiteness would have some continuity and stability.

Whatever the merits or demerits of the argument and the theory (on which see McDowell [5], pp. 123–8), we need to ask what part it plays in the dialogue. What Plato seems to be doing is attempting to establish a similar two-way entailment to what we found in the previous section. Thus the relativism which is built into the flux theory from the start (152d) is not, or not exclusively, Protagorean relativism, which is relativism to an individual percipient. The suffixes 'for me', 'for you', 'for each individual', etc., play no part in this section until 154a, by which time the consequences of the secret doctrine are being drawn out. According to the flux theory, the qualities of things may be relative in time, space, to one another, etc. (compare *Symposium* 211a), *and* to individual percipients. In other words, the flux theory of the impermanence of all things is taken to guarantee the privacy (and hence incorrigibility) of perceptions.

So the reason for the introduction of the radical theory of flux is again to establish a two-way entailment. To call this Protagoras' 'secret' doctrine implies that Protagoras' explicit doctrine entails it; and now we have found that it is taken to entail Protagoras' explicit doctrine too. Plato is presenting Heraclitus as an 'inchoate' relativist (to use Jackson's felicitous term – [38], p. 246), as Aristotle would later (e.g. *Metaphysics* 1012a–b, 1062b–1063b). The prime purpose for the introduction of the strictly unnecessary doctrine of flux (for surely relativism could have been more economically established in some other way) is the thoroughness of Plato's critique. He has now set up a series of two-way entailments between Theaetetus' definition, Protagoras and Heraclitus, so that whichever one of these notions he attacks, he is attacking the others. On the interrelations between the three theses, see Burnyeat [86], Marc-Wogau [106] and Sayre [52], pp. 61–77.

However, we have yet to examine the implicit idea that Protagoras' overt doctrine entails the secret doctrine; so far we have seen only that the reverse entailment is contained in this section. In fact, the idea that 'Things are as each individual perceives them to be' entails only that things are relative in this single respect, not that they have the out-and-out relativism of the flux theory (see also pp. 189–90). So although

in calling this Protagoras' secret doctrine Plato is claiming
that it is what Protagoras should have taught, given his overt
doctrine, his thinking is weak here; however, he is possibly
following Heraclitus himself in describing relativism as flux
(see Irwin [96]): the idea is that since the wind may be either
cold or warm (to different perceivers), it *is* neither in itself.

In fact, the flux theory as stated actually contradicts Protagorean relativism: Protagoras claims that each individual is
infallibly correct (see also 167a–b); the flux theory claims
that *no* identification is correct (152d). Hence, perhaps, Plato
contrasts Protagoras' overt doctrine as 'riddles' with the secret
doctrine as 'truth' (152c). In attributing the secret doctrine
to Protagoras, Plato is in effect modifying Protagoras' overt
doctrine from 'Each individual's perceptions are infallible' to
'Each individual's perceptions might as well be called infallible.' From this modified proposition, the flux theory may
follow; but since the modification was a consequence of the
flux theory in the first place, if this was Plato's justification
for assimilating the secret doctrine to Protagoras' written
doctrine, it is a circular justification.

At any rate, Plato believes he is thoroughly supporting
Theaetetus' definition. Perception is infallible, because no one
can gainsay anyone else's perceptions; the picture of the world
in flux (or at least the idea that the qualities of things are in
flux – but the things of this world are taken to be no more
than bundles of qualities: see p. 153 and p. 40, n. 3) supports
this privacy, because it guarantees that perceptions will not
be repeated.

Plato is arguing that the common, everyday situation
described on p. 148 is implicitly committed to a rather extraordinary picture of the world. I think he is intending to begin to appal common sense – if this is what it takes to
support Theaetetus' definition, then perhaps we are better off
without it – and he certainly continues with this tack in
the next section.

❧ Puzzles of Size and Number (154b–155c) ❧

The first puzzle is that six can be called 'more' (than four), but also 'less' (than twelve); the second is that Socrates can at one point be 'taller', at another point 'shorter', than the same person. In both cases 'everyday language' (that is, common sense) takes it that neither the six nor Socrates have changed (hence at 154d Theaetetus wants to answer 'Yes' to the question whether something can become 'more' without being increased).

However, when common sense (the 'contents of our hearts' of 154d and the 'phantoms' of 155a) is spelled out, it includes the proposition that 'It is impossible for something later to be which once was not, without having come to be', which apparently conflicts with the supposed equality or sameness of the six or Socrates: how could Socrates at one time be 'more', at another 'less', without having undergone the change of having come to be less?

The theory of perpetual flux, then, must be supposed to accommodate these puzzles by taking into account this apparent conflict in common sense and stating that Socrates is *not* in fact equal to himself: he is undergoing constant change, including increase and decrease, and so is the person whom at one time he perceives himself to be taller than, at another time shorter than. That is why these puzzles are introduced immediately after the idea that both the perceptible object and the perceiver are constantly changing (154b) and why the flux theory of perception is said to account for them (155d).

It should be noted that all this is not the unsophisticated, not to say idiotic, idea that Socrates may be five feet and six inches tall today, and just five feet tall tomorrow. The point, as before, is a logical one. To say that Socrates is equal to or the same as what he was yesterday, or even a moment ago, is taken to imply that there are things that can consistently and securely be said about Socrates.

In effect, Plato is pressing home an implication of the secret doctrine. On Protagoras' overt doctrine, as stated in 152a–b,

the *same* wind may be perceived by different people as possessing different qualities. This is a statement of fact, but the
overt doctrine apparently gave no explanation of the fact.
The secret doctrine does offer an explanation; the puzzles of
size and number illustrate *how* the secret doctrine allows the
possibility of Protagorean relativism. But the secret doctrine
is stricter than the overt doctrine: strictly speaking, the wind
should not be called the same. If it could be called the same,
then it would be, as it were, a substrate, which gains different
qualities in different relations, while itself remaining identifiable. The secret doctrine is committed to there being no
such substrates, but only perceptions of qualities. This is how
it is supposed to support the overt doctrine and Theaetetus'
definition: perception is the *only* means of getting at what is –
it is knowledge.

From our point of view, these puzzles are pretty trivial.
They arise only from talking about someone or something
being 'more' or 'less' without taking into consideration what
they are more or less *than*. Kirwan [100] points out that this
is a lingering piece of short-sightedness in Plato, but there is
no reason to suppose that Plato had not seen through it by
the time of writing *Theaetetus*, at any rate. After all, he does
criticize the idea that nothing in this world is identifiable, at
181c ff. I suspect that they were well-known sophistic puzzles
(see the references to the sophists at 154d–e); we can easily
imagine the sophists of Plato's *Euthydemus* pushing them
for all they are worth (hence Theaetetus is familiar with
them and they make him dizzy (155c)). *Phaedo* 100e–102e
shows Plato dealing with them in his middle period. Here,
however, no comment is passed on them beyond the fact that
they are supposed to tell against common sense and in favour
of the secret doctrine: nothing can be said to *be* more, or less,
than anything. No comment is required, because all Plato is
trying to do at the moment is be thorough in establishing the
flux theory: it is backed up (a) by corollaries (153a–d); (b) by
the acknowledged individuality of perceptions (153d–154a);
(c) by conflicts in common sense.

❧ A Fluxist Theory of Perception (156a–157c) ❧

The upshot of the secret doctrine is that nothing *is* anything in a stable manner: everything becomes qualified in a certain way according to its relation to an individual perceiver or some other relation. Nothing is a thing-in-itself; there are only these fleeting qualities. This is now applied to perception in general. On the question whether Plato believed this theory of perception, see pp. 159–63.

Plato establishes a fourfold model (*pace* Nakhnikian [111]) to account for the fact that perceptible qualities are by now supposed to have been established to be undergoing a process of *generation*. Suppose I am looking at a white stone. *Ex hypothesi* even my eye and the stone must be changing, but since they are not apparently doing so, they may be said to be undergoing slow change: the stone will eventually become sand, my eye will eventually become dim. When the stone and my eye get close enough to meet (have sexual intercourse), they engender whiteness and sight as their offspring: the stone becomes white and the eye sees. Until then the stone, as it were, did not exist and the eye was blind. Since this engendering is instantaneous, and is lost as soon as the eye moves on, the colour and the perception may be said to be undergoing quick change. So two slow-changing things (eye, stone) engender two quick-changing things (sight, whiteness), in the space between them. In terms of the different types of change distinguished in 181c ff., we could say that the eye and stone are predominantly undergoing alteration, while their offspring are undergoing motion in space.

Why is the perceived object called active and the sense-organ passive (see 156a with 159c)? At first sight, it makes more sense to talk of the eye as active (as Plato himself did in the preliminary sketch of a flux theory of perception at 153e–154a): the eye, as we say, 'falls upon' the stone. But Plato is thinking here of how, as we may put it, the stone *causes* the eye to 'see white'. But this tends to suggest that there is whiteness in the stone independent of any observer, which becomes observable when the stone causes the eye to 'see white'. Did Plato intend the theory to mean this, or that the qualities of things arise *only* in relation to an individual percipient? Taken on its own, this section of the text contains no clear answer. But since the theory is supposed to stress relativism above all, it must be that the dependence of qualities on perceivers is uppermost in Plato's mind (see also p. 38 n. 3).

The theory is a very clever and elegant construct. The notion of the quick motions travelling in space reminds us not to assimilate it too much to the views of Berkeley or Locke, whose 'ideas', like Hume's 'impressions', are mental entities, but it must have struck Plato's contemporaries as a 'state-of-the-art' theory. It enables a Protagorean relativist to explain the relativism of his changing world. However, it is less clear how the model is meant to work with perceptions other than sight, though Plato clearly wants it to (156b–c, 156e–157a); it is particularly unclear how 'pleasure, pain, desire and fear' (156b) are accounted for. One could say that when I face the prospect of a difficult interview, it becomes 'fearful' and my mind becomes 'fearing' – but this is a purely mental occurrence. Where, then, do the quick motions arise? Many commentators are also worried by the introduction of mental phenomena in the first place; but, as mentioned on p. 144, the Greek term *aisthesis* (perception) covers them, so their introduction is legitimate.

❧ A Possible Objection (157e–160c) ☙

Theaetetus' child is almost born. There remains, however, a possible objection to the Protagorean infallibility of impressions: dreams and hallucinations are rarely, if ever true (corresponding to reality). Theaetetus is impressed by the objection (158a–b), but Socrates comes back with the obvious answer that even dreams and hallucinations are private and incorrigible, and thus satisfy the Protagorean criterion, which, in combination with a theory of flux, guarantees that there is no external reality for truth to be correspondence to.

If the answer is so obvious, why does Plato take so long to state it (158b–160c)? Partly, no doubt, to illustrate the flux theory of perception in action – to show that the theory copes well with people disagreeing over the perceptual qualities of things – and perhaps partly because the distinction between health and illness and their effects on impressions (159b ff.) will play a part later (166d ff.). But the main reason is to confirm the dialectical mutual entailment of the secret doctrine, Protagoras' overt doctrine and Theaetetus' definition: hence, once this section is over, the conclusion is that these ideas are identical. Theaetetus' definition was taken to be the Protagorean infallibility of perception; Protagoras' position was taken to entail and be entailed by the secret doctrine; therefore it is relevant for Plato to take time to show that the secret doctrine guarantees infallibility.

The relevant bit of the argument, however, is so abstract as to be abstruse. I take it to be as follows: (1) since the perceiver is different (a consequence of the absolute-difference requirement of 158e, on which see below), the perceived quality is different (159c–e, 160a); (2) since the perception (of the perceived quality) is different, the perceiver is different (159e–160a). Even this is not an exaggeration, given the instantaneous uniqueness of each perception and the absolute-difference requirement. This establishes the required absolute relativism (that the perception and the perceived quality are peculiar to just such an instantaneous perceiver-and-object combination), so that Plato concludes, (3) the perceiver and the object are relative to each other, not to themselves nor to anything else (160a–b). His desire for thoroughness here makes him reject two ideas which are impossibly remote anyway: (a) the perception and the perceived quality are each relative to themselves; (b) the perception and the perceived quality are relative to nothing, or nothing extraneous (i.e. extraneous to a total event such as Socrates drinking wine).

It may not be going too far to find a second purpose in the section, and to glimpse the beginning of the *reductio ad absurdum* of Protagoras (at any rate, this is the effect to which Aristotle puts the argument at *Metaphysics* 1010b). His position undermines the common-sense distinction between madness and sanity, dreaming and waking. If it is right to see this response to Protagoras here, it is an *ad hominem* response

– but we will find that Plato is not averse to such arguments.

There is a further hint of a possible *reductio* in the stress laid in this section on the *absolute* difference between Socrates ill and Socrates healthy (158e ff.). Although it looks peculiar to say that they are completely different, Plato is being true to the flux theory of perception, which requires total impermanence, so that the whiteness I perceive now is different from the whiteness I perceived a moment ago, because both I and the whiteness have changed. It is already implausible to deny that Socrates is in *some* sense the same (though again we find the denial of substrates: see p. 153); and another absurdity occurs in 159a, where as a consequence of the absolute-difference requirement it is said that, 'What is growing similar is becoming identical, and what is growing dissimilar is becoming different.' To take the first half of this assertion, we say that owners come to resemble their pets, but not that they become identical! In other words, the theory Plato is displaying fails to recognize middle terms between the extremes of identity and absolute difference.

However, it has been argued that Plato is confusing moderate and extreme Heracliteanism. When Plato turns to explicit criticism of the theory (181c ff.), he assumes what Crombie ([25], p. 12) calls 'rampant' Heracliteanism – that everything is, even now, changing. But are we not here dealing with a less extreme version? Even if everything is the *result* of change (153a–d), we may still be able to identify any given thing: it is not slipping away from us even as we try to identify it. Doesn't Plato's talk of whiteness and other qualities mean that we *are* able to identify these qualities, so that the criticism of 181c ff. is misplaced? I think, however, that the distinction between rampant and normal Heracliteanism is of limited use. As I argue on pp. 181–3, Plato's point in 181c ff. is precisely that even 'normal' Heracliteanism is committed to the rampant version, otherwise it is no more the case that everything is changing than that everything is stable. Thus even at 152d, in introducing the theory, Plato describes it as the view that 'you cannot correctly identify anything or say what it is like'.

If this idea is correct, that Plato is assuming the logical point that even normal Heracliteanism precludes secure identification, then we can see that Plato is being careful in his support of Protagorean relativism. For if even *some* identifications were secure, then there would be no guarantee either that perceptions are private to individuals, or that events may not repeat (and therefore deserve the same or a similar description from one moment to the next). Plato guarantees the privacy of perception by making any perceived quality the interaction of just this object with just this perceiver at just this moment. The same construct eliminates (or at least makes highly unlikely) the idea that events repeat. The overall logical point is that, at any given moment, one might as well describe an object as F or as not-F: this entails the incorrigibility of any individual's perceptions, in a highly sceptical fashion.

Just how strictly Plato takes this consequence can best be seen from 157b, where Plato draws the conclusion that no terms which suggest stability should be allowed to enter our speech; among such terms he includes 'his' and 'mine'. These might seem to be allowable, and even guaranteed by the privacy of each person's perceptions. But the point must be that by the time I have laid claim to anything as 'mine', it has changed and is no longer the thing I laid claim to. If nothing is in any stable sense, you cannot properly refer to it at all. While in 157b Plato excludes obvious indicator words such as 'this' and 'that', a later passage (183a–b) seems to suggest that he is thinking even of general words such as 'man' as indicator words.

It is interesting to note in passing that in his own earlier metaphysics, which accepted the flux of the physical world, Plato allowed for the repetition of events. At *Timaeus* 49d–50a he says that even if what we call 'fire' is never precisely the same, because it is in flux, it is similar enough to deserve the same identification as 'fire'.

Theaetetus' child is now stated to be born (160d–e). The child, then, is not just the definition, which was given in

151e, but also its implications – Protagoreanism and Heracliteanism. It might not be too gross an extension of the image to picture Protagoreanism and Heracliteanism as the placenta and umbilical cord, say, of Theaetetus' definition: they support the embryo and give it life. If they are demolished, the child is likely to be still-born. In his role as midwife, Socrates will next test the new-born idea to see if it is sound – that is, he next turns to criticism. First, however, it is worth asking whether Plato himself holds any of the theory he has just been using to support Theaetetus' definition.

◦৺ Is There a Platonic Theory of Perception in *Theaetetus?* ৺৹

An affirmative answer is often given to this question: see especially Cornford [2], Modrak [109], Nakhnikian [111] and Reed [114]. Despite slight variations and more or less elaboration (and omitting Nakhnikian's more outrageous views), the claim is essentially that the fluxist theory of perception (hereafter FTP) was believed by Plato. The evidence adduced for this claim is as follows:

    1. That FTP is paralleled elsewhere in Plato's writings.
    2. That it is never refuted in *Theaetetus*.
    3. That it is a consequence of premises that Plato believed to be true.

    1. The chief relevant passages are *Timaeus* 45b–46c and 67c–68d, which are admirably summarized by McDowell [5], p. 139:

> There is a sort of fire in us which, when there is daylight outside, issues from our eyes and coalesces with the daylight to form a 'body' stretching away from the eyes: this efflux of fire from us is called 'the flow of seeing', or simply 'seeing'. Visible objects, on the other hand, emit flames made up of various kinds of particles: these effluxes are identified with the different colours. The particles emitted by objects cause disturbances in the 'body' stretching away from the eyes; this has an effect on the eyes, and thereby, ultimately, on the mind.

Reed has clarified the issues, but despite his attempt to

align the two theories, two difficulties remain. In the first place, FTP makes no mention of particles. This is perhaps not decisive in itself, since *Timaeus* may still be claimed to be compatible with FTP, as a mechanistic account of the same phenomena. However, secondly, it is not impossible on the account in *Timaeus* for the various colours, which are products of the size and shape of particles, to exist independently of being observed. At 67d we hear of the effect of colour-particles meeting the visual ray: the effect is to make the eye see whatever colour it has to, given the action of the particles on the visual ray. But it is not said that a colour exists only for an individual percipient at a particular moment of perception. These particles would, as far as we can tell from *Timaeus*, have the same effect on any number of percipients. It is obviously implausible to suggest that particles come into being at an instant of perception.

2. It is undoubtedly true that in refuting the claim of perception to be knowledge, Plato is not committed to the falsity of FTP: it is just that it doesn't tell us anything much about knowledge. But this point gets us nowhere: FTP could still be a construct of Plato's for the purposes of *Theaetetus*, or even a theory he has borrowed from other thinkers. Modrak's thesis is more to the point. He points out that in 184b ff. Plato makes certain points about perception which are undoubtedly Platonic in that Plato exploits them to refute the claim of sense-perception to be knowledge. Specifically, there are two relevant points: the doctrine that each sense has its proper objects (on which see especially Holland [94]); and the distinction between mind and the sense-organs. Modrak claims that these points are either found in, or are not incompatible with, FTP; therefore FTP is Platonic. Compare the more cautious account of Crombie [25], pp. 14 ff., on the relation between FTP and 184b ff.

The proper-object doctrine occurs in FTP in its talk of compatibility at 156b–c (see also 153e): perceptions and perceived things must be compatible. In addition, a phenomenalist account of perception, such as FTP, could even be said to underpin the proper-object doctrine, in the sense that a perception and a perceived quality arise *only* in relation to each other.

The distinction between mind and the sense-organs is not found in FTP, but Modrak was not the first to claim that it is not inconsistent with FTP and even represents a useful addition.

Leaving aside the proper-object doctrine for the moment, it must immediately be noted that this last point is incorrect. The introduction of mind in 184b ff. is incompatible with FTP (see Burnyeat [84]). FTP talked specifically about the eye doing the seeing (e.g. 156e); this, incidentally, is also the way Plato used to talk in earlier dialogues. But 184b ff. says that this is wrong: it is the mind, not the eye, which does the seeing. The single mind is introduced specifically to replace an account of multifarious senses. Moreover, FTP cannot be adapted to take a single mind into consideration: its singleness alone is anathema to FTP. It would have to be an infinitely changeable and changing mind, and that would reduce 184b ff. to the idea of the plurality of the senses which it is trying to avoid.

This, in turn, shows how 184b ff. is generally incompatible with FTP. In 184b ff. we hear of the 'hardness of hard objects', as if these qualities were objective, not just qualities which arise in relation to a particular perceiver at a particular moment. And 184b ff. makes plenty of play with 'being', which is expressly excluded by FTP.

It has been claimed that Plato can talk of 'being' in 184b ff. because he has by then shown that there must be *some* stability in the external world. This is true, but misses the point. The exclusion of being is *essential* to FTP; to adapt FTP until it takes being and public, not private, objects into consideration is to deny FTP altogether.

We are left with only the proper-object doctrine as common to both parts of *Theaetetus*, but this by itself is inconclusive evidence. Indeed, it is arguably not a philosophical theory so much as a (dubious) matter of common sense: what else can perceive smells except the nose?

3. FTP is a consequence of Protagorean relativism and Heraclitean flux, or perhaps of Heraclitean flux alone. The claim that Plato believed these premisses cannot hold water. The 'digression' of 172c–177b is Plato's declaration that at the time of writing *Theaetetus* he was no kind of relativist, let alone a Protagorean one (nor was he ever, in fact). Although Plato had believed in his middle period in a version of flux as regards the things of this world, it is clear that he no longer believed this at the time of writing *Theaetetus*: the implication of 181c–183b is that the world must have enough stability to allow for meaningful conversation (see pp. 181–3, 242–3). Even in his middle period, it may be doubted whether Plato would have thought that the whiteness of a white stone comes into being only when it is being perceived (Runciman [49], p. 19). It is true that his earlier quasi-Heraclitean view of the world leads him, at *Timaeus* 49d–e, to make some similar linguistic remarks to those of *Theaetetus* 183a–b; but the contexts are drastically different. In *Timaeus* he is stating consequences of his own theory; in *Theaetetus* he is reducing an alien theory to absurdity. (Besides, I happen to follow Owen [45] in seeing *Timaeus* as a middle-period dialogue: see Waterfield [55].) Finally, to say that Plato believed the premisses of FTP is to ignore the way the whole of the early drawing out of implications of Theaetetus' definition is *hypothetical* (Sayre [52], p. 74): Plato is saying, '*If* Theaetetus' definition is to be sound, *then* Protagoreanism is required; *if* in turn that is so, *then* Heracliteanism and FTP are required.' Plato is in no way committed to FTP.

So, what are we left with? FTP is part of a 'secret' doctrine in *Theaetetus*, which probably means that it is a Platonic construct, to suit the purposes of the dialogue. In this sense it is Platonic, but in no other. Plato reckons that this is what Theaetetus' definition is committed to, so he articulates this underlying commitment into a theory. On the other hand, FTP may even be the construct of some historical fluxists (though precisely who must remain uncertain). In either case, it is noticeable that Theophrastus, summarizing in *c.* 320 his predecessors' views on sense-perception in his *On Sense-perception*, relies entirely on *Timaeus*, never on *Theaetetus*, for Plato's views. Perhaps he saw that FTP is inconsistent with *Timaeus* and is refuted by Plato in *Theaetetus*. However, Plato's clues about his own theory of sense-perception in 184b ff. are not incompatible with *Timaeus*, and in a dialogue written later than *Theatetus*, Plato possibly alludes to some such theory as that of *Timaeus* (I am thinking of the talk of effluxes or rays at *Sophist* 266c). FTP is not Platonic, nor can we unearth a Platonic theory of perception from *Theaetetus*; but the account in *Timaeus* may have survived Plato's rejection of other views of that dialogue.

❧ Plato's Criticism of Protagoras (160e–179b) ❧

The basic ordering of Plato's demolition of Theaetetus' equation of perception and knowledge is to begin by criticizing Protagoras, then turn to Heraclitus, and finally deal with the definition itself. Little of the criticism of Protagoras or of flux would be relevant to an epistemological inquiry if Plato had not established the mutual entailments between the three theses. But the very fact that Plato does view the three theses as identical slightly obscures the course of this critical section of the dialogue. Thus in the middle of arguments aimed specifically against Protagoreanism, he inserts arguments aimed chiefly against Theaetetus' definition (163a–165d). And the argument against flux (181c–183b) is also taken to be an argument against Protagoras, since flux is supposed to be his 'secret' doctrine.

❧ Pigs, Baboons and Protagoras (161b–163a) ❧

Plato's first foray against Protagoras employs an *ad hominem* argument he also uses in other dialogues (*Cratylus* 386c–d, *Euthydemus* 286b–287b). Pigs and baboons are 'measures' just as much as people are; and if every person is the measure of the truth of his impressions, then why did Protagoras set himself up as a teacher? In effect, not only teaching, but any intellectual inquiry, is made redundant. Protagoras himself is brought in (162d–e) to reply that this is merely captious; then Plato can get down to less superficial criticism. Thus when the same general point – that Protagoras' position is self-defeating – recurs later in the dialogue (at 170a–171c), it is no longer *ad hominem* in the same way, but is supposed to rely on a genuine inconsistency which has been uncovered in Protagoras' doctrine as expounded, or more probably expanded, by Plato (see pp. 168, 188). The tactics are excellent: to provide your opponent with the strongest possible foundation for his claims, before investigating those claims. If the suggestion is correct that Plato is expanding, rather than merely expounding, Protagoras' doctrine in 166d–167b, then it is probable that the historical Protagoras was more open to the initial *ad hominem* attack of this section than the Protagoras of Plato's *Theaetetus*. However, it is also likely that the historical Protagoras would have *accepted* the consequence that there are no teachers or experts (on a Platonic understanding of the terms), and even claimed that the main point of his 'teaching' was to communicate the idea that there are no such teachers. His message is, '*You* are the measure.'

Socrates is frequently made to use *ad hominem* arguments in the dialogues, and there are good reasons for this. Nowadays, such arguments are considered *infra dig.*: they do not deal with the philosophy, only the philosopher. But many ancient philosophers, and especially Socrates, blurred this distinction; beliefs were to be lived by and were not merely academic exercises. Socrates requires his interlocutors to state their true beliefs, and it is a presupposition of his dialectic that they do so. Hence he describes his dialectic at 161e not only as investigating beliefs, but as testing the people who hold these beliefs. The point is familiar to readers of the early Socratic dialogues.

Whether or not we judge the argument superficial, however, it has a part to play in the progress of the dialogue. It may well be true to say, as Plato himself had implied in mentioning dogs and other animals at 154a, that where their mere sense-perception is concerned, humans, gods and animals are equally authoritative. So this section serves to begin the distinction Plato wants to make between sense-perception and everything else which the Greeks had lumped together under 'perception' (see pp. 143–4). We may say that this section has two implicit thrusts: (1) Are there any grounds for distinguishing between humans and other animals as far as sense-perception is concerned? (Answer: perhaps not.) (2) Are there any grounds for distinguishing between experts and laymen as far as intellectual activity is concerned? (Answer: yes.)

◈ Arguments on the Equation of Perception ◈ and Knowledge (163a–165d)

The first argument (163b–c) is that if perception is knowledge, then we should be incapable of hearing a foreign language that we do not know, and we should be said to know a foreign language, even if it is the first time we have heard it, just because we are hearing the sounds. The purpose of this argument seems clear: if perception is taken to be sense-perception alone, this unduly restricts the kinds of things we can be said to know, and the ways in which we can be said to know. When Theaetetus goes the whole hog and accepts the implications of this, Socrates hints that he has laid himself open to further objections, which are presumably those of 184b–186e; but these objections are not developed at present.

It should be noted in passing that this argument cannot be taken as evidence that 'perception' means sense-perception throughout the dialogue. Socrates launches the argument by asking, 'Are we going to say that everything we perceive *by hearing or seeing* we also simultaneously know?' In other words, he is qualifying perception as sense-perception in this argument, and is not addressing the whole range of perception. This argument is not taken further, and merely sows seeds for 184b–186e.

It is more difficult to understand what is going on in the two immediately subsequent arguments. The second argument (163c–164b) is that if perception is knowledge, then we should be incapable of having a piece of knowledge in our memories when our eyes are closed (i.e., by extension, when none of our senses is functioning).

At first sight, this looks like another argument with the same point as the first. If perception is knowledge, that excludes memory from the range of 'knowledge', just as the first argument excluded understanding a language.

However, this cannot be the point that Plato intends this second argument to be making. There are two factors which show this. The first is that Theaetetus is being portrayed as doing his best to defend his equation of perception and knowledge. Thus, in the first argument of this section, he goes the whole hog, as above, and denies that we can be said to know a foreign language by having learned it (163c), which shows that he is prepared to make a stand against common parlance, to say the least. Yet in this second argument he readily admits that we can be said to know something by remembering it. Given his equation of perception and knowledge, it looks as though he is treating memory as a kind of perception. If this is the case, then the point of the argument cannot be that the equation of perception and knowledge unduly restricts the domain of knowledge by ignoring memory.

The second factor which proves the same point arises out of the third argument's relation to this second one. Immediately after ending the second argument, Plato accuses it of being superficial and sophistic, and insists that correct attention to words would defuse it. He then provides a third, deliberately sophistic argument, to demonstrate the casuistry (164d–165d). Presumably, then, the obvious flaw of this third argument should be the (less obvious) flaw of the second argument. The third argument is: If one eye is covered, while the other is not, then according to Theaetetus' definition, the same person is simultaneously knowing and not knowing the same thing.

This argument is sophistic because it employs the common sophistic fallacy of *secundum quid* (for many examples, see *Euthydemus*) – that is, of dropping qualifications. Theaetetus correctly wants to insert the qualifications: 'I will say that I can't see *with the one eye*, but can *with the other*' (165c). Socrates, playing the sophist, overrules him, to insist that he has admitted that one can simultaneously see (know) and not see (not know) the same thing.

What qualifications, then, are lacking in the second argument? Plato must be wanting it to be defused as follows: 'I do not know something *by seeing it*, but I do *by remembering it.*'

Now, in the first place, all this shows that the point of the second argument is not that Theaetetus' definition unduly restricts 'knowledge', but that it generates an apparent paradox, that of simultaneously knowing and not knowing the same thing. In the second place, if this paradox is to harm the equation of perception and knowledge, then memory must be assumed to be a kind of perception. For if memory is not being taken to be an instance of knowledge which the equation accepts – i.e. as an instance of perception – then the paradox simply falls flat.

Thus two factors show that memory is included in the broad range of 'perception'. This point is worth stressing, because it shows clearly that perception is not being restricted to sense-perception in *Theaetetus* (see p. 144).

A further series of sophistic arguments is adumbrated in 165d, such as that the equation of perception and knowledge entails the absurdity that knowledge can be clear and hazy. Because of their incompleteness, it is not easy to guess at the course of these arguments. Again, they look as though they might be objections to an equation of *sense*-perception and knowledge, on the grounds that knowledge cannot be both clear and hazy, as the senses can. This would align them with the first argument of this section. But since they are said to be 'further questions of the same kind' as the *third* argument, then probably they are best read as generating apparent paradoxes by employing the fallacy of *secundum quid*. Thus, for example: 'I see the same thing clearly at one time and hazily at another time; therefore [dropping the temporal qualifications], I see the same thing clearly and hazily; therefore (by the equation of perception and knowledge), I know clearly and hazily.'

If such an argument seems ludicrous, the reader is again

referred to *Euthydemus*, where a couple of sophists come up
with several arguments which are just as silly, to our way of
thinking.

Since it is clear that Plato was aware of how to defuse the
apparent paradox of the second and third arguments, why
does he mention it at all? I suspect that there are two reasons.
In the first place, he is giving a thorough survey of arguments
relating to perception; I have no doubt that he has simply
lifted these arguments from some sophist or other. In the
second place, there is irony in using sophistic arguments
against Protagoras, the father of all the sophists.

❧ *Protagoras Defends Himself* (166a–168c) ❧

Socrates now puts into Protagoras' mouth a fascinating and
important defence of the man-measure principle, of the
equation of knowledge and perception, and especially of his
right to be a teacher. The application that we find in this
section of the man-measure principle to mental activities and
hence to politics is undoubtedly genuine Protagoreanism.
Gosling [26], pp. 146–7, and Glidden [92] construct plausible
arguments for how Protagoras might have extended his
doctrine from sense-perception to beliefs, but I am denying
that any such arguments are necessary: the term *aisthesis*
already covered the full range of perception from sensation to
belief. Nevertheless, Plato most probably does extend the position of the historical Protagoras, when he has him considering how to cope with the notion of expertise; but we
shall see that even this extension is based firmly on genuine
Protagoreanism. The core of the speech which constitutes
this section is in effect a defence of the role of sophists. On the
ironies in Socrates' impersonation of Protagoras, see Lee
[101].

First we get some general remarks (166a) on fairness in
argument, which continue Plato's worries about dealing with
a dead author who cannot reply for himself (see also 164e).
Socratic dialectic dealt with living people (see p. 164).

Next Protagoras is made to deny that he would have been
troubled by the paradox of the previous section, that it is

possible for the same person simultaneously to know and not to know the same thing; he systematically demolishes this paradox. First he says that memory is *not* concerned with 'the same thing' as seeing, as the paradox claims: strictly, one should say, 'I know X by seeing and I know Y by remembering', even where Y is a memory-image of X. Of course, we want to complain that the memory-image of X is not completely different from X; but on a fluxist theory it may well be. Second, he again draws on the theory of flux to deny that 'the same person' is involved in the paradox, because a person does not remain the same over any two instants, or even in the same instant. Thus he has demolished the three aspects of the apparent paradox – 'the same person', 'simultaneously' and 'the same thing'.

To repeat the point emphasized on pp. 166–7, notice that these are adequate responses, on Protagorean-fluxist lines, to the paradox of the previous section, but they do not take those arguments to be excluding memory from the domain of perception.

Next Protagoras comes to the crucial part of the defence (166d ff.). Plato must provide a way for Protagoras to reconcile the subjective truth of impressions with his claim to be an expert, especially since experts are commonly held to have objective knowledge. Protagoras is made to allow that impressions differ, not in respect of truth and falsehood, however, but in respect of goodness and badness. An expert is then described as someone who can make a person or thing have good impressions instead of bad ones. What does this mean? By what standard are some impressions better than others? It is not immediately clear.

If we follow the example of the doctor (166e–167a), it would seem that 'better' means 'more pleasant'. The doctor, by curing my illness, can make food, which appears (and truly is) unpleasant to me, appear and truly be pleasant to me.

The example of the farmer (167b–c) is opaque, but since Protagoras is prepared to say that plants have perceptions, then he would presumably be prepared to say that they can feel better or worse, and that the farmer is a plant-doctor, substituting pleasant impressions for unpleasant ones in his tender patients.

However, the examples of the politician and the sophist (167c–d) tend in a different direction: 'better' here, where the issue is society's rules, say, can only mean 'more beneficial' or 'more expedient'.

It is difficult to reconcile these conflicting ways of spelling out 'better'. It is tempting to suppose that Protagoras is assuming that what is more pleasant is in fact more beneficial. But there is no reason for a community with 'unsound' ethical beliefs not to revel in them and find them more pleasant, even if they are not in fact more beneficial; and this suggestion also imports an *objective* utilitarian standard of benefit, which is alien to Protagoras' relativism, and should only be attributed to Plato's Protagoras here as a last resort. It is perhaps more accurate to think that 'better' may be spelled out in many ways, according to context; and that the unifying factor is that the perceiver will *prefer* the 'better' impressions to the ones he had before. Protagorean relativism is preserved because what one person or community prefers is not, of course, what another prefers.

However, it is often said (for instance, by Cole [87]) that Protagorean relativism *is* implicitly compromised in this passage. Isn't he saying that strawberries, say, *should* taste pleasant? Isn't he saying that some sets of rules objectively are more beneficial for a community than others, and that a wise politician knows this and steers the community towards benefit? It is certainly possible to read the passage in this way at first sight, but it would have the awkward consequence that if a community judges its unsound rules to be beneficial, when they actually are not, judged by the standard of objective benefit, then the community has false beliefs, despite Protagoras' insistence that it cannot.

However, on a second reading, there is no reason to see the defence as inconsistent in this way (see Glidden [91]). Provided that we remember the radical nature of Protagoras' doctrine, he can be seen as saying that a politician simply makes a community perceive different rules as beneficial. There is no standard of objective benefit: the community just feels better now. This is a highly cynical view of politics and education in general, but it is one which squares with Protagoras' denial of objective facts, knowledge of which distinguishes experts from non-experts, on a normal and Platonic account of expertise; it also squares with what we know from elsewhere about Protagoras (see pp. 193–4).

However, Kerferd [98] points to two sentences which appear to tell against the relativist position I am attributing to Protagoras in this section. At 166d, Protagoras says, 'I actually define wisdom as the ability to make good things appear and be for someone instead of bad things.' This sentence does not represent Protagoras as saying that bad things appear good, but that good things appear: couldn't these be objectively good things? But the sentence is more open-ended than Kerferd allows, and can bear an interpretation between the two extremes of 'make bad things seem good' and 'make objectively good things appear'. I take it to mean 'make whatever appears appear good'. The same considerations apply to the other sentence Kerferd rightly picks on, in 167c, about the politician making 'sound notions be and appear' for a community.

If the inconsistency was present in Protagoras' defence, it would have been obvious to Plato, who wrote the defence, and he would have used it to argue against Protagoras' position. Throughout the ensuing argument against Protagoras, however, Plato can be seen to assume thorough-going relativism, until he is in a position to do otherwise. If Plato was covertly importing objective standards, he would unfairly be attributing to Protagoras something which the historical person would hardly have said. Some commentators suggest that Plato is here drawing on 'incomplete Protagoreans', those who could not go the whole hog into radical relativism. But Plato claims he is being fair to Protagoras (166a–b, 166c). If the defence can be read as assuming radical relativism, then that is surely the best interpretation.

∽ *Protagoras Defeats Himself* (169d–172b) ∾

In 161b–163a an *ad hominem* objection to Protagoras was raised and dismissed; in 163a–165d it was suggested that the equation of perception and knowledge has paradoxical consequences, but this suggestion has twice been answered, once implicitly by Plato in 163a–165d, and once explicitly by 'Protagoras' in 166b. Protagoras has also defended his right to be called an expert. Now, however, the criticism begins in earnest. In the course of the next few sections, Plato will attack in turn relativism, flux and finally Theaetetus' definition.

This section, 169d–172b, which has been very intensely studied by the commentators, and indeed requires careful commentary, takes up Protagorean relativism. Plato's thesis, which was adumbrated in 161b–163a (but more particularly at *Euthydemus* 286c ff.) is that Protagoras' doctrine is self-defeating. The starting-point is still the issue of expertise or wisdom, as in 161b–163a. Since then, we have seen that Protagoras allows for experts, but in a highly cynical fashion, which is in harmony with his relativism. It is in harmony with his relativism because it relies on the proposition that every person's beliefs are true for that person, and thereby does not entertain the possibility of external, objective knowledge, which some may be privy to and have true beliefs about, while others do not. However, both the Platonic and the common-sense view of expertise is precisely that there is such knowledge and there are such experts. Cole [87] neatly expresses the difference in the political sphere as that a Protagorean expert makes people see something as good, whereas the Platonic expert makes people see the good in something.

We must first consider the specific context of the argument of this section. The preamble, at 169e, is rather puzzling. Plato claims that what should be investigated is whether the concession he attributed to Protagoras, that there are experts, is valid. The subsequent argument, in short, is that Protagoras is committed to the existence of experts with objective knowledge. Is Plato then saying, despite the fact that it is possible to interpret Protagoras' 'concession' as thoroughly relativist, that he has already committed Protagoras to the existence of objective experts, and is now simply confirming this commitment?

The preamble can certainly be read this way, and of course is by those who attribute to Protagoras (or to 'incomplete Protagoreans') some objective standards. But it is not necessary to read the preamble in this way. All Plato says is that the crux is Protagoras' concession that there are experts *of some kind* – that is, that the term 'expert' is part of Protagoras' vocabulary (as it must be, since Protagoras is a teacher). He then goes on to argue that Protagoras is committed to the truth of others' beliefs, and that others believe that the proper description of experts is that they have objective knowledge. From these premises he concludes that, since the term 'expert' is part of Protagoras' vocabulary, he must accept that the term is properly applied to those with objective knowledge.

At any rate, the context shows that Plato's concern is the issue of expertise. This is clearly borne out by the conclusion of the argument (171b–c): 'Therefore ... even Protagoras himself will concede that no dog and no ordinary person is a measure of anything at all, unless he understands it.'

That this is the conclusion Plato is aiming for is also clearly announced in the run-up to the main argument (170a–d). First we get a statement of the Protagorean position:

(P) What appears to each person also is for the person who has the impression.

That is, everyone equally has access to (private) truth. This is immediately contrasted with the normal view:

(Q) Only experts grasp truth, not everyone.

So the run-up begins by contrasting P, which contains the Protagorean qualifier 'for the person' and is equivalent to the denial of objective knowledge, with Q, which asserts objective knowledge. The run-up concludes (170c–d) by saying that the idea that man is the measure is committed, in fact, to the notion that beliefs may be both true and false. Note the lack of Protagorean qualifiers: Plato is throwing down the gauntlet. He is announcing the aim of his argument as deducing Q from P! No wonder Theodorus asks Socrates how this is possible. And notice that if Plato can substantiate this claim, that P entails Q, he is clearly saying that Protagoras refutes himself. Since Protagoras is a relativist, it is hard to convict him of self-refutation (see Waterlow [122]). But what he can never do, as a relativist, is commit himself to a non-relativist position like Q. This tells fatally against the thesis of Waterlow that Plato is *not* trying to convict Protagoras of inconsistency.

The run-up is over, and we now come to the argument itself:

(1) Suppose a person A has a belief x; according to P, x is true for A.

(2) But x can have some truth-value for others, and may be false for them; x may be false for B, C, etc.

(3) When this happens, x is true for A, but false for B, C, etc.

Notice that the Protagorean qualifiers are still firmly in place, so that all Plato deduces from this is that it is true for B, C, etc., that x is false (170e). This is not yet a complete recoil argument in its own right, and brings Plato nowhere near Q yet.

Next Plato substitutes the Protagorean thesis P for x:

(4) P is true for Protagoras.

(5) P is false for others.

(6) Therefore P is 'more false than true, in proportion to the extent that the unbelievers outnumber the believers' (171a).

The talk of believers and unbelievers is just another way of retaining the Protagorean qualifiers, so that we could express (6) as precisely parallel to (3). Theodorus' comment immediately following (6) also stresses the presence of the qualifiers.

Plato now marks the final stage of the argument (note that I am finding a single argument here, not several, as others do) by saying that he is going to point out an 'exquisite' consequence.

(7) Protagoras believes P.

    (8) Therefore it is true for Protagoras that it is true for others that P is false.

    (9) Therefore it is true for Protagoras that P is false for others.

    (10) Therefore it is true for Protagoras that P is false.

The moves from (7) to (8) and (8) to (9) are clearly valid. What about (9) to (10)? Here Plato drops the qualifier (that is, to use the locution of 171a–b, he doesn't mention 'the opinion' that P is false, just that it is). What might allow Plato to make this crucial move?

Most recent commentators (such as Lee [101], pp. 242–9, McDowell [5], pp. 169–71, Passmore [113], and Sayre [52], pp. 87–90) claim that there is no justification for Plato's move from (9) to (10). In this I believe that they are correct: the qualification 'for them' should have been added in (10), as Grote [28], pp. 137–8, was the first to notice (though commentators until recent years overlooked Grote's point).

Plato could perhaps retort: 'But we are not Protagoreans. When we say that a belief is false, we do not mean that it is false merely for those who believe it is false; we mean that it is objectively false.' However, Protagoras could easily reply that no such thing has been proved: it remains true for him that it is true for others that P is objectively false, and this formulation still follows from P.

Plato has been careful about inserting the qualifiers all through the argument, wherever they are necessary. Why does he suddenly drop them? Burnyeat [83] is surely right to suggest that Plato is arguing that there are awkward consequences for Protagoras even on the properly relativistic statement (9). P has been reduced from what it purported to be, a theory of truth that is universally valid, to a theory that is valid only for Protagoras and any other whole-hearted Protagoreans. And should Protagoras, a relativist, be making absolute statements in the first place (see Burnyeat's interesting remarks, [83], pp. 192–5)?

However, Burnyeat also seems to believe that this validates Plato's argument; but he ignores (10), or rather assumes that it implicitly contains the relevant qualifiers – a plausible idea, except that it makes (10) a redundant restatement of (9). Even granted Burnyeat's point that P entails that everyone occupies their own private world, and that Plato is arguing that relativism is a part of very few such worlds, and even granted that Protagoras is forced to admit that P is false for others, it does not follow, as Burnyeat says it does ([83], p. 188), that P is false for Protagoras as well: Protagoras can still claim that the argument is *formally* invalid by insisting that the statement 'Relativism is irrelevant for 99 per cent of mankind' is a genuine consequence of P, and by insisting that the qualifiers certainly must be inserted in any statements about what is true for him, as (9) and (10) are. The qualifiers could be dropped only if Plato could justify the suggestion at 170e (where it is hypothetical) that P is true for no one, including Protagoras. He claims at 171c to have done just this, but the claim is a consequence of (10), which is invalid.

So the formal invalidity of the argument remains, and it cannot be said that Plato has successfully convicted Protagoras of refuting himself. Protagoras may well be unassailable, from this angle (short of more sophisticated argument, such as that of Pears [46], p. 58). But Plato has reduced Protagorean doctrine to being dogmatic and even solipsistic; and he has emphasized just how counter-intuitive the notion is that there are no false beliefs, which is the issue to which he will return in 177c–179b.

Anyway, given that Plato thinks that he has successfully turned the tables on Protagoras, it is easy for him to conclude that Protagoras is committed to Q: if Protagoras admits that beliefs may be either true or false, then he must recognize the authority of those who have true beliefs in any area – the experts (in a Platonic sense of the word). Hence, when he comes to take the issue up again, in 177c–179b, he will assume that the modified Protagoreanism outlined in 171d–172b is also Protagoras' position.

❧ A 'Digression' (172b–177c) ☙

Plato pauses from hard argument against Protagoras and inserts a few pages of glorious, impassioned writing contrasting the mentality of philosophers with that of the worldly-wise. Is the irony of using rhetoric to denigrate its usual practitioners intentional? At any rate, as a rhetorical passage, it needs little commentary: its merits are on the surface.

The way of life outlined as philosophic is highly other-worldly and ascetic; but more moderate versions of the claims occur in other dialogues. *Gorgias* is worth comparing on the contrast between philosophy and rhetoric/politics (see also *Phaedrus* 259e ff. and *Philebus* 58a–d); *Republic* on the relation between justice and happiness; *Phaedo* 64c–69e on the philosopher's detachment from mundane affairs.

In so far as it has been maintained that this section presupposes Plato's middle-period theory of Forms, it is discussed on p. 242. The only question I want to raise at the moment is: What is the digression doing here, at this point of the dialogue?

It is generally agreed that Plato calls it a 'digression' (177b), not because he thinks the points he is making are irrelevant to the issues of the dialogue, but because to argue for them, rather than express them rhetorically, would take him too far from the chief issue of perception and knowledge. As McDowell says ([5], p. 174), a modern writer might have made the digression an appendix to his book.

It is also generally agreed that the points Plato raises in the digression are counterblasts to the relativism of Protagoras and even to modified Protagoreanism. He is guarding against the impression that he agrees at all with even the modified version: to say that morality is merely in the eyes of the beholder is, in fact, anathema to him. Since he has just said (172b) that 'everyone' is in a sense a modified Protagorean (see also p. 148), he immediately feels compelled to point out that he does not include himself.

The first contrast in this section is between philosophers

and lawyers/orators/politicians. Why does Plato pick on this
group? They were an intrinsic part of the democracy of
Athens; they were the leaders, the demagogues; they formed
people's opinions. Democratic procedure, according to Plato
and other critics of Athenian democracy, entails relativism.
A number of views would be put to the populace, and the
populace then decided which view to adopt: that is how the
rules Plato is talking about in 172a – the laws of a community – are formed. What appears to the populace is true
for it. According to the critics, this is an arbitrary process:
rules may change even from day to day. Socrates and Plato
in particular decried the lack of reliance on experts. In the
present context, the suggestion would be that experts, with
access to objective knowledge, would remove the arbitrariness
of Athens' political procedure. For a judicious and thorough
discussion of Socrates' political views – with which Plato's
largely coincided – see Kraut [69].

Plato's emphasis on lawcourts may strike a modern reader
as strange, but they were an integral part of the Athenian
democratic process. Apart from criminal and civil cases,
which we too might expect to find in a lawcourt (though not
as often, proportionally, as in litigious ancient Athens), any
holder of public office would expect to find himself in court to
account for his actions during his period of office.

The first contrast, then, is between popular leaders, who
further the implicit relativism of ordinary people, but are
therefore slavishly dependent on the populace's whims, and
the freedom of philosophers. But it is noticeable that when
Plato turns to characterize philosophers (173c ff.), he ex-
aggerates, and thereby implicitly extends the first contrast
into a second one. He portrays philosophers as *completely*
other-worldly, which is to contrast them not just with political
leaders, but with anyone who is at all interested in mundane
matters – who may plausibly be supposed to be 'everyone'.
Thus the mundane matters are not so much affairs of state as
tittle-tattle (173d).

The rest of the digression needs little comment: it stands on
its own. But it is worth pointing out the distinction at 176b–d

between the quasi-Protagorean view of favouring a reputation for morality (that is, of it appearing and being true
to others that you are good) and true virtue. In 176d Plato
turns the tables: 'They are exactly the sort of people they
think they are not, and all the more so for not thinking it.' In
other words, 'It seems to me that I am F' is denied to entail 'It
is true that I am F'. On strict Protagorean lines, that should
have been 'It is true for me that I am F'; but Plato's rhetorical
point is clear enough.

At any rate, it seems that Protagorean doctrine is being
alluded to throughout the 'digression'. Lee [101] interest-
ingly also finds elements in the harsh portrait of lawyers
which are meant to apply to Protagoras, and elements in the
portrait of philosophers which Protagoras conspicuously
lacks. As an example of the latter, notice that the philosopher
is meant to distinguish human nature from all others (174b),
whereas Protagoras conflated humans and animals (162e);
as an example of the former, Protagoras' defence (166a–
168c) is concerned with himself and his 'property', as,
according to Plato, lawyers always are too (172e). I would
add that the relativist 'expert' politician of Protagoras' defence, as interpreted on pp. 170–71, is simply pandering to the
community, as Plato says here, at 173a, that politicians do.

❧ Final Refutation of Protagoras (177c–179b) ☙

I call this the final refutation of Protagoras, though since
Protagoras has been saddled with the 'secret' doctrine of flux,
it is in fact only after flux has been criticized in the next
section that Protagoras is said to be refuted (184c) and
Theodorus (who became the chief interlocutor for the duration of the criticism of Protagoras) is allowed to return to the
background. But this is the last section in which Plato deals
with Protagoras' overt doctrine – his historical position.

The argument of this section is not independent. It assumes
the correctness of the conclusion of the recoil argument, that
Protagoras must modify his position to allow for experts and
that there may be some false beliefs. This section merely justifies this conclusion by pointing to a particular instance –

the future – where experts must be taken to be authoritative.

Thus at 177c–178a Plato repeats the distinction between benefit and other qualities which forms the basis of modified Protagoreanism, and dismisses as trivial the idea that as long as the mere word 'beneficial' remains in use, then there is benefit. He prefers the idea of objective benefit and claims that Protagoreanism is now committed to this objectivism. But in fact the true Protagorean expert of unmodified Protagoreanism *was* concerned merely with words: his job was to make a community describe a set of rules as beneficial, so that they felt better about those rules (see pp. 170–71). Plato prefers the twin objectivist theses, that the word 'beneficial' can only be applied to something that is truly beneficial, and that this is what communities aim for in legislation (see *Hippias Major* 284d–e).

Finally, Plato points out that talk of benefit is covert talk about what will actually occur in the future and correctly argues that experts with objective knowledge must be allowed to be more authoritative about the future than laymen. But notice again that Plato could use this argument only on the basis of modified Protagoreanism. An unrepentant Protagorean could insist that the formula, 'It *now* seems to me that I will have a fever tomorrow', is unassailable; whatever happens tomorrow will be another relative reality. For Plato, however, the truth of a present assertion about the future depends on whether or not the event will in fact occur (*Philebus* 37a–40c).

Since judgements about the future can be made even where standard Protagorean qualities such as 'hot' are concerned, we are meant to read this section as whittling away even more of Protagoras' thesis: given the implicit commitment to *some* objective knowledge, it follows that there can be objective knowledge even about relative qualities, at least in the special case of the future.

It is worth noting at this point, now that Protagoras has been dealt with, that the assault on his relativism has been conducted at the level of beliefs or opinions (*doxai*). As mentioned on p. 144, there is overlap between *doxa* and *aisthesis* (perception). In isolating *doxai*, Plato is trying to deal with the claim of that aspect of *aisthesis* to be knowledge: the definition cannot cope with the expert's knowledge of the future. Plato's criticism has been very carefully orchestrated: in order to reach the conclusion that the definition is incorrect because it cannot cope with the expert's predictive knowledge, he first had to establish, in the face of Protagoras' denial of the fact, that there *are* experts; only then can the conclusion follow.

❧ A Reductio of Flux (181b–183b) ❧

Plato now turns to fulfil the promise of 178e to deal with present and past 'perceptions'. In fact he deals only with present ones, since it is the immediacy of perception which constitutes its main claim to be knowledge. The privacy and immediacy of perception was taken to be a consequence of flux. Plato's assault on this theory is in some ways similar to his criticism of relativism in 169d–172b: he reduces it to being no kind of *theory* at all, and certainly not one which guarantees the infallibility of perceptual judgements such as 'It is hot'. In fact, flux prohibits any kind of identification whatsoever. So perception cannot be infallibly correct, and it does not grasp being because no judgement such as 'It *is* hot' is possible at all in an impermanent world. Incorrigibility and grasp of being were, you will remember, the two marks of knowledge stated at 152c.

Notice how we are moving from beliefs (169d–172b, 177c–179b) to the cognitive aspect of sense-perception (this section); in the next section, I will argue, Plato is dealing with mere non-cognitive sensation. Plato is being thorough in dealing with everything which might have been understood by a normal Greek to be meant by 'perception'.

Since the argument of this section is a *reductio ad absurdum*, it makes sense to ask how much of the flux doctrine Plato thinks is absurd. On the view of Cornford [2], he is arguing that the things of this world are in flux, so that there can be no knowledge of them, and intends us to remember the stable world of Forms, which are therefore the objects of knowledge.

But this is really reading rather a lot into the argument. Given that what is rendered absurd is the idea that everything in this world is in total flux, and given that Plato is rejecting this view, then Plato is suggesting that there must be some stability in *this* world. On Cornford's view, Plato would have to accept the consequence that we are condemned to speechlessness about this world, which Plato would never have done. On the issue of Forms and *Theaetetus*, see further pp. 239–46.

McDowell ([5], pp. 180–84) argues that Plato concentrates on the absurdity of saying that the 'offspring' – seeing and whiteness, for instance (see p. 154) – are in total flux, and suggests that Plato means us to reject the idea that despite moving in space, they are also altering in quality. But in the first place, Plato does *not* talk only about the offspring: at 182d he talks of something 'flowing white', which must be the parent – the white stick or stone – since it makes no sense to talk of the offspring, whiteness, as flowing white. It is worth remembering that on the flux theory there are, strictly speaking, no external objects, only bundles of qualities (see 157b–c and pp. 153, 157). This licenses the amalgamation of objects and their qualities (see 160c with p. 46, n. 2). When Plato talks mainly about the offspring in this section, he is *also* talking about the parents.

In the second place, if McDowell were right, Plato would only have modified Heracliteanism to allow for identification to be made in any given instant of perception. From this modified position, the Protagorean privacy and infallibility of perception could still follow, from which Theaetetus' definition could still follow; Plato would have undermined his whole careful refutation of Theaetetus' definition.

Heraclitus himself, it should be noted in passing, allowed for identification: the difference between his position and the extreme Heracliteanism of Cratylus (see also p. 38, n. 2) is neatly brought out by comparing Heraclitus' claim (Fragment 91) that you can't step into the same river twice, with Cratylus' that you can't step into the same river even once (Aristotle, *Metaphysics* 1010a 13–15). So McDowell's interpretation could be rephrased as that Plato is accepting the Heraclitean position while rejecting the Cratylan one.

However, if there is an interpretation which does not convict Plato of commitment to speechlessness or of carelessness, we should adopt it. In the first place, then, what he is rejecting is certainly the view that we cannot sensibly talk about the world we live in. In the second place, the way in which he is rejecting it is, I suggest, as follows. He is not, or not primarily, making the empirical point that identification *is* possible; the mode of argument is logical. The two types of change – alteration and locomotion – are distinguished in order to argue that the Heraclitean is committed to total change, if he is committed to change at all (181c–e); from this it follows that nothing perceptible is F rather than not-F (182a–d) and therefore that perception cannot be infallible (182d–e). Indeed, language itself is made useless (183a–b). In other words, Plato is repeating a point we met earlier (p. 151; see also p. 158), that a Heraclitean *might as well* call something 'white' as 'not white'. So the conclusion of his reflections on language is that Heracliteans should only say '"not like this either" ... provided they go on and on saying it'.

This interpretation, apart from coping well with the text, has the advantage of linking this section with the earlier sections where flux was introduced, where it was the *logical* puzzles of size and number which were taken to ratify the flux doctrine; and it has the advantage of having Plato make a point which applies as much to less extreme Heracliteanism as to the Cratylan version. Notice the point that if a Heraclitean is committed to change at all, he is committed to total change: on any flux theory, one might as well talk of 'seeing X' as 'not seeing X' (182e), whether flux is taken to be instantaneous or from identifiable moment to the next identifiable moment. For the history of this type of argument and the adoption of the Heraclitean position in later Scepticism, see Delacy [89].

✎ Final Refutation of Theaetetus' Definition (184b–186e) ✎

Here Plato argues that to define knowledge as perception unduly limits knowledge: perception grasps the immediate properties of things, but what about properties (like being, sameness, difference) which are common to more than one thing? They are not grasped by perception, but by mental reflection. This criticism emerges naturally from the criticism of flux in the previous section. As Runciman puts it ([49], p. 25): 'If observer X perceives object O at time t, he cannot assert that a subsequent perception is of the same object, for the subsequent perception is of O_2 by X_2 at time $t + n$, and to trace a connection between the two is something which cannot be done by perception itself.'

There are three main lines of interpretation of this section. The first, exemplified especially by Cornford [2], claims that Plato initially establishes that perceptible things cannot be the only objects of knowledge, and then that non-perceptible things are in fact the only objects of knowledge. The main problem with this interpretation is that it ignores the fact that Plato's distinction between perception and mental activity is based less on their respective objects than on the different processes involved: it is the difference simply between thinking about things and the mere use of senses.

The other two main lines of interpretation accordingly emphasize this basis of Plato's distinction. They differ in how much cognitive ability they see as being granted to perception. One group, consisting mainly of Cooper [88], Modrak [109] and White [123], claims that what Plato is calling sense-perception involves 'simple perceptual judgements' such as labelling experiences (e.g. 'This is hot'); the other group, consisting chiefly of Bondeson [129], Burnyeat [84], Shea [116] and partly Xenakis [125], claims that what Plato is calling sense-perception here has no cognitive ability at all, but is merely inarticulate and instinctive intake of sensible qualities.

Given this primary difference between the two groups, they will clearly also differ in interpreting the other half of Plato's distinction, that is, what mental faculties Plato is distinguishing from sense-perception, and how, therefore, sense-perception fails to be knowledge.

The group that attributes some cognitive ability to sense-perception finds evidence as follows: (1) in the fact that the mind is explicitly involved in sense-perception (e.g. 186b); (2) in the fact that the independent use of mind is illustrated only in cases of reflecting on properties common to more than one sense, which suggests that simple judgements concerned with just one sense are being attributed to sense-perception; (3) in the emphasis at 186b–c that long education is required for the independent use of mind: it would be unrealistic of Plato to suggest that long education is required for simple perceptual judgements.

I cannot here do justice to the complexity and excellence of an article such as Cooper's, but let us at any rate notice that this evidence is not overwhelming. (1) This is evidence only if it is assumed that the mind is *only* reflective; but it is not. The mind (*psyche*) is necessarily involved, according to Plato, even in mere sensory awareness. At *Philebus* 33d–34a Plato argues that the body on its own is completely insensate. (This also, incidentally, explains the otherwise odd talk of 'perceiving experiences' at 186b–c: an 'experience' may not be perceived – that is, 'penetrate through to the *psyche*', as *Philebus* puts it.) (2) The emphasis on common properties is explicable by the fact that one of Plato's avowed aims (184d) is to demonstrate that there is something in people that is singular, rather than the plurality of the senses. When he argues that there is something which deals with properties common to the objects of more than one sense, all he is doing is arguing for the existence of this single something (mind). It does not follow that the mind does not make judgements about the objects of a single sense. (3) The mention of long education can be understood as referring to the *complete* ability to manipulate abstract concepts such as being and benefit. This ability, as twentieth-century psychologists have observed, does take a long time to form, and, of course, may never be complete from a philosopher's point of view. Thus the ability to make simple perceptual judgements may be acquired relatively early and easily; but the complete ability to make all kinds of judgements takes a long time.

There is certainly no unambiguous evidence in favour of the view that sense-perception has some judgemental aspect. There are also serious difficulties with it. In the first place, if sense-perception is capable of judgements like 'It is hot', then Plato's talk of 'being' as one of the common properties which only the mind can grasp has to be understood as talk of 'existence', since judgements about existence are more reflective than those which simply say '. . . *is* hot' or whatever. But it is impossible for 'being' to mean 'existence' here. The existential use of 'to be' (see p. 146) has been remarkably absent throughout the preceding discussion, whereas the predicative use has been pervasive. More telling, however, is that the common properties of, say, a sound and a colour include not just 'being' but 'not being' (185c). It is not said that we judge that they are *or* are not, but that they are *and* are not, just as we judge that they are the same (as themselves) *and* different (from each other): see 185a. If existence is one of their common properties, how can they also be non-existent? 'Being' is obviously predicative: it is one of their shared properties because it is possible to say of both that they *are* what they are; not being is one of their shared properties because it is possible to say of both that they *are not* any number of things.

Moreover, if 'being' is 'existence', Plato has undermined his whole careful argument (as White [123] in fact complains). To deprive sense-perception of access to existence, and therefore conclude that it is not knowledge, does not affect the claim of sense-perception to have access to the 'being' which it originally had (152a–c) and which constituted its claim to be knowledge; the claim of perception to be knowledge was supported by the fact that it grasps being precisely in the sense that it makes simple perceptual judgements like 'The wind is cold'. If Plato now assumes that sense-perception does make these sorts of judgements, and talks about an entirely different sense of 'being', he is more than careless.

Note also that the novel recognition of the sense-organs (184d) assists a distinction between cognitive and non-cognitive aspects of perception, since the organs on their own are non-cognitive.

Finally, it is worth noting aspects of Plato's general tactics. In the first place, this section leads immediately into a discussion of the cognitive aspects of the mind: the clear contrast is with sense-perception as non-cognitive. Secondly, as I argued on p. 181, Plato has by now dealt with the cognitive aspect of sense-perception; it remains for him only to refute the claim of non-cognitive sensation to be knowledge, then he has dealt with everything that a normal Greek might have ascribed to *aisthesis* and might have understood Theaetetus' definition to entail.

The upshot of all this is that it is possible to read 186d–e as Plato having Theaetetus acknowledge the restriction of the term *aisthesis* to mere sensory awareness in this section.

I conclude that the interpretation that sense-perception is entirely non-cognitive in this section is correct; it does not make even simple perceptual judgements. So here at last we have the distinction between sensation and perception. There are no grounds for thinking that the distinction occurs earlier in the dialogue, nor does it occur earlier in the history of philosophy (though it may be adumbrated in *Republic*: see Hamlyn [35], pp. 11–12). The point Plato successfully makes in this section is that since mere sensation cannot even say 'It is hot', it has no grasp on being, and therefore no grasp on truth, and therefore cannot be knowledge. Notice the implication that truth may be a function of propositions, i.e. statements of sufficient minimal complexity to include the verb 'to be'. Strictly the implication is only that sensation has no grasp on being, not that knowledge necessarily does; knowledge may grasp truth through propositions, but Plato is not precluding knowledge by direct acquaintance (see further pp. 195, 212–14).

Therefore, Plato concludes, sensation fails to have both the relevant marks of knowledge (see 152c): it doesn't grasp being, and since it doesn't grasp truth, it cannot be infallible.

Plato has now argued that, given the Protagorean and Heraclitean implications of Theaetetus' definition, none of the aspects of 'perception' which may have been read into the definition have the two marks of knowledge: beliefs may be false, simple perceptual judgements are no more infallible than fallible, and mere sensation won't do either.

❧ *Theaetetus* and the Historical Protagoras ❧

The second part of the dialogue is complete. A historical issue finally needs some treatment. Plato assimilates Theaetetus' definition to Protagorean relativism, which in turn is assimilated to a theory of flux. Protagoras is criticized, defended and criticized again. How much of all this is reliable evidence for the actual views of the historical person Protagoras?

There is no doubt that Protagoras was a relativist; the difficulty is to decide what sort. There is little evidence outside of Plato or not dependent on Plato, and the Platonic evidence is not clear-cut.

We should first assess the parameters to considering Plato's evidence. There is no doubt that he knew Protagoras' book well: at 152a he quotes from it, and Theaetetus is made to claim that he has often read it. Moreover, throughout the Platonic corpus, Protagoras is treated with respect; Plato may disagree with him, but we should not expect Plato to be a hostile witness. Finally, he is careful in our dialogue to mark when he is extending Protagoras' written doctrine: he calls the flux theory a 'secret' doctrine of Protagoras (152c, 155d); he revives the dead philosopher to defend his 'orphaned' written doctrine (162d, 164e, 166a). In other words, these are points at which he is consciously extending Protagoras' written doctrine: neither the secret doctrine of flux nor Protagoras' defence were in the book. However, at both points Plato feels he is drawing out legitimate consequences of Protagoras' written doctrine. He feels that Protagoras could consistently have held a fluxist position, and made the points the defence makes. *Prima facie*, then, it makes sense to consider Plato a reliable source, if treated with caution when he warns us to treat him with caution.

The starting-point is the man-measure fragment (Fragment 1), quoted at 152a: 'Man is the measure of all things – of the things that are, that they are; of the things that are not, that they are not.' I take it that there is now consensus that 'Man' refers to individuals, rather than mankind as a whole (which is obvious on reading the next piece of doctrine attributed to Protagoras as an actual quotation: see p. 30, n. 4); that 'things' are not specific (that is, not restricted to sensible qualities, and not necessarily implying externally existing physical objects); that the being and not being that people are supposed to measure are not exclusively whether or not things exist, nor exclusively that things are the case, nor exclusively what properties belong to things (see p. 146); and finally (which is again obvious on my reading of the text: see p. 30, n. 4), that the inference that 'Things are for each person as they appear to each person' is genuinely Protagorean.

Here, then, is the core of his relativism. But what sort of relativism is it? Plato's illustration of the wind (152b) is clearly fair given the points agreed on in the last paragraph, but it is ambiguous: that the wind may be cold to me and warm to you is capable of three relativistic interpretations:

1. That the wind in itself is neither cold nor warm. These properties come into existence when and only when they are perceived to exist. This has traditionally been called the 'subjectivist' view (S), and I shall use this name, though (3) is really the subjectivist view.

2. That the wind in itself is both cold and warm. Both properties coexist in the wind: I perceive one of them, you perceive the other. I shall call this the 'objectivist' view (O).

3. That there is no such thing as the wind itself. There is only the wind as it appears to me, and the wind as it appears to you. I shall call this view 'V', since its most recent proponent is Vlastos [121].

Notice that, whichever of these three views is correct, Protagoras is rejecting the view that the wind is either cold or warm, and that one of the two percipients is simply wrong.

If we accept that Plato is accurately paraphrasing Protagoras, we have to reject V: Plato says that 'the *same* wind' is involved. But it should be noticed that V is the view of the secret doctrine, with its dismissal of substrates; so in denying V we are denying that Plato is correct to have attributed the secret doctrine to Protagoras, even as a consistent consequence of his written doctrine.

How are we to decide between S (favoured, for instance, by Glidden [91] and Guthrie [93]) and O (favoured, for instance, by Cornford [2] and Kerferd [98])?

↛ Late Greek Evidence ↜

Sextus, *Outlines of Pyrrhonism* I.216–19, seems to favour O. Sextus quotes the man-measure fragment, claims that Protagoras' 'things' are external events, attributes the doctrine of flux to Protagoras, and continues: 'He says that the reasons for all appearances subsist in matter, so that matter, as far as it is capable, can appear to be whatever it appears to be to anyone.' He then summarizes the argument from dreams and hallucinations (*Theaetetus* 158b ff.) and concludes: 'Therefore man turns out to be in himself the criterion of what is.'

This is scarcely reliable evidence. In the first place, it is dependent on *Theaetetus* and therefore begs the question of how we are to interpret *Theaetetus*. Secondly, the conclusion that man *in himself* is the measure does not follow from the statement that the 'reasons for all appearances' have objective existence, but rather from the doctrine of flux. Sextus is in fact confusing S and O and is no more evidence for one than for the other.

Another late passage is sometimes adduced as evidence for O. In *Against Colotes* 1108F, Plutarch reports that Colotes criticized Democritus for holding that no external object is describable in one way rather than another. Plutarch says that this criticism is obviously misplaced, since Democritus himself criticized Protagoras on this very issue.

Again, this could be evidence for either S or O, since both of them mention external objects like the 'wind in itself'.

✦ *Aristotle's Evidence* ✦

It is better to leave later writers aside. Closer to hand, let us look at Aristotle. In two passages of *Metaphysics* (1007b 18–23 and 1062b 12–19), Aristotle stresses that Protagoras' doctrine is effectively a denial of the law of non-contradiction; this is perhaps easier to understand as a consequence of O, with its talk of co-existent contradictory properties, than of S. However, the latter passage is vitiated as evidence by obviously being Aristotle's own deduction: 'He said that man is the measure of all things, by which he means that what appears to each person also assuredly is. If this is so, it follows that the same thing both is and is not, and is bad and good, and that the contents of all other opposing statements are true.'

In fact, it is not the case that the denial of the law of non-contradiction follows only from O; it might just as well follow from S. Or rather, it is the case that it follows from neither, strictly speaking, since the law of non-contradiction is a universal law and necessarily omits the Protagorean qualifiers, as Aristotle does in the passage quoted above. The law of non-contradiction says, 'A thing cannot be both F and not-F'; Protagoras, on either S or O, says, 'A thing is F for one person and not-F for another.'

However, there is one piece of Aristotelian evidence which points towards S rather than O: at *Metaphysics* 1047a 4–7, he describes 'Protagoras' theory' as the view that 'Nothing is either cold or warm or sweet or has any perceptible quality unless it is being perceived.'

✦ *Platonic Evidence Apart from* Theaetetus ✦

Protagoras' political views as reported in *Protagoras* fit in well with the view attributed to him on pp. 169–71 he seems to say that political decisions about what is advantageous for the community are decided by general assent without resort to experts with objective knowledge (Taylor [119], pp. 83–4). However, he does allow that some skills are unevenly distributed, so that some people are better flute-players than others, for instance (323a–b, 327b–c). But even this is not inconsistent with the subjectivist position I attributed to him on pp. 169–71: a good flute-player will simply be someone whose playing seems good to people.

Plato's *Euthydemus* attributes to Protagoras the view that falsehood is impossible and therefore disagreement is impossible (286c); as we have seen in discussing Aristotle on non-contradiction, this does not allow us to decide between S and O.

✺ *Other Fragments of Protagoras* ✺

'Teaching relies on natural talent and practice; one must learn from youth' (Fragment 3). This is unclear. Does he mean that a teacher requires the pupil to be talented and to practise a lot? This is how the fragment is usually understood (in which case see above on the flute-players in Plato's *Protagoras*). But why then did Protagoras say 'teaching' rather than 'learning', which would have made the point clearly? It is perhaps better to take the fragment literally, since both *Protagoras* and *Theaetetus* suggest that Protagoras was concerned to justify the teaching role of sophists in general and himself in particular. In this case, there is nothing in this fragment which is inconsistent with the cynical teachers espoused by a subjectivist Protagoras in Plato's defence (pp. 169–71): even such teachers need to practise and learn their art.

Fragment 4 (quoted on p. 50, n. 1) tells us nothing about S and O, though Mansfeld [105] makes some interesting comments on its relation to the epistemology of the man-measure fragment.

Finally, Protagoras' famous claim that there are two sides to every argument, which was central to his role as a teacher of rhetoric, is obviously ambivalent as between S and O. In fact it is important to remember that although Plato cites the man-measure fragment as coming from a book entitled *The Truth*, which sounds like a work of philosophy, Sextus reports it as coming from Protagoras' book on rhetoric. If the latter was accurate, then of course Plato would have to tease out the philosophical aspects: Protagoras perhaps meant the fragment more as a gnomic utterance to support the relativism of his rhetorical teaching. He claimed to be able to teach his students to present a winning case – even 'to make a weaker argument defeat a stronger' (Aristotle, *Rhetoric* 1402a 5–28). Whatever appeared to their audience would be true for their audience.

❧ Plato's Defence of Protagoras ❧

We must now return to Plato's defence of Protagoras (166a–168c), bearing in mind the claim of, for instance, Kerferd [98] and Cole [87] that objectivist standards are imported there. If there are experts with objective knowledge about what is good for people and communities, then O is supported because these experts pick out, as it were, the good properties of things, and have the ability to make others see these good properties. S cannot tolerate such experts, because according to S external objects do not intrinsically have properties which are there to be picked out: an object only has the properties which I perceive it to have, and I may perceive 'good' properties to be 'bad', or vice versa.

I point out on p. 170 that the objectivist reading of the defence forces Protagoras into the inconsistency that *not* every belief is true. Since the truth of every belief is firmly attested for Protagoras by our ancient evidence, we should reject the interpretation that makes him contradict it. And in the defence, Plato repeatedly assures us that he is being fair to Protagoras.

But if we reject this reading of the defence, we saddle Protagoras with a highly cynical view of teachers: they are those who have the ability to make something seem better to their students, whatever the 'facts' of the matter. Is there any external evidence that Protagoras could have held such a view of expertise? There is in fact one slight clue tending in that direction: at *Metaphysics* 997b 35–998a 4, Aristotle reports that Protagoras argued against geometry that a straight line cannot be *perceived* to touch a circle at only a point. This looks like a fragment of an argument that, contrary to expert and objective knowledge, people's perceptions are authoritative.

At the end of this discussion, we can see that there is some reason to attribute S to Protagoras, but no clear evidence that points to O. We should finally consider the fact that Plato attributes radical flux to Protagoras. On either S or O, this is an incorrect attribution, since both S and O claim that there are external objects (though S claims that they have no objective properties), whereas the radical doctrine of flux claims that, strictly, a so-called external object is just a bundle of qualities, none of which exists until it is perceived. But it is obvious that S is closer to flux than O is. Plato seems to have thought he was being fair to Protagoras in attributing a doctrine of flux to him; he is more likely to have thought this if S was Protagoras' view.

PART THREE:
❧ KNOWLEDGE AND BELIEF (187a–201c) ❧

In the last section of the second part of the dialogue (184b–186e), Plato demolished the claim of mere sense-perception to be knowledge. However, he has not yet argued that beliefs are not knowledge; in so far as beliefs have played a part in the second part of the dialogue, he has only argued that they are not bound to be true, as Protagoras claimed. Naturally enough, then, Theaetetus next suggests that knowledge might be belief and, equally naturally, settles on true belief rather than false belief (187a–b).

As in his treatment of Theaetetus' first definition, Plato's tactics are again oblique. The investigation of the idea that true belief is knowledge is postponed in favour of another so-called digression (see the reference at 187d to the first digression of 172b–177c), on how false belief is possible. This is very much a sign of a philosopher at work: Plato is not content with the patent fact that false belief is possible; he wants also to be able to explain it and to discover why people might hold that false belief is impossible. This digression takes us all the way up to 200c; then, at 200e–201c, he very briefly and in an authoritative fashion dismisses the claim of true belief to be knowledge.

At face value, this is the most aporetic part of the dialogue: not only does true belief fail to be knowledge, but Plato also fails to account for false belief, despite several attempts. However, we also learn a great deal about Plato's epistemology from this point of the dialogue, and it will help to preface a survey of its arguments with an epistemological distinction.

One of the few weaknesses of the English language is that it lacks a distinction between different senses of 'know'. The same is also true (though more controversially: see pp. 236–7) for Greek. Basically, we use 'know' in two ways. We say that we know people and objects, meaning that we recognize them. For this the French is *connaître*, the German is *kennen* and the Italian is *conoscere*; I shall use the phrase 'knowledge by acquaintance'. We also say that we know facts, or that something is the case. For this the French is *savoir*, the German is *wissen* and the Italian is *sapere*; I shall use the phrase 'propositional knowledge'. Russell [50] remains the starting-point for reading about these two types of knowledge.

As the discussion progresses, the question whether Plato distinguished these two types of knowledge will exercise us. At any rate, this distinction has been held to be relevant to discussing *Theaetetus*, so it will help to bear it in mind. For the moment, I introduce the terminology just to make the discussion of this third part of the dialogue easier to follow.

❧ Puzzles about False Belief (187d–189b) ❧

Having agreed with Theaetetus that there is such a thing as false belief and that it should be investigated (187d–e), Socrates introduces two dichotomies which he sees as relevant to the problem. The first is between knowing and not knowing, the second between being and not being.

❧ Knowing and Not Knowing (188a–c) ❧

The argument of this section plays a dual role. In the first place, Socrates sees the dichotomy itself as immediately generating an impediment to explaining false belief; but in the second place, it sets the parameters for much of the following discussion of false belief. At crucial points in the discussion the consequences of the dichotomy between knowing and not knowing are shown not to have been escaped (196b–c, 200b), and the dichotomy sets the terms for most of the ensuing arguments. It is important, therefore, that we understand what is going on in this brief section.

The argument is that if everything is either known or unknown, then it is impossible to mistake something known for something else that is known or for something that is unknown; and it is equally impossible to mistake something unknown for something else that is unknown. Therefore, if everything is either known or unknown, false belief is impossible.

The paradox that false belief is impossible was a favourite among the sophists. It is probable that the argument of this section is sophistic in origin. We know from *Meno* 80d–e and *Theaetetus* 163a–165d that the dichotomy between knowing or not knowing was sophistic. At 188a Socrates excludes any intermediary states between these two extremes: in so doing, it has been claimed, he is simply following the dictates of a familiar casuistic argument.

It looks at first sight, then, as though this argument need hardly delay us long (so, for instance, Guthrie [30]). There is such a thing as false belief, so the argument is wrong, and Plato hints that it is wrong because it fails to take account of intermediary states. But this view is superficial, because (as already noted) at 200a–b, at the end of the discussion of false belief, Plato finds that he has been unable to account for it precisely because the best view that he can come up with is still liable to the quandary of this section, even though the argument is sophistic. This means that, even if the argument is invalid (as it must be, given its paradoxical conclusion), Plato is unable to pinpoint the invalidity and deal with it. In other words, he shares common ground with whatever assumptions generate the puzzle and (if our analysis of 163a–165d on pp. 165–8 was correct) although he knows that some qualifications have to be inserted into the bare dichotomy

of either knowing or not knowing, he cannot see what qualifications will do in this instance. This in turn means that in
excluding intermediary states such as learning, he is following
his own viewpoint, as much as that of any sophist, and is not
hinting that this is the flaw in the argument. So we find, at
191c–d and 197e, that learning is the acquisition of knowledge: something unknown becomes known through learning. Plato is committed to the view that everything is either
known or unknown (Lewis [134], pace Fine [131]); and he is
genuinely puzzled by the problem of how I can have something before my mind and yet fail to know what it is.

Given all this, it makes sense to consider the argument
more carefully; it will inform us of Platonic assumptions about
knowledge. The argument is plausible only on the assumption
that making a mistake about something rules out having
knowledge of it (188b) – in other words, that to know something is either to know everything about it, or at least to
know enough about it to be able to distinguish it from
everything else. And this in turn, in our terminology, only
becomes plausible if knowledge is taken to be knowledge by
acquaintance. Propositional knowledge, such as knowing
that there is a plant called Japonica, does not preclude me
from having false beliefs about Japonica, or even from mistaking it for some other shrub.

To put the issue another way, the model Plato here establishes for error is misidentification: one thing is wrongly identified as another thing. But this is a restricted kind of error. The
wider class of false beliefs associated with propositional states
has to do with, say, applying an inappropriate predicate, as in
'Japonica has yellow flowers'. This false belief is nothing to do
with misidentifying yellow flowers for red (or white) ones. I
need not be acquainted with Japonica at all to hold the true
belief that there is a plant called Japonica, and yet the false
belief that it has yellow flowers.

Yet Plato concludes not that a certain limited set of false
beliefs – false identity beliefs – are impossible, but that *all*
false beliefs are impossible. (As a matter of fact, he will later
(191a–b) correctly point out that this bare, unqualified

argument does not rule out even all false identity beliefs.)
Plato obviously recognized that, grammatically, propositions
could follow the verb 'to know'; it looks as though he is either
carelessly or deliberately assimilating the two types of knowledge. This, as I said before, is an issue which will exercise us
from time to time. For the moment, we have uncovered the
assimilation, and we will watch out for it in what follows.

For more detailed analyses of this section, see McDowell
[136], Williams [138], Lewis [134] and Fine [131].

❧ Being and Not Being (188c–189b) ☙

The argument in this section that false belief is impossible is
familiar from elsewhere in the Platonic dialogues (*Euthydemus*
283e–284c, *Republic* 478b–c, *Cratylus* 429d–e, *Sophist* 240d–
241b). It arises out of the ambiguity of the verb 'to be' (see
p. 146) and was undoubtedly a central problem of Greek
philosophy, until Plato paved the way for its solution in
Sophist. However, *Theaetetus* pre-dates *Sophist*. As with the
previous argument, this route to the paradox was well
trodden by the sophists, chiefly Protagoras; but since again
Plato does not defuse the argument, we have to suppose that
at the time of writing *Theaetetus* he was still puzzled by it. The
underlying puzzle is: How can I think at all and yet fail to
have an object before my mind? Hintikka ([37], Chapter 1) is
well worth reading on the depth background to this puzzle.
He argues that a teleological approach to belief, speech, etc.,
had a very strong hold on Greek thought: each has a job to
do, and does it.

The argument of this section may be paraphrased as follows: Belief (like sense-perception) is always of something;
but false belief is belief of what is not (that is, on the veridical
sense of 'to be', what is not the case); 'what is not' is nothing
(that is, on the existential sense of 'to be', 'what is not' is non-
existent); therefore, since *ex hypothesi* belief is always of something, false belief is not belief at all.

It is interesting to note that Plato gets close to defusing this
argument. In 188d he twice qualifies 'believing what is not'
as 'believing what is not *about* something'. If he had followed

this through, he would perhaps have reached the conclusions of *Sophist*, that this 'something' is the subject of a sentence, and that false belief may be analysed as attributing an inappropriate predicate to this subject. But Plato has plainly not developed this analysis of the logic of sentences, with the result that at 189b he amalgamates 'what is not about something' with 'what is not' in an absolute sense.

I have so far analysed the argument in terms of the ambiguity between the veridical and existential senses of 'to be'. At the risk of complicating the issue, it is worth noting that it is not impossible that the predicative sense of 'to be' is involved as well. The risk is worth taking because it shows how radical the ambiguity of 'to be' is in this argument. Consider the analogy, supposedly established in 188e–189a, between sense-perception and belief. Both have an object, something which is. There is clearly existential import involved, since 'something which is not' is eventually glossed as 'nothing'; but up until that gloss the argument could be relying on the predicative sense, so that 'something which is' means 'something which is F', where F is some predicate such as 'black'. Then to deny the possibility of believing 'something which is not' is to deny the possibility that there is (exists) anything about which one cannot say, 'It is F.'

The argument for an analogy between sense-perception and belief is also interesting in the light of the fact that Plato has already shown himself aware, in 184b–186e, that belief may be more complex than sense-perception, particularly since it is cognitive and may be propositional. However, even acknowledging a possible propositional content for belief does not preclude Plato from thinking that it shares with sense-perception at least the common ground that it is of 'something which is'. And again we find, as we did in the last section, that the propositional nature of mental states is not clearly distinguished from the immediate grasping of individual things which characterizes perception and other mental states. Otherwise he might have seen that the analogy between believing and perceiving is false: one cannot say, 'He saw X, but X wasn't there' (except in the sense of 'He thought he saw X'); but one can say 'He believes X, but X isn't so.'

This section is somewhat loosely tied into the rest of the discussion of false belief. At 189c, Plato merely suggests that whatever the object of belief, it must be possible to say of it that it is: this is all he takes the argument of this section to establish. In other words, in the context of *Theaetetus*, it is best read as a kind of appendix to the argument about knowing and not knowing: if false belief is wrongly thinking that *a* is *b*, then whatever else obtains, both *a* and *b* must exist. His problem is that, despite having admitted at 186c–e that mental states have access to being, he must find a way to explain mistakes.

◆ Three Models of False Belief (189b–200d) ◆

Plato proceeds to try out three different models to see if any of them overcomes the problem raised by the dichotomy of knowing and not knowing.

◆ *False Belief as Cross-belief* (189b–190e) ◆

A common-sense view of the falsity of false belief is that it is due to lack of correspondence with external reality: the belief is inaccurate, or goes awry, as a Greek would put it. If I think that fresh snow is black, I am wrong. This looks like a promising view of false belief, and is in fact essentially the one Plato will later adopt in *Sophist*. However, he here rejects it; we need to see why.

The first part of the argument analyses the common-sense view as the view that false belief takes *a* to be *b*, that is, takes what is externally the case (white) to be something else (black). The second part of the argument claims that this analysis is absurd. For something to count as a belief, it must be the end-result of a whole process of (perhaps unconscious) deliberation. I look at the snow; I run through a range of colours; I conclude that it is black. It is not that I am in the perverse position of claiming that white snow is black: that the snow is white has not been formulated by my mind as a belief. Plato argues that the analysis of false belief as taking *a* to be *b* requires that both *a* and *b* are beliefs present to my mind, which puts the believer in precisely that perverse and ridiculous position. It is rather the case, as Plato says at 190c, that if a madman takes something to be a cow, it doesn't matter what the external facts are; he will still never be in the position of saying that this 'cow' is a horse (notice the hint of Protagoreanism: see p. 155). Plato therefore concludes, unfortunately, not that his analysis of 'taking a to be b' is wrong, but that this formula is wrong, or has not yet been explained.

It is Plato's analysis of the formula that is at fault. In this section he appears to be concerned with thinking, not the strong knowledge of 188a–c, and in particular with beliefs that attribute some predicate to something. This looks promising. But instead of analysing 'Taking a to be b' as applying a predicate b to a subject a, he analyses a and b as things of equal status and equally present to the mind. In other words, in the first place he does not have the awareness, which he gains in *Sophist*, of the breakdown of sentences into subjects and predicates; and secondly, he misconstrues the part the external world plays in the falsity of a false belief. It is not that I perversely think 'This white snow is black'; I think 'This snow is black'. It is only an external observer who is in the position of filling in *both* the blanks in the formula, and saying, 'He thinks that this snow, which is in fact white, is black.' So Plato remains on the basis of thinking that mistakes are misidentifications. In fact, the argument here usefully shows precisely why he reached the conclusion of 188a–c, that all false beliefs, not just those involving what we would call misidentification, are impossible: he takes even the attribution of inappropriate predicates to be a type of misidentification.

It might be wondered why Plato comes up with this analysis of the cross-belief formula. What is the temptation to do so? It is due to an ambiguity in the notion of 'cross-belief'. The ambiguity is subtle, and it is not implausible that Plato could have got confused. Consider the sentence, 'I think that white snow is black.' This can be taken either to be a direct and literal report of my belief, or a reconstruction of my belief. Plato starts with the common-sense view, which is obviously the latter, that I do not actually believe that white snow is black, but my belief can be reconstructed this way; but he ends with the claim that both *a* and *b* must be present to the mind, which turns 'I think that white snow is black' into a literal report, not a reconstruction, of my belief. As a literal report it is, as Plato says, absurd.

The temptation to take 'cross-belief' in this way is offered to Plato by the puzzle of 188a–c (Fine [131]). If in order for something to figure in my belief, I have to know all about it, then I must know that snow is white, and must be in the perverse position Plato argues for in this section.

The simple grammatical device of quotation marks can often resolve this fallacy – but Greek lacked quotation marks. Chisholm ([24], p. 37) gives an amusing illustration:

> A Frenchman, believing that 'potatoes' is English for apples, may use 'There are potatoes in the basket' to express the belief that there are apples in the basket; from the fact that he has a mistaken belief about 'potatoes' and 'apples', it does not follow that he has a mistaken belief about potatoes and apples.

In other words, it is wrong to say that this Frenchman thinks that potatoes are apples, which is what Plato is effectively saying; he thinks that 'potatoes' are apples.

For other and more detailed analyses of the section, see McDowell [5], Williams [138], Lewis [134] and especially Fine [131]. The two models which follow in the next two sections are best read not as distinct models, but as attempts to discover how cross-belief might be possible (see especially the reference to cross-belief at 193c–d, and also 199b).

❧ The Wax Block (190e–196d) ☙

This is a long and closely argued section. In order to make the densest part of the argument somewhat clearer, I have inserted numerals in the text (192a–d). It will also be convenient to use shorthand: I use *a* and *b* in the text for objects; here I shall also use K for the case where something is known, –K where it is unknown, P where it is perceived, –P where it is not perceived. Thus '*a*K–P and *b*–K–P' would be shorthand for a case where object *a* is known, but not perceived, and object *b* is neither known nor perceived. This will make the task of understanding this section infinitely easier.

In 191a–e the background is established. The claim, at 188c, that something unknown cannot be taken to be something known, is arguably wrong. Something perceived from a distance, but otherwise unknown, can be taken to be something known, but not currently being perceived: *a*–KP and *b*K–P, in our shorthand. Socrates claims that there may be several cases where the right analysis reveals the possibility of false belief; the model he uses for analysis is that of a wax block which retains the memory-impressions of things we have learned or otherwise come to have known. The model allows the possibility of treating cases where there is a relation between stored knowledge or its lack and current perception or its lack, which Plato believes may reveal the possibility of false belief.

We are first (192a–c) given an apparently systematic list of cases where false belief is impossible:

[1] *a*K–P and *b*K–P

In the next three cases, Plato does not mention perception at all; but since he later recapitulates [2] and [3], at 193a–b, as neither involving any current perception, we may take him to be assuming that we carry –P over from [1]:

[2] *a*K–P and *b*–K–P
[3] *a*–K–P and *b*–K–P
[4] *a*–K–P and *b*K–P

Notice that [2] is the same as [4], except that *a* and *b* have swapped statuses.

The next four cases do not mention knowledge at all, but since we know from 191e that all the cases involve some knowledge or its lack, it is easy to supply lack of knowledge in all four, just as we supplied lack of perception where necessary in the first four cases:

[5] *a*–KP and *b*–KP
[6] *a*–KP and *b*–K–P
[7] *a*–K–P and *b*–K–P
[8] *a*–K–P and *b*–KP

Notice that [7] is the same as [3] and that [6] is the reverse of [8].

The repetition and two reversals that we have already noted might lead us to wonder how systematic Plato is being. We next get three cases where Plato stresses a match between the memory-mark and the perception. We will have to come back to this feature. Ignoring it for the moment, we find:

[9] aKP and bKP
[10] aKP and bK–P
[11] aKP and b–KP

And we end with three further impossibilities:

[12] a–K–P and b–K–P
[13] a–K–P and b–KP
[14] a–K–P and bK–P

Now, each of these is a repetition: [12] is the same as [3] and [7]; [13] is the same as [8]; [14] is the same as [4].

If we glance ahead to the three cases where Plato reckons false belief *can* arise (192c–d), we find:

[15] aK–P and bKP
[16] aK–P and b–KP
[17] aKP and bKP

The main puzzle that greets us here is that [17], a case where false belief is said to be possible, repeats [9], where it is said to be impossible! But it is also worth nothing that [15] is [10] reversed, and that [16] is the case Theaetetus mentioned in 191b.

The upshot of all this is clearly that it is best to read the passage as discursive: its systematic appearance is deceptive. Of sixteen possible cases (each of a and b can have four statuses: KP, –KP, K–P and –K–P), four are not mentioned at all, one is mentioned three times and three are mentioned twice! Nor is it the case that any of the omissions can be excused as reversals of cases that *are* mentioned: of the six possible reversals among the sixteen possible cases, three have both sides mentioned, two have only one side mentioned, and one has neither side mentioned (neither 'aKP and b–K–P' or 'a–K–P and bKP' are mentioned). Nor can the omissions be explained as not worth mentioning because they are in some way obvious: nothing could be more obvious than that [3] does not yield false belief, yet it is repeated twice.

Faced with all this, it might be thought that it was after all wrong to supply, for instance, –P in [2] to [4]. Perhaps if Plato says [4] aK and bK, that is all he means us to consider. This would make the passage even less systematic, of course, since a system based on this would contain sixty-four possibilities, but it would get rid of the repetitions (except for [9] and [17], but that is obviously a special case anyway). However, not only does Plato introduce the passage at 191e by saying that both knowledge and perception have some status in every case, but this is also reiterated in 192e.

Short of the hypothesis of drastic textual corruption, it is impossible not to conclude that Plato is not being systematic. His distinction of cases where false belief is impossible is to a degree random. The passage, then, is best read as a piece of discursive philosophy, making points which Plato feels are relevant to what he is considering. Read in this way, it is not so much *which* cases are claimed or not claimed to allow for false belief that becomes important, as the emphasis in 192b on matching, or aligning memory-traces with perceptions. Plato is here making some point about the mechanics of false belief.

But first let us summarize the rest of the argument. The general principle, that both knowledge and perception can have two statuses each, is repeated (192d–e); the whole paragraph of 192a–c is summarized (192e–193b); cases [17] and [15] are spelled out (193b–d); [9] and [17] are distinguished (193d–194a); [15] is repeated (194a); and finally we get a somewhat sketchy summary of the conclusion (194a–b).

The principle which allows Plato to distinguish [9] and [17], and which is stressed several times between 193c and 195a, is that of matching or mismatching perceptions to memory-traces. If I successfully match what I see with what I remember (know), then I have true belief; if I do not, I have false belief. It becomes clear that this is the principle which has been assumed throughout. In other words, none of the fourteen cases where false belief is said to be impossible allows the possibility of mismatching; where there is a possibility that they might (in cases [9], [10] and [11]), it is stressed that such cases do not allow for false belief *when* there is no mismatch (192b).

From this it follows that the three cases where false belief is said to be possible should be the only cases where such a mismatch is possible. However, he has probably overlooked one:

[18] *a*KP and *b*–KP

This is a repetition of [11], but surely (like [9]) it is a case where mismatch is not automatically excluded by the statuses of knowledge and perception. I see two people in the distance; the one on the right I actually know, the other I don't know; but I get them the wrong way round and say to myself that the one on the left is the one I know, while the other is a stranger.

So again we find that Plato is not being systematic: not even all the cases where false belief can arise are mentioned. Again we must conclude that it is the principle of matching or mismatching that concerns him more than the listing of cases.

Plato now turns to criticize the model (195b–196c); the criticism is straightforward. Plato has identified a certain class of mistakes which are concerned with the mismatch of current perceptions and stored knowledge. But it has been agreed (191d, 195a) that our memories contain purely mental information, abstract concepts: the model fails to cater for a false belief such as '7 + 5 = 11'.

The point is correct, but the argument is weak. To Theaetetus' claim that, just as nobody is going to mistake a man for a horse when both are merely being thought about, so nobody is going to think that the abstract number 11 is 12, Socrates responds by substituting 7 + 5 for 12, and pointing out that mistakes in calculation are possible. But this is the same fallacy we have met before (pp. 201–2): if I mistakenly say that 11 is the sum of 7 and 5, I am not mistaking 11 for 12 – that is a *reconstruction* of my belief. At any rate, having made the substitution, Plato reckons that the Wax Block falls foul of the problem we met in 188a–c: both 11 and 12 are known, so how can they occur in errors?

The substitution of simple knowables such as '11' and '12' for the more complex 'the sum of 7 and 5' shows that in the Wax Block Plato is still operating with a model of false belief as misidentification of things known by acquaintance. This is important to realize, because otherwise there is a temptation to find, as one of the strengths of the Wax Block, that it appears to do away with the strong conception of knowledge which was assumed in 188a–c. It is no longer the case, apparently, that the only choice we are being offered about an object is either to know it or to be totally blank about it: uncertainty of perception and even unclarity of memory are taken into consideration. When considering the strong conception of knowledge of 188a–c, we might have entertained the hope that if this conception came to be weakened, Plato would consider the logic of propositional knowledge, since blankness is the opposite of acquaintance, whereas falsehood is the opposite of propositional knowledge. There are grounds for claiming that the Wax Block begins to fulfil this expectation: it accommodates descriptions along the lines of 'That person whom I now see in the distance is Socrates', rather than merely 'Theodorus is Socrates'. This is explicit at 191b. The extra complexity of descriptions could have led towards a loosening of the hold of the simple model of misidentification, and towards a consideration of propositions, because descriptions are more obviously to do with facts, not things knowable by acquaintance.

However, the substitution of the simple '12' for the description 'the sum of 7 and 5' shows that reflection on descriptions is no part of Plato's programme. Nor, it need hardly be added, is he distinguishing between *a priori* statements, such as '7 + 5 = 12', and contingent statements, such as, 'That cat is the one I saw yesterday.'

What we have, in fact, is a situation where Plato has not really altered his conception of knowledge, but has simply changed the rules of the game. Belief has become a relation between an immediate perception of a simple identity and an equally simple memory-imprint. The talk of unclarity of memory is not so much intended to alter the concept of knowing as explain how a mismatch can occur (194c–195a). The description 'The sum of 7 and 5 is 11' is broken down into two simples, '12' and '11'. Similarly, the description 'That person whom I now see in the distance is Socrates' is presumably to be broken down into 'Theodorus' (assuming Theodorus to be the person in the distance) and 'Socrates'. There is no weakening of the hold of knowledge by acquaintance; and Plato is still assuming that if two terms (such as '7 + 5' and '12') refer to the same thing, they must *obviously* refer to that same thing: the object is known, so its descriptions are known.

◆ The Aviary (196d–200d) ◆

The third and final model that Plato proposes for false belief, presumably as the best he can do, is just as fascinating a description of our mental apparatus as the Wax Block, but just as disappointing an effort to solve the paradox of false belief. The Wax Block could have been allowed to stand as a model for some false beliefs and we might have hoped, especially given the nature of Plato's criticism of the Wax Block, that he would next turn to consider more complex beliefs and even propositional belief. Instead, however, since the Wax Block fell foul of the recurring problem of 188a–c – how something known can be unknown – it is rejected *in toto*, and the Aviary represents a fresh start, trying to deal with all false beliefs *en bloc*. And it turns out to be hampered by the same assumption, that false belief is misidentification of simple identities, which has run throughout this part of the dialogue. As Lee [133] points out, commentators look in vain for any attempt to deal in the Aviary with more complex beliefs.

The model depends on the distinction between potential or dispositional knowledge and actual knowledge. We are to imagine that we have aviaries within us, in which we store what we have learned and from which we recover what we want to recall. Thus even someone who knows (potentially) all numbers is said to be able to make mistakes by making actual the wrong piece of potential knowledge. In considering the question 'What is the sum of seven and five?', he actualizes the answer 'eleven' instead of 'twelve'. It is clear that Plato's concern is still to explain how something known can be unknown (that is, can enter into a false belief); it is also clear that knowledge is still being seen as acquaintance, a kind of grasping, and that the objects of knowledge and belief are individuals, like the individuals of 188a–c.

It is worth noting that the Aviary is not a complete model for human mental apparatus, but only of memory. It is empty at birth and stocked by learning, which involves separate apparatus (197e). But it is unclear whether what is learned is, say, the sequence of numbers, or also sums such as '7 + 5 = 12'. If the former is the case, then faced with the question 'What is 7 + 5?', we go into the aviary to look for the bird which we think is the correct answer; if the latter is the case, then we go straight in search of the 12-bird.

Whichever of these two is correct, it is important to see that our aviaries contain only simple birds such as '11', '12', etc. It is repeated in 198a–b that what the mathematician knows are numbers; in other words, he knows sums only in a secondary sense, because his stored knowledge of numbers enables him to do calculations. One does not store complex birds such as 'the sum of 7 and 5'. Such complexities are either part of the question which sends one into the aviary to search for the answer, or are part of the learning process which originally stocked the aviary with its simple numbers. In either case, they are part of an apparatus which is distinct from the aviary itself.

Plato is still thinking of false belief as cross-belief. Even someone who knows how to count, and therefore potentially knows that 7 + 5 = 12, can actualize the wrong piece of knowledge. He is mistaking a for b in the sense that, faced with the question, he mistakes the 11-bird for the 12-bird, because they are similar (199b) – that is, they are similar as answers to sums, not in themselves (see 195e).

Here again, of course, is the same fallacy we have found

recurring throughout this section (see pp. 201–2, 206). Plato wants to say that the mistake is describable as 'thinking that 12 is 11'; but this should correctly be seen as a reconstruction of a belief, not the believer's actual belief.

Plato distinguishes the two levels of knowledge precisely so that he can defend the view that mistakes involve mis-identifying *a* for *b*. Since he fails to distinguish between beliefs and reconstructed beliefs, he is bound to see mistakes in this way. This in turn leads him to be puzzled, since in many cases both *a* and *b* are known – and how can one known be mistaken for another known? Plato has still not escaped his initial quandary.

At 199d he begins to criticize the Aviary model. He starts by claiming that it is counter-intuitive to say that a piece of knowledge can make one ignorant (e.g. when '11' figures in an error). This appears to be a rather superficial criticism, since it ignores the issue of the *appropriateness* of actualizing a given piece of knowledge as an answer to a given question. For Plato, however, if an object is fully known, the occasions on which it is appropriate to actualize the object are also known. So reflection on this criticism could have been more productive: it is counter-intuitive that knowledge causes ignorance only if it is assumed that knowledge entails knowing all or enough about something (see p. 197). If that is the case, then 'eleven' can never figure in a false belief – and it is difficult to see how anything else can. In other words, reflection on this criticism could have led Plato in the direction of questioning the conception of knowledge that has been predominant ever since 188a–c.

The second objection, which immediately follows, is that the idea of interchange, of taking *a* to be *b*, in itself provides no guarantee that the correct answer will *ever* be produced. One could go on exchanging *a* for *b*, *b* for *c*, and so on. The process of making a mistake has not been explained, on this model or on either of the previous two models.

Again, however, Plato expresses this point as that knowledge could go on making one ignorant. Theaetetus picks up on this to suggest that 'pieces of ignorance' should be included in the Aviary to explain false belief (199e). What does this mean? What would a 'piece of ignorance' be like? One possibility is that it is simply gobbledegook (or perhaps an 'objective falsehood', a statement which contradicts a necessary truth), which is never appropriate as an answer; but these are not the terms of the Aviary. 'Eleven' is not gobbledegook; it is just incorrect as an answer to some questions. Another possibility is that a piece of ignorance is a false belief like '7 + 5 = 11', but we have already seen that the aviary contains only simple birds such as '11'.

In fact, Theaetetus' suggestion seems to be no more than an alternative labelling of birds. 'Eleven' is to be labelled a piece of knowledge when it is the appropriate answer, but a piece of ignorance when it is not. But this raises further problems (200a–c). Either the original difficulties of 188a–c have not been overcome, and the question still remains how I can mistake a piece of ignorance for a piece of knowledge, or confuse two pieces of knowledge or two pieces of ignorance; or the extra labelling of birds raises the question how can I be sure that what I have got hold of is a piece of knowledge. In short, how can I know that I know? The regress involved is a constant problem in epistemology (see Pears [46], pp. 3–4).

As usual, I have given short shrift to many of the scholarly issues of this section, and must be content with referring the reader to the bibliography; Lewis [135] is the starting-point.

So, at the end of this so-called digression, false belief remains unexplained. We have seen that it does so because of the confusion of actual and reconstructed beliefs, and because of the strong acquaintance model of knowledge which Plato assumes. Error cannot be explained on such a model, because the opposite of error is not acquaintance, but factual knowledge: error has to do with facts, but the opposite of acquaintance is ignorance.

Plato may have failed to explain false belief, but we are in a position to learn quite a bit about his conception of knowledge. I have discussed the arguments so far in terms of the traditional modern distinction between knowledge by

acquaintance and propositional knowledge: from this point of
view the fundamental weakness of the digression on false
belief is its emphasis on knowledge by acquaintance to the
exclusion of propositional knowledge. This is a fair and accurate criticism, I believe, but we also need to go a little further.

We need at this point to distinguish three possible interpretations of Plato's position on these two types of knowledge:

1. He (mistakenly) fails to recognize the existence of
   propositional knowledge. This is the orthodox view
   of, for instance, Robinson [47] and Runciman [49].
2. He deliberately fails to acknowledge the existence of
   propositional knowledge. This is the view of Bondeson
   [129], Gosling [26] and Fine [131].
3. He (mistakenly) finds the distinction irrelevant to his
   purpose.

There are plenty of reasons to support the orthodox view
(see Gosling [26], p. 121). In *Theaetetus*, we have already
seen that it is plausible, because Plato is evidently unaware of
the analysis of propositions, and he consistently regards false
belief as misidentification. Since propositional knowledge is
factual knowledge, it perhaps needs to be said that the
orthodox view is not that Plato denied that knowledge of
facts was a type of knowledge, but that he took it to be a kind
of acquaintance.

However, Gosling ([26], Chapter 8) has shown that, appearances notwithstanding, Plato does not simply fail to recognize
propositional knowledge. It is rather the case that his
grammatical (and hence conceptual) framework is alien to
ours. For instance, while it is an axiom of modern philosophy
that belief is always propositional or covertly propositional
(see, for example, Woozley [59], pp. 25–6), yet the Greek
verb *doxazein* is as capable of taking a direct object, implying
acquaintance, as it is of governing a propositional construction. The same goes for verbs meaning 'know'. At 147b, for
instance, Plato moves freely between describing the project of
the dialogue as 'to know knowledge' and 'to know what
knowledge is' (see p. 22, n. 1). In short, while there is no

reason to suppose that Plato simply overlooked the existence of propositional knowledge, there is plenty of reason to suppose that there were major impediments to his getting clear about its differences from knowledge by acquaintance.

Despite, however, recognizing that Plato acknowledged the existence of propositional knowledge, those who hold the second interpretation above find it inescapable that in the discussion of false belief Plato overlooks it. This oversight, then, has to be deliberate, and requires some special explanation. Accordingly, Fine, for instance, reckons that the target of the arguments is Theaetetus' definition of true belief as knowledge. If this definition were correct, she argues, then knowledge would have to be knowledge by acquaintance; but if knowledge is knowledge by acquaintance, then false belief is impossible. The 'digression' on false belief thus becomes one prong of a two-pronged assault on Theaetetus' definition, the second prong being the eyewitness argument of 200d–201c.

The basic problem with these interpretations is that they are uneconomical. They require passages which look like puzzlement to be read as clarity, so that if Plato affirms something, we are in fact to take him to be denying it. Clearly, we need very strong grounds before adopting such an interpretation; and the mere fact that Plato recognized that belief and knowledge could be propositional does not afford such grounds. We need to be sure that Plato was able to distinguish knowledge by acquaintance from propositional knowledge so completely that the paradox of false belief can be solved. This would require, at least, the recognition that propositional knowledge, not knowledge by acquaintance, is knowledge of facts, and that therefore it alone is opposed to falsehood, whereas the opposite acquaintance is ignorance or blankness. And this in turn would require the recognition that a proposition, stating a fact, involves descriptions: propositions are *about* things, and they require distinguishing what they are about, as subject, from what is being said about or predicated of the subject. In other words, clarity about propositions requires that the predicative sense of 'to

be' is distinguished from other senses (see p. 146), and
that a statement 'I believe that *a* is *b*' is recognized as a
description of *a* as *b*, rather than asserting the identity of *a*
and *b*.

There are no signs of any of these insights in *Theaetetus*,
and therefore it is uneconomical to interpret the dialogue as
taking such insights for granted. If the discussion of false
belief is in effect a *reductio* argument, why doesn't Plato say
so, either explicitly or in so many words?

As an aside at this point, however, we must acknowledge a
certain attractiveness in Fine's view. We have seen that in
the context of Socratic midwifery, a definition does not count
as a birth until its implications are also realized: Fine's view
provides such implications for Theaetetus' second definition. I
suggest, however, that it is more plausible to see the implications as suggested on p. 200: if belief has access to being,
as argued at 186c–e, at the end of the previous part of the
dialogue, how can it ever be false?

To return to the issue of Plato's position on the two types of
knowledge: the third interpretation is, I suggest, more plausible. We have plenty of reasons to suppose that Plato acknowledged propositional knowledge; we have plenty of reasons to
suppose that he was not clear about it. But it is uneconomical
to regard the passage on false belief as less than a record of
genuine puzzlement.

Plato's difficulty in explaining false belief may be seen as
generated solely by his conception of knowledge as a reliable
grasp on something (see 152c). This rather vague conception
does not exclude the 'something' being a proposition. Plato's
problem is that if knowledge is a reliable grasp, how can
anything which is present to the mind not be reliably grasped?
This is the question which generated the difficulty of 188a–c,
which, as we have seen, is also the difficulty underlying the
whole section on false belief. The answer to the question, of
course, is to get clear on propositional knowledge and to
distinguish it from knowledge by acquaintance; for I can
have a reliable grasp on a fact without being fully acquainted
with what the fact is about, and so still be liable to error.

There is certainly no reason to suppose that Plato perversely or unconsciously ignored propositional knowledge, nor is there any reason to suppose that he was clear on the distinction of the two types *before* writing *Theaetetus* (we will find later that it is rather the case that without the work carried out in *Theaetetus* he may not have been able to perform the better analysis of *Sophist*). What Plato has explicitly undertaken in *Theaetetus* is the Socratic task of defining knowledge as something single. It is a result of this project that he fails to elaborate possible distinctions within knowledge. The distinctions are irrelevant to his purpose. Thus, while it is illuminating for us to see his arguments in terms of the distinction or its lack, this must not blind us to Plato's own concerns.

❧ True Belief is Not Knowledge (200d–201c) ❧

Before the digression on false belief, Theaetetus suggested that true belief was knowledge. Plato now turns to refute this suggestion.

The brief and plausible argument of this section is that a jury, even if they have true belief (reach a correct verdict on a case), were not eyewitnesses to the crime, and therefore fail to have knowledge. The result of the type of persuasion that goes on in a lawcourt is belief; knowledge is the result of leisurely teaching. Plato's general point is clear enough: belief – even true belief – may take no account of facts, but either teaching or eyewitnessing gives reliable access to facts. Plato is not far off expressing the point recognized by modern philosophers that a true belief cannot be a case of knowledge, because it may be deduced from a false belief (see, for instance, Russell [50], p. 76).

It has been argued that it is unfortunate that Plato presents this as a single argument, when in fact its two elements tend in different and contradictory directions (see especially Burnyeat [130]). Plato argues for a distinction between rhetoric and teaching based on the constraints of the former, but he also argues that hearsay cannot yield knowledge – that only eyewitnesses have knowledge. The latter argument appears to make the former one redundant, because by the latter argument, even if the constraints on rhetoric were removed (so that it became proper teaching), it would still fail to yield knowledge. The first argument suggests that knowledge *can* be transmitted from one person to another; the second denies that knowledge is transmissible. The first argument, it should also be noted, is concerned with propositional knowledge; the second is concerned with knowledge by acquaintance.

However, I think that this reads too much into the passage and generates difficulties where none need exist. Plato's point is not that hearsay *never* yields knowledge (and there is plenty of evidence from elsewhere that Plato thought knowledge was transmissible: *Meno* 87b, *Gorgias* 454e–455a, *Symposium* 175d–e, *Republic* 518b–c, *Timaeus* 51d–e, *Theaetetus* 198b), but that it cannot in the short time allotted in the lawcourts (201a–b). It is true that the two aspects of the argument tend in opposite directions, but there is no need to extend them to their ultimate limits. What Plato is after is reliable access to truth: being an eyewitness provides this, and so does being properly taught. The two directions do not necessarily end in contradiction, provided that they end in reliable access to truth. Thus there is no need to try to decide, as Burnyeat has to, which type of knowledge – propositional knowledge or knowledge by acquaintance – Plato is committed to. He is committed to both types – or rather, he is committed to trying to find a single knowledge that encompasses both types. There is no need to conclude (as Burnyeat does, p. 180) that Plato is now denying that transmissible knowledge is knowledge at all, rather than merely justified true belief (though this gives a very neat solution to the problem raised on pp. 233–4).

❧ PART FOUR: KNOWLEDGE AS TRUE BELIEF ❧ PLUS AN ACCOUNT (201c–210d)

We come now to the most intensively studied few pages of the dialogue. There are two chief reasons why they have

been subjected to so much scrutiny: they are difficult, but
rewarding; and they seem to anticipate modern accounts of
knowledge. A fairly standard account of knowledge today
would be that someone knows that *p*, if *p* is true, if that
person believes that *p*, and if that person has sufficient justification for that belief (but see Gettier, in Griffiths [27]). So
when Plato says that knowledge is true belief plus a rational
account (*logos*), could he be groping towards this conception
of knowledge?

Plato is assuming in this section that if I say that Smith has
true belief, and that Jones has knowledge, I am saying that
Jones has everything Smith has, plus something extra. This is
what entitles Plato to ask the question what it is which,
when added to true belief, converts it into knowledge. This
approach – the idea that knowledge is some kind of special
state – has been criticized by modern philosophers; but see
Chisholm ([24], pp. 15–18), for a defence of the approach.

Theaetetus' third definition of knowledge is proposed as
tentatively as the other two; this time it is not even offered as
his own idea, but as an aspect of someone else's theory. The
course of this part of the dialogue is as follows: the definition
is stated (201c); the theory of which this definition is said to
be a consequence is laid out (201d–202c); the theory is criticized (202d–206b); finally the definition itself is refuted
(206c–210a). The dialogue then ends aporetically. This part
of the dialogue requires a fairly long, and sometimes fairly
technical, discussion; but we will learn from it a great deal
about Plato's epistemology.

৵ Socrates' Dream (201d–202c) ৶

We must first see what the theory is, of which Theaetetus'
third definition is said to be a consequence. When Theaetetus
is unable to explain the theory, Socrates offers his version,
which he says he heard in a dream (201d). Socrates recalls
dreamed theories elsewhere in the dialogues (*Cratylus* 439c,
Philebus 20b). In each case it is unclear what, if anything, is
added by calling the theories 'dreamed'. In each case they
are theories which probably seem to Plato to have greater

plausibility than the ones which precede them in each dialogue; but calling them 'dreams' perhaps indicates that they are obscure or somehow imprecise (Burnyeat [141], pp. 103–6; Rorty [155], pp. 229–30).

The theory rests on a distinction between *stoicheion* and *syllabe*. *Stoicheion* is the Greek scientific word for 'element', but its primary meaning is 'letter' or 'unit of sound'; *syllabe* means literally 'combination' or 'complex', but in a grammatical context 'syllable', that is, a combination of letters. Throughout these sections Plato is using the words in both senses at once, but sometimes one sense is more prominent than the other, and I have translated the words accordingly.

The theory is that the elements are the 'bottom line' of analysis. Things, like syllables, are complex, but the process of analysing them ends when you reach their elements, which are not further analysable. These elements are not knowable, in the sense that, strictly, all one can do is name them, not give a rational account (*logos*) of them, and a rational account is a prerequisite of knowledge. Theaetetus' definition of knowledge as true belief plus a rational account is a consequence of this theory because the theory insists that for anything to be knowable it must be accessible to a rational account.

There are many questions which arise about this theory. Perhaps the central one is: What is meant by *logos*? It is a dilemma for a translator that the word has to be presented in translation, which prejudges the issue. I have translated *logos* as 'rational account', and this requires justification. In discussing this question, we will deal with some other issues along the way.

The Greek word *logos* is often hard to translate. It covers a range of meanings, from mere 'statement' to 'argument', 'speech', 'theory', 'definition' and so on. Quite a few commentators on our dialogue want to take it as 'statement' or 'proposition', and there are initially plausible grounds for this.

1. A *logos* is contrasted with a mere name; that is, stating seems to be distinguished from naming (202a–b).
2. Belief and knowledge are undoubtedly expressed in sentences.

3. In *Sophist* sentences are seen as woven-together complexes of nouns and verbs: compare the image of weaving at 202b.

4. There are echoes of the refutation of the claim of sense-perception to be knowledge (184b–186e), where, as we saw (p. 187), knowledge may be propositional, that is, expressed in statements or sentences.

This view has found favour with Ryle (chiefly in an un-published paper, but echoed in [156] and [51]), McDowell [5], Crombie [25] and Galligan [146], at least (and Runciman [49], pp. 41–2, Gulley [29] and Bondeson [140] seem to think that this is what Plato starts off with, but shifts to another sense of *logos* later), and it is an attractive view. It has Plato making the vital distinction between names, which merely pinpoint, and statements, which say something *about* a named subject; it has Plato recognizing that knowledge of truths is propositional knowledge; and it has Plato implicitly acknowledging that the Forms – which were in his middle period the objects of knowledge – are simple nameables and are therefore inadequate for knowledge. I shall call this interpretation Ryle's view.

There are, however, insuperable difficulties with this view. We have so far found little reason to suppose that Plato recog-nized propositional knowledge as a prime instance of know-ledge; but this is controversial and cannot weigh on its own against Ryle's view. Even apart from this consideration, there are insuperable difficulties.

In the first place, as Ryle himself admits, Plato cannot have been very clear about the distinction between naming and stating. What he says at 202a–b and again in 202d–206a implies, on the view that *logos* means 'statement', that a statement is merely an accumulation of names. In other words, if he had grasped this important distinction, we would have to call it at best an intuitive grasp, since it fails to recognize the different functions of different parts of a sen-tence, but calls them all 'names'. So, whatever the metaphor of weaving means in *Theaetetus* (and it is taken no further), it cannot be aligned with the weaving together of nouns and verbs in *Sophist*, since it fails to distinguish verbs from nouns.

Secondly, even if Plato did have some intuitive grasp of the distinction, why does he go on to criticize the theory? At the very least, he cannot have seen its importance, and we would have no grounds for attributing to him modern epistemological insights.

Thirdly, at 206d–e, Plato summarily dismisses as irrelevant to the definition precisely this meaning of *logos*. What converts true belief into knowledge is said at 202c to be the ability 'to give and receive a *logos*' – the ability to give and receive *sentences* can hardly be a sufficient condition of knowledge.

Fourthly, it is a consequence of Ryle's view that no statement whatsoever should be possible of elements. But at 203b Theaetetus says of the element or letter S that it 'is one of the soundless letters, but makes a noise as if the tongue were hissing'. So far from being damaging to the theory, this statement is being offered in support of the theory. The 'things' which are said to be composed of elements are 'human beings and everything else' (201e) – that is, everyday things of the material world. Are these the only things we can form sentences about?

Fifthly, at 202b–c, the dream theory says that there is true belief about complexes; but it does not say, nor does it imply, that there is no belief, true or otherwise, about elements. And how would such belief be expressed, if not in sentences? In fact, the dream theory does not imply that one cannot utter sentences true of elements; it only implies that such sentences do not yield knowledge. Thus Theaetetus' sentence about the letter S redescribes S, but does not explain it. One cannot explain elements: it is like trying to describe the taste of a ginger biscuit without offering some redescription of 'gingery'!

I have criticized Ryle's view fairly thoroughly not just because it is fundamentally mistaken, but because the objections against it afford us insights into what *is* going on in the dream theory. The last three points in particular show that whatever *logos* means, it must be such as to yield knowledge. For this, the translation 'account' seems to be the minimum required and to beg the fewest questions. Since *logos* has connotations of rationality, I have used the translation 'rational account'. Plato *is* concerned with sentences, but only those which are accounts.

We can go further and say what type of account is involved. As the terminology of complexes and elements reveals, and as Plato's discussion in 207a–208b suggests too, the type of account the dream theory involves is analysis into elements. Thus if I have a true belief about X and can also analyse X into its elements, the dream theory claims that I know X.

We are now in a position to understand the most puzzling part of the dream theory (201e–202a):

> Each of them [the elements], taken just by itself, can only be named, but nothing else can be said about it. You can't say that it is, or that it is not: that would already be to attribute being or not being to it, but nothing extra should be assigned to it at all, if that thing itself is independently to enter a discussion. In fact, you shouldn't even use 'itself', 'that', 'each', 'independent', 'this' or any other extra, since these attributes run around and get applied to everything, and are different from what they are attributed to. If it were possible for a primary to be spoken of, if it had its own appropriate account, all these attributes should be avoided in speaking of it.

If the dream theory, as suggested, holds that for something to be known it has to be fully analysed, then this process of analysis has to end somewhere, otherwise there is no possibility of ever attaining knowledge. This is the central point of the dream theory, and we should naturally expect the theorist to have given instructions as to how to identify an element. The passage quoted above gives those instructions (Burnyeat [141]). About any given thing we must ask ourselves whether, taken on its own, there is only a name for it, or whether it can be further analysed into elements (compare *Cratylus* 422a–b). Ryle's contrast between things which are

only nameable and things which are statable is too severe:
the exclusion of 'this' and 'is' and so on is not a denial that it
is possible to say 'This is X' of an element (otherwise, as we
have seen, Theaetetus' description of S at 203b would be
excluded); it is saying that terms like 'this' and 'is' are
common and indiscriminate – they do not help us to distinguish elements from complexes. One can equally well say
'This is a human being' and 'This is a quark'.

We are also in a position to deal incidentally with two
further problems which have exercised some commentators,
namely why the elements are said to be perceptible (202b),
and what true belief might be like, according to the dream
theory, when it is unaccompanied by *logos*.

On Ryle's view, Plato is distinguishing between propositional knowledge, as true knowledge, and knowledge by
acquaintance. 'Perceptible' has to be taken to mean 'cogniz-
able' or 'knowable by acquaintance'. This is extremely
unlikely: Plato could not have introduced such a restricted
meaning for 'perceptible' in an apparently throw-away phrase.

Others restrict 'perceptible' to sense-perception. The basic
problem is that all these views, like Ryle's too, take perceivability to be a criterion for distinguishing elements from
complexes. But we have seen that the complexes the theory is
concerned with are things like human beings: are they not
perceivable? The theory has already done the work of distinguishing elements from complexes: it depends simply upon
whether or not further analysis is possible. Perceivability is
not a criterion. The appearance of the phrase, as a throw-
away, is correct: the dream theory is just saying that the
elements may not be analysable, but they are there – they
must be, or knowledge is impossible (Burnyeat [141]). This
fits in with what we have seen earlier in the dialogue, that an
unannounced and unqualified use of 'perceptible' should
simply mean 'apprehensible' and cover the full range of what
the Greek term *aisthesis* means, from sense-perception to
cognition.

As for the question what true belief might be like without
logos, there is no need to suppose that it is some simple,

inarticulate impression. It could come in any form whatsoever, provided that it fell short of full analysis; and its objects
could be complexes or elements, though in the latter case it
could never be converted into knowledge, because elements
are *ex hypothesi* unanalysable.

There is plenty more of philosophical interest in the dream
theory, which bears crucially on the question of where
Theaetetus leaves us with regard to Plato's views on knowledge. Discussion is most conveniently approached via the
historical question of what the source of the dream theory is.

The reason it is attractive to look for a source external to
the requirements of the dialogue is not just that the dream
theory is written up as if Plato had garnered it from elsewhere
(see especially 201c–d), but also because its inclusion is
strictly gratuitous. Theaetetus states his third definition of
knowledge; this is said to be a consequence of the dream
theory; the dream theory is criticized; finally, Theaetetus'
definition is criticized. Patently, the two middle elements of
this sequence could be dropped without noticeable loss.

There is a sense in which its inclusion need not disturb us,
since the strategy is on a par with Plato's treatment of the
other two definitions. Neither of Theaetetus' previous two
definitions was immediately dealt with either: the first led to
a long discussion, also perhaps strictly unnecessary, on
Protagoreanism and flux; the second led to a discussion of
false belief. The broad context is Socrates' midwifery: in order
for a definition to count as a birth, it must not only be stated,
but set in context too. Plato takes it that the context of the
first definition is Protagoreanism and flux; that the context of
the second definition is the paradox of false belief (see p. 214);
and that the context of the third definition is the dream
theory.

However, this only rephrases the question. Why did Plato
adopt this strategy with regard to the third definition? To
this, one common answer has been that he wanted to criticize
the doctrine of some other thinker or school of thinkers.

Without going into all the details, it is perhaps sufficient to
repudiate this notion by pointing out the uncertainty of

attribution of the theory. For interest rather than elucidation, here is a list: some Pythagoreans such as Ecphantus
or Philolaus (Taylor [54]); Antisthenes (Campbell [1], Gillespie [148], Guthrie [30]); mathematicians in general (Morrow
[154]); some unknown Academician (Hicken [151]); Democritus the Atomist (Centore [142]).

Others (such as, in their respective ways, Ryle (see p. 219),
Moline [42], pp. 157–65, and Lesher [152]) seek the target in
Plato's own middle-period theory of Forms. This is more
plausible, on two counts. First, given the uncertainty of finding an external source, it makes sense to look for an internal
source (and it is also worth mentioning that the analogy of
letters and syllables was a favourite of Plato's: he uses it for
various purposes at *Philebus* 17a–b, 18b–d; *Cratylus*, *passim*;
Sophist 253a; *Statesman* 277c–278d; *Republic* 402a–c).
Second, as we shall see later, *Theaetetus* does undermine certain aspects of Plato's middle-period philosophy.

However, this is not the place to find such criticism. As
Annas remarks ([139], p. 98): 'The terminology of the dream
theory would not suggest Forms to anyone not determined to
find them.' Moreover, the belief that knowledge required *logos*
of some kind is a constant feature of Plato's epistemology
(*Meno* 97e–98a, *Gorgias* 465a, *Phaedo* 76b, *Symposium* 202a,
Republic 533b–c), so, since Forms were – at least in the last
three dialogues referred to – the objects of knowledge (one
could only be said to know the Form Justice, since it, not any
particular instances of justice, is stably what it is), the
common description of them as incomposite (as the elements
are in the dream theory) cannot mean that they are inac-
cessible to *logos*. This view leads to too great a contrast between Plato's earlier and later metaphysics. In later dialogues
(*Sophist*, *Statesman*) Plato talks of how Forms interrelate, but
it is not certain that Forms were incapable of interrelation in
earlier dialogues too (Waterfield [55], pp. 282–3).

There are other views about the origin of the dream theory.
The most popular recent view is that Plato is not so much
criticizing as considering aspects of his own earlier epistemology – by 'aspects' here I mean consequences of his basic

assumptions, such as that knowledge requires a *logos*. This view has generated three excellent articles by Burnyeat [141], Fine [145] and Annas [139]. My own account of this part of the dialogue has already been and will continue to be indebted to these papers.

Such a view, however, requires taking the attribution (by Theaetetus, especially) of the theory to an external source as part of the whimsy of describing it in the first place as a dream. This is not impossible, and has been persuasively argued by Burnyeat [141], pp. 103–7. Note also in particular that what Socrates says at the beginning of 202d patently implies that this is all a newly made-up theory. If this is so, then in order to discover the purpose of the inclusion of the dream theory in *Theaetetus*, we need to get clear not only on what it is saying (which we have already done), but on what Plato finds wrong with it.

❧ The Dream Theory Criticized (202d–206b) ❧

Plato's criticism of the theory is clearly summarized at 205d–e:

> If a syllable is a whole and is the same as its constituent letters (however many there may be), then, since we found that a complete set of parts is the same as a whole, a syllable and its letters are equally knowable and expressible in a rational account. If, on the other hand, a syllable is single and indivisible, then it is just as inexpressible in a rational account and as unknowable as a letter.

In other words, he sets up a dilemma. The first horn of the dilemma is argued at 203c–d:

1. If a complex is the same as its elements, then if the complex is knowable, so are the elements.

This is plausible, but it is obviously not universally true that a whole has the same properties as its parts, and vice versa. As Plato himself had argued in the fairly early dialogue *Hippias Major* (297e–303d), a group of small people is not necessarily a small group of people.

This horn of the dilemma, which argues against the dream

theory's contention that elements are unknowable, is also said to be supported by experience (206a–b): in disciplines such as literacy and music, we learn the 'elements' first and foremost.

The basic argument of the second horn of the dilemma is as follows (203e–205d):

    2a. Any whole is the same as its parts.

    2b. The parts of a complex are its elements.

    2c. Therefore the complex is the same as its elements.

But this is liable to the first horn of the dilemma. So we have to maintain:

    2d. A complex does not have parts.

In which case it is a simple entity like an element and is *ex hypothesi* unknowable.

The crucial premiss is 2a, which is argued for at length (204a–205a): the complete set of a thing's parts is the totality of that thing; the totality is the same as the whole; therefore the whole is the complete set of parts. However, the argument is not expressed as straightforwardly as this, because it is expressed as an argument against the thesis that a totality and a whole are *different*. The crowning argument against this thesis is rather weak: identity of result implies identity of cause; both a whole and a totality cease to be what they are if anything is missing; therefore a whole is the same as a totality. Clearly the weak link here is the idea that identity of result implies identity of cause. On the whole argument, for both horns of the dilemma, see McDowell [5], pp. 241–5, and Sayre [52], pp. 130–32.

Despite the lengthy argument for 2a, the principle that a whole is the same as its parts can hardly be taken to be established. The argument may have shown that a whole is [consists of] its parts, but not that a whole is [is identical to] its parts. This equivocation on 'is' spoils the argument.

A lot of weight is placed on this principle. However, at *Parmenides* 157c–e (which was written prior to *Theaetetus*), Plato shows himself aware that the principle is not unassailable: a whole may be seen not only as consisting of parts, but as an epiphenomenon – a single identity in its own right. The fundamental law of synergy, as we might put it today, is $2 + 2 = 5$. In terms of letters and syllables, the syllable BOX does not simply consist of the letters B, O and X: if that were the case, these three letters could appear in any order, since OXB consists of the same elements. BOX consists of the same letters as OXB, but is an entity in its own right, because it has a different *organization*. In a passage which reads as though this bit of *Theaetetus* is the background (*Metaphysics* 1041a–b), Aristotle makes the same point.

If Plato was aware that a whole is not necessarily the same as its parts, why does he assume that it is in this argument against the dream theory? Either he is arguing unfairly, or the dream theory is committed to the notion that a whole is the same as its parts. In fact, there is no sign that the dream theory is not committed to the idea: it makes no mention of any principle of organization of elements. If a whole is *not* seen as identical to its parts, then the dilemma, on the horns of which Plato has impaled the theory, is not exhaustive. The dilemma is effective against the dream theory only if the theory is committed to its exhaustiveness. In other words, Plato's argument can be teased out into a criticism of the dream theory's lack of regard for the principle of organization.

Fine ([145], pp. 382–4) makes these points with admirable clarity, and holds that Plato is criticizing the dream theory on this score. But there is a problem. If this was part of Plato's criticism of the dream theory, why does he go about it in such an oblique fashion? Why doesn't he come right out and say that the idea that a whole is the same as its parts is false? The only reasonable explanation that occurs to me is that it is not his main concern. We have inferred this point from the dilemma argument, but it is not the point the dilemma argument is designed to make. This needs bearing in mind.

We need to review the situation again, to see what Plato might be getting at. The central insight of the dream theory, as we have seen (p. 221), is that if knowledge is to be finite and therefore a possibility, the chain of entailments has to stop somewhere. If I know *a* only if I know *b*, and know *b* only if I know c, and so on, then a vicious regress is generated. The dream theory ends the regress by positing ultimate elements. The peculiarity of the theory is that it makes these elements unknowable. Fine ([145], pp. 375–8) gives an interesting discussion of the strengths and weaknesses of this view as opposed to the more familiar notion of Descartes and Russell that the 'elements' are knowable. Whatever its strengths and weaknesses, however, it is at least odd to suggest that knowledge is based ultimately on unknowables – and this is precisely Plato's criticism in the first horn of the dilemma argument against the theory and at 206a–b.

Plato is attacking the notion that the elements are unknowable while the complexes are knowable, which has been called the principle of 'asymmetry of knowledge' (AK). For Plato, as we have already mentioned (p. 138), knowledge must be based on knowledge (KBK). Now, AK in the theory is the result of two prior principles: that knowledge requires a rational account (KR) and that if a rational account is a weaving together of elements, then there is no rational account of elements: in other words, there is 'asymmetry of rational account' (AR). KR and AR generate AK. So in attacking AK, Plato is attacking at least one of KR and AR. Which? Or is it both?

At 202d, KR is apparently endorsed. Socrates says, 'I mean, surely a rational account and true belief are prerequisites of knowledge?' At 205d–e, quoted on p. 225, Plato concludes the dilemma argument by impugning AR as well as AK.

So if KR and AR entail AK, and KR is endorsed, while AR and AK are criticized, it looks as though Fine is correct in saying that AR is Plato's underlying target. But if that is the case, then on the terms of the dream theory Plato is committed to the view that the so-called elements are just as analysable as complexes – or rather that there are no elements. In other words, he is committed to the vicious regress outlined on above.

In order to avoid this consequence, Fine argues that Plato substitutes a circular model for the linear model which generates the regress. Instead of an infinite regress $a, b, c \ldots$, she reads Plato as proposing that all knowables are interrelated. This is certainly a possible view of dialogues that post-date *Theaetetus*. Is it a plausible view of this part of *Theaetetus*? Fine finds it in 206a–b, where Plato talks of letters of the alphabet and musical notes. But while it is of course true that letters and notes are interrelated, that is not the point Plato makes in 206a–b, which is that each letter is learned *separately* (that is, that they are distinct and knowable).

Secondly, we need to remember (see p. 227) that it is unrealistic to take the dilemma argument as an assault on the notion that a whole is identical to its parts. Plato may well be aware that this is false, but it is not his concern to say so. Fine argues that the dilemma argument is such an assault, because that would corroborate her view that AR is Plato's main target: appeals to order and organization of complexes undermine AR by interrelating the elements of a complex and thus making them accessible to a rational account, an account of their interrelations.

Thirdly, at 203a–b, Plato appears to endorse AR in having Socrates agree with Theaetetus that one cannot 'say what the elements of an element are'.

We seem to have reached an impasse. Plato attacks AK and in so doing should be attacking at least one of AR and KR which entail AK. Yet both are apparently endorsed. At this point it might be sensible to conclude that Plato is not clear on the issues involved, and in a sense I think this is correct. But there is one further consideration.

Whether Plato made up the dream theory on his own or inherited it from someone else, he is the author of the dialogue. That is, he is aware of the issue, which the dream theory addresses, of a possible regress being involved in some accounts of knowledge (and Aristotle, *Posterior Analytics* 72b 5–18, shows that there was discussion in the Academy on this topic). Arguably, then, he was aware of the possibility of a regress in his own earlier assumptions about knowledge. Two principles that we are safe to attribute to Plato's earlier epistemology are KBK – that knowledge is based on knowledge (see p. 228) – and KR – that knowledge requires a rational account (see p. 224). These two principles could entail a regress: to know *a*, it must be explained in terms of *b*, which must in turn be known, that is, explained in terms of *c*, and so on *ad infinitum*.

Now, Plato's criticism of AK in the dilemma argument of 202b–206d is an affirmation of KBK: in attacking the principle that knowledge is based on unknowable elements, he is affirming that knowledge is based on knowledge. So, from this point of view, assuming that Plato is aware that KBK and KR together can generate a regress, and given that he affirms KBK, it looks as though KR has to go, or be qualified.

So, of the two endorsements, the one at 202d of KR is perhaps not seriously intended; it is noticeable that it is phrased as a rhetorical question, and questions notoriously do not commit the questioner to any view on the subject.

However, the fact that we have had to work so hard to reach even this tentative conclusion shows that these issues are not on the surface of the dialogue, and perhaps that Plato was not fully clear about them; it would be foolhardy to conclude that the purpose of the inclusion of the dream theory is to impugn KR, but we may say that it is *implicitly* impugned. The purpose is to air certain ideas for examination; there is no reason to suppose that Plato was more definite than that about anything, at the time of writing *Theaetetus*. However, it is noticeable that, while in dialogues later than *Theaetetus* Plato has little to say on epistemology, KR seems not to appear. Of the two places where it has been said to appear after *Theaetetus* – namely *Timaeus* 51e and *Seventh Letter* 342a–e – *Timaeus* was probably written earlier than *Theaetetus* (see Owen [45]) and the authenticity of the seventh letter is greatly in doubt.

❧ The Third Definition Criticized (206c–210a) ❧

Having cleared away the idea that a rational account might produce knowledge by relying on unknowables, Plato turns to look more closely at the actual role it might have in turning true belief into knowledge. He considers three types of rational account:

1. The expression of one's thoughts (206d–e).
2. The enumeration of the elements of something (206e–208b).
3. The stating of a mark which uniquely differentiates something from everything else (208c–210a).

The first type of rational account, as Plato says, will clearly not convert true belief into knowledge; since anyone can express his or her thoughts, this rational account affords no way to distinguish true belief from knowledge.

The second type of rational account is also correctly argued not to be a sufficient condition of knowledge. To know something one must be able to carry over a true belief about it to any other cases where it is appropriate; but one can have a true belief about the elements of something without having this ability. One can have a true belief about how to spell 'Theaetetus', but have gained this true belief by chance rather than systematic knowledge. Since this is the type of rational account assumed by the dream theory, Plato no doubt also means us to remember his earlier criticism, that knowledge cannot be based on unknowable elements. Fine [145] again finds here hints of an interrelation model of knowledge (see pp. 228–9); but this is less than obvious. If Plato approves of an interrelation model of knowledge, he would hardly make it so obscure, or simply bury it in the course of an argument rejecting a certain definition of knowledge.

The argument denying the suggestion that the third type of rational account converts true belief into knowledge needs a little more discussion. Plato again employs a dilemma argument. Either the ability to state a mark which differentiates something fails to distinguish true belief from knowledge, or the definition of knowledge as true belief plus this ability is a circular definition.

The first horn of the dilemma argues that the ability to state the differentiating mark cannot be a sufficient condition of knowledge, since it is also a necessary condition of true belief. On this we need only comment that while in order to have a true belief about X it is certainly necessary to be able to distinguish X, it is not necessary to be able to *state* what it is about X that enables you to distinguish it.

Plato complicates this essentially straightforward argument by offering, at 209b–c, three suggestions as to what it must be to have an account of Theaetetus' uniqueness. The third suggestion, which is the one he endorses, is difficult to understand.

> (a) 'Theaetetus is a human being, with nose, eyes, mouth, etc.' – this doesn't differentiate Theaetetus from other human beings.
>
> (b) 'Theaetetus is the one with bulging eyes and a snub nose' – this doesn't differentiate Theaetetus from Socrates (see 143e).
>
> (c) 'In order to have an account of Theaetetus' uniqueness, his particular snubness of nose (and all the other features which make him what he is) must have been recorded in my memory as different from all the other snubnesses I have seen, so that on any occasion I can distinguish Theaetetus from anyone else.'

The emphasis here seems to be on *my* experience, which is bound to be limited; all Plato is saying is that I have enough material to distinguish Theaetetus from others in my experience. In (a) and (b), however, Plato was operating with a stricter notion: that Theaetetus' unique mark must *necessarily* distinguish him from all other people both within my experience and outside of it. So, if the emphasis here is on my experience, Plato is tacitly relaxing this strictness.

Still, this is a minor quibble: the essential argument for the first horn of the dilemma is correct (and shows, incidentally, that the artist of 145a, who has knowledge, is *not* the only one who can pronounce upon Theaetetus' and Socrates' physical similarity). In order to have a belief about X, I already need to be able to distinguish X. Or perhaps one should say I already need to know X: here is the second horn of the dilemma. If this ability is an expression of knowledge, then knowledge is now defined as true belief plus knowledge of distinguishing marks – but this is a circular and meaningless definition, as it stands.

The dialogue then concludes that none of the three

proposed definitions of knowledge is acceptable. Commentators have queried the correctness of this conclusion; that is, they have queried Plato's implication, at 206c and 208c, that the three senses of 'rational account' which he considers are exhaustive, or at least exhaustive as regards the types of rational account that may convert true belief into knowledge. I have already mentioned (p. 218) that *logos* is a word with wide and diverse meanings, and there is one meaning in particular whose absence is claimed to be peculiar.

At *Meno* 85c, Socrates has just finished eliciting a correct answer to a mathematical proposition from an uneducated slave; he says that the slave cannot yet, having gone through the issue only once, be said to have knowledge rather than belief, but that repetition will strengthen the belief and convert it into knowledge. At 98a the same topic is still being discussed: Socrates says that what converts true belief into knowledge is 'working out the reason'. In other words, once the slave understands *why* the mathematical proposition is correct, he can be said to know it, rather than just truly believe it.

Now, *Meno* is a relatively early dialogue, and if this were an isolated notion, we would probably not have grounds for placing much emphasis on it. However, the notion recurs at *Symposium* 202a, and the idea that knowledge involves understanding reasons underlies the recommendations Plato makes about knowledge in *Phaedo* and *Republic* (see McDowell [5], pp. 229–30, though it should also be noted that in these dialogues Plato is not talking about converting belief into knowledge – the gap between them is too great – but just about knowledge itself).

At any rate, we have good grounds for supposing that for Plato knowledge involved understanding why. This alone might lead us to expect to find this notion in *Theaetetus*; but we also have good grounds (*pace* Nehamas [44]) for supposing that, for Plato (when he considers that the gap between belief and knowledge is not unbridgeable), what converts true belief into knowledge is the ability to justify one's true belief by answering the question why the thing believed is as believed.

Here, then, is the source of the query referred to above. To quote just one instance of this query, Burnyeat ([130], p. 180) says:

> [The final part of the dialogue] does not take the (to us) obvious step of suggesting that true belief becomes knowledge when it is supported by adequate grounds. What [it] adds to true judgement or belief is *logos* in the sense of an explanatory account which answers the question what something is (cf. 203a–b, 206e, 208c–d): not an account that answers the epistemological question 'Why, on what grounds, do you believe that *p*?' Neither here nor anywhere else in the dialogue does Plato so much as mention the now familiar analysis of knowledge in terms of justified true belief.

However, not to beat about the bush, I believe that this view is mistaken and is a major impediment to understanding this final part of the dialogue, and hence Plato's epistemological inquiry in *Theaetetus*. There are many cases where an answer to the question what something is can simultaneously serve to justify one's belief as to what that thing is; the two latter senses of *logos* are such cases, or at least we have no reason to think that they are not intended by Plato to be such cases. If I believe that the person sitting in the corner is Theaetetus, what type of *logos* is required to justify my belief other than an account of Theaetetus' uniquely differentiating mark or marks? In explaining *what* Theaetetus is, I have also explained why I hold the belief. It is true that, by *our* standards, in explaining what Theaetetus is I have only contingently justified the belief; but the point is that there is no reason to think that *Plato* is not using *logos* in senses which are supposed to act as such justifications.

The general issue here, that if I know that *p*, I have adequate grounds, or the right to be sure that *p* (see Ayer [19], pp. 28–35), is expressly raised by the eyewitness example of 201a–c, and it would indeed be surprising if Plato did not follow it up.

Having summarily dismissed this problem, we still need to

ask what Plato finds unsatisfactory in such explanatory accounts. Why is he rejecting the suggestion of *Meno*? The
notion of knowledge of causes is scarcely prevalent in *Theaetetus*, and could no doubt have usefully been explored at
greater length: why does he give it such short shrift? The
answer is not far to seek, since Plato himself provides us with
it. It is that, as far as Plato can see at the time of writing
Theaetetus, such a definition of knowledge is circular (see
Chisholm [24], Chapter 1): it entails that the term 'knowledge' occurs not only in the definiendum, but also in the
definiens.

When Plato brings up the issue of circularity of definition
at 209e–210a – which is significantly the very last issue
considered in the dialogue – he is considering precisely the
problem of justified true belief. If in addition to truly believing
that *p*, I have an account which gives me adequate grounds
for *p*, what are these adequate grounds? Mere belief is not
adequate, because by definition belief is uncertain; only knowledge can yield adequate grounds, but then the definition is
circular. So *any* justification which gives adequate evidence is
bound to be circular. So the notion of knowledge of causes is
touched upon, only to be immediately dropped.

Having seen that *this* is Plato's problem, we are in a position
to assess where *Theaetetus* leaves us as regards Plato's epistemology, and to tie together our discussion of this final
section of the dialogue. Let us first ask the question: What
could allow Plato to retain his notion that justified true belief
is knowledge and to avoid a circular definition?

The most plausible answer is that the clear distinction of
propositional knowledge and knowledge by acquaintance
would do the job. For if in the apparently circular definition
'Knowledge is true belief plus knowledge', the term in the
definiendum (on the left of the equation) meant, say, propositional knowledge, and that in the definiens (the right of the
equation) meant knowledge by acquaintance, then circularity
is avoided. Plato could retain the definition, and the notion
(KBK) that knowledge is based on knowledge. He would come
to the Cartesian or Russellian position that the ultimate

justification for (propositional) knowledge is intuition or acquaintance.

Since this issue has reappeared, and in such an important context, we need briefly to return to it. I argued earlier (pp. 212–15) that there is no reason to think that Plato had fully analysed these types of knowledge (in the sense, say, of having analysed the logic of propositions, or having realized that error is not the opposite of acquaintance), and at the same time no reason to think that he perversely failed to recognize that propositional constructions can follow epistemological terms and therefore that, in this limited sense, there is such a thing as propositional knowledge. It is not, of course, the case that either belief or knowledge is thought of exclusively as non-propositional. Belief is defined as an internal statement (189e–190a) and is distinguished from sense-perception in a way that allows it to be propositional (184b–186e; see p. 187). Knowledge of the future (177c–179b) must be propositional. Grammatical forms of epistemological terms which govern propositions are employed freely throughout the dialogue. The point made before (pp. 215) was that Plato has ostensibly undertaken the Socratic task of trying to define knowledge. Socratic definition (see p. 137) involves a single phrase which is universally substitutable for the definiendum: to define knowledge is to find a single term or phrase which can be substituted for 'knowledge' every time one uses the term. We see here that Plato is not considering types of knowledge at all; he is looking for a universal definition which transcends types, and this is precisely what prevents him from making the necessary analyses, from seeing, for instance, that only propositional knowledge is knowledge of facts.

Two further aspects of this issue should be noted at this point. There are some (e.g. Hamlyn [34], Lesher [152]) who argue that Plato actually had different words for propositional knowledge and knowledge by acquaintance, at least in this concluding part of the dialogue. But this is false. It is true that there is more than one word in Greek for knowledge, but any attempt to distinguish between *gnosis*, as knowledge by acquaintance, and *episteme*, as propositional knowledge,

founders on Plato's own disregard for any distinctions between these terms (for instance, the sentence which starts
210a is: 'I mean, to know (*gnonai*) is to have got hold of
knowledge (*episteme*), isn't it?') and on Lyons's meticulous
study of Plato's epistemological vocabulary ([40]), which
shows that, apart from minor differences in grammatical
construction, the two terms are synonymous.

Secondly, it should also be noted that in attempting to find
the distinction between the two types of knowledge in
Theaetetus, there is a danger of naively assuming that they
are mutually exclusive. They are not, of course (see Ayer
[19], pp. 12–14): if I know X by acquaintance, I also know
facts about it; and Plato makes no distinction between
'knowing X' and 'knowing what X is' (see, for example, 147b
with p. 22, no. 1). Similarly, the start of the whole dialogue is
concerned neither with propositional knowledge nor with
knowledge by acquaintance, but with skills (146c–147c),
which involve a third type of knowledge, namely knowing
how to do things. But again, a cobbler's skill does not exclude
him having knowledge of relevant facts, but even entails him
having such propositional knowledge, and knowledge by
acquaintance as well. Pears concludes his discussion of this
topic by saying ([46], p. 38), 'There are intricate connections
between all the three types of knowledge.' So, although it
would be foolish to praise Plato's lack of distinctions (the
Socratic assumption that there is some single core meaning
to terms often hinders his attainment of a definition), there is
a sense in which it is not an utterly idiotic approach.

To return to the chief issue. I am suggesting that, just as
Plato's failure to distinguish types of knowledge vitiated his
discussion of false belief, so it also forces him to conclude that
the definition of knowledge as justified true belief is circular.
Moreover, it is not impossible that these problems in *Theaetetus*
could have led Plato to make the necessary distinctions later.
It is worth noting that there is what we might call a tendency
in the dialogue towards isolating propositional knowledge:
the discussion of perception ends by rejecting the claim of
sense-perception (i.e. acquaintance) to be knowledge; and the

discussion of belief ends by considering propositions at least
in the sense of analyses of elements (see especially Matthews
[4], pp. 20–23, on this tendency in the dialogue). We have
no grounds for thinking that Plato had clearly distinguished
these types of knowledge before *Theaetetus*; but *Theaetetus*
could have led him in this direction.

We can now briefly survey the concluding part of *Theaetetus*
as a whole. The main issue, as we have seen, is the possibility
of a regress in accounts of knowledge, including Plato's own
earlier assumptions about knowledge. The dream theory
offers one way of ending the regress, by the strange stratagem
of positing unknowable elements. In rejecting this theory,
Plato reaffirms that knowledge must be based on knowledge.
But having reaffirmed this principle, he is left with a further
problem – that this very principle entails a circular definition,
since a justification for a claim to knowledge itself makes
reference to knowledge. So although the giving of adequate evidence is another way of stopping the regress (see Pears [46],
p. 12), and one of which Plato was well aware (see *Phaedo*
101d–e), he now thinks that this stratagem too is untenable.

Thus the sequence of thought of the final part of the
dialogue is straightforward, interesting and relevant. The
other main issue of interpretation which exercised us (pp.
227–30) led us to the tentative conclusion that the principle
KR – that knowledge requires a rational account – was being
weakened. Again, we are now in a position to see both why
this should be so, and why it should be so hard to uncover
Plato's thinking on this point. It was hard simply because, as
suggested on p. 230, Plato is not clear; if he had been clear,
then he would already have entertained the Cartesian or
Russellian account of knowledge, according to which KR is
shed in the last analysis. At the same time, the fact that he *is*
implicitly impugning KR is another thread in the tendency
we have noted for it to be one of the *after*-effects of *Theaetetus*
to distinguish the two types of knowledge.

Finally, if Plato in *Theaetetus* is after a single knowledge,
what might it be? I do not have any positive suggestions on
this question, because I do not think Plato had anything

definite in mind. It is tempting, given the tendency just noted
to isolate propositional knowledge, to suppose that Plato, like
modern philosophers, recognized propositional knowledge as
knowledge *par excellence*; but given Plato's certain unclarity
about the nature of such knowledge, it would be rash to
conclude that he had such recognition before or during
Theaetetus. Nehamas [44] argues that knowledge of essences
is the single knowledge Plato has in mind. But the point is
that neither the thrust nor the interest of *Theaetetus* lies in its
ostensible aim to search for a single knowledge. It is certainly
not clear from *Theaetetus* that he has anything as definite as
knowledge of essences in mind; it is rather the case that he is
raising and exploring epistemological issues, and that these
issues tend towards distinctions within knowledge, rather
than any single knowledge. In *Theaetetus*, as in other dialogues, the assumption of univocality – that there is a single
core meaning to terms – is simply the motivation for philosophical discussion. Again, if Plato came to realize the difficulties in this assumption, he could have been led to an
interest in types of knowledge, and thence to the masterly
analysis of propositions that we find in *Sophist*, which despite
being composed possibly several years later is attached by its
dramatic setting to *Theaetetus* (p. 131, n. 1).

THEAETETUS AND PLATO'S MIDDLE-PERIOD PHILOSOPHY

Having explored *Theaetetus*, there are one or two loose ends,
which may usefully be pulled together in the context of
considering the dialogue's relation to Plato's earlier epistemology and the famous theory of Forms. In the nature of
things, this cannot be a thorough survey of Plato's earlier
views; I shall have to be content to list dogmatically and
skimpily the salient features, with a recommendation to read
especially Crombie [25], Gosling [26], Ross [48] and White
[57].

Following clues which he found in Socrates' search for
definitions, Plato in his middle period of writing developed a

two-world ontological theory. The things of this world are unreliable: something good in one respect is bad in another; nevertheless it is possible to name the qualities of things and it must be possible to define such qualities. If the things of this world are unreliable, however, then what we are defining on any occasion does not belong to this world; in fact, when we call something 'good', the term really applies to the Form, an inhabitant of another world. It is only by participation in the Form Goodness that a thing is good. Moreover, there is only one Form Goodness, so that all the multifarious things which we call good participate in the same unique Form, and resemble one another by virtue of this participation in the same Form. In order to substantiate the reliability of Forms, we must call them incomposite (so that they are not liable to generation and destruction) and eternal. Thus they truly are what they are: they have *ousia* (being) whereas the things of this world have only *genesis* (becoming).

At this time, Plato's epistemology was inseparable from his ontology; the two main epistemological consequences of this theory are as follows. First and foremost, since knowledge is *ex hypothesi* certain, its objects are Forms; the things of this world are not knowable, but are the objects of belief (*doxa*), which has the unreliability and mutability appropriate to its objects. In fact, Plato actually defines knowledge by its objects: if an object is a Form, there is knowledge (on the background to such definition of a faculty by its objects, see Hintikka [37], Chapter 1). The extreme separation of knowledge and belief (and their respective objects) can best be illustrated by the fact that Plato felt compelled to deny that our knowledge of Forms is even acquired by reflection on the things of this world; at best they may remind us of Forms, but our knowledge of Forms is acquired prenatally (this is the famous theory of recollection: all so-called learning is actually recollection of prenatally acquired knowledge).

Secondly, as we have seen, he distinguishes sharply between knowledge and belief. While in the earlier (and possibly Socratic) *Meno* there is the possibility of true belief being converted into knowledge, by the time he wrote *Republic* the gulf between the two has widened. They deal with different objects and are irreconcilable.

Now, all of these views came to be modified in the light of a self-critical dialogue, *Parmenides*. This view is controversial, but it is now generally accepted that *Parmenides* does initiate a modification of Plato's metaphysics. In particular, *Parmenides* objected to the separation of the two worlds of Plato's middle-period philosophy: the notion of participation is incomprehensible (131a–e); if the Form Goodness is itself (reliably) good, a regress ensues (131e–133a); and separation tends to make Forms unknowable (133a–134e). The arguments of *Parmenides* are not unassailable, but the point is that we have no reason to believe that Plato did not think them valid against his earlier theory. Therefore the question of the relation of *Theaetetus* to Plato's middle-period philosophy could also be phrased as a question whether or not *Theaetetus* was written after *Parmenides*.

Clearly there is little sign of these issues and points in *Theaetetus*. From where, then, has the need arisen to mention them when commenting on the dialogue? The chief culprit is Cornford [2]. In this influential book, he developed a thesis which has aptly been named a 'conspiracy theory': that the very lack of mention of Forms by Plato in *Theaetetus* is meant to alert us to how necessary he feels they are for a satisfactory epistemological inquiry. This extreme and, at face value, implausible view (by this methodology, textual exegesis becomes indefinite, to say the least) has given rise to two responses (where it has not won acceptance). The first, exemplified by Runciman [49] is a *non liquet*: 'The reason that the Forms are unobtrusive in the *Theaetetus* is that they are not very relevant' (p. 28); 'There is nothing in the *Theaetetus* which entails the conclusion that Plato had discarded the epistemology of the *Republic*, but equally there is nothing which makes it certain that he could not have modified it' (p. 52). The second, exemplified by Owen [45], is a positive counterblast to Cornford: 'The *Theaetetus* states and explodes the thesis that *genesis* excludes *ousia* ... Plato, unlike his commentators, does not resuscitate it' (pp. 323, 325).

A starting-point, at least, is clear enough: we shall have to decide where *Theaetetus* stands on these issues entirely by what *it* says. The dialogue is Plato's last essay on epistemology: later works give only hints, which could tend in various directions (Runciman [49], pp. 52–7).

Now, it is in the nature of a thesis like Cornford's to be extremely flexible: a commentator determined to find hints of Forms will find them all over the place. So here I shall deal only with the most plausible passages, and especially those where Cornford claims that Forms are blatant. And it can be stated at the outset that the thesis that Forms are the *invisible* background to *Theaetetus* is undermined when the same commentator claims to find *explicit* mention of them in the dialogue.

There are three main passages where Cornford finds reference to Forms. First, in the 'digression' of 172c–177b, Plato characterizes the philosopher as an inquirer into questions like 'What is it to be a human being?' (174b) and 'What right and wrong are in themselves' (175c), the latter question being one which a non-philosopher has to be 'hoisted up' to consider. Cornford reckons these are Forms; but this is quite unnecessary. As Robinson says ([47], p. 46): 'The whole of this description [of the philosopher in the 'digression'], except for the imitation of God, could be truly said of a nominalist and positivist philosopher; for the essence of it is that the philosopher is a theorist, a generalizer and a spectator of the whole.' To be specific, the theory of Forms has nothing in itself to do with what behaviour is peculiar to a human being, which is how the question of 174b is glossed, nor how doing right leads to happiness and wrong leads to misery, which is how the question of 175c is glossed. The digression is not wholly incompatible with the theory of Forms, and the impassioned nature of Plato's writing recalls his writing about his theory, but the digression does not imply the theory. Even if we did feel compelled to read Forms into the passage, this would still have nothing to tell us about the general thesis of Cornford's, that the Forms are still the only possible objects of knowledge for Plato.

Secondly, from the refutation of flux at 181c–183c, Cornford wants us to derive the moral that 'Unless we recognize some class of knowable entities exempt from the Heraclitean flux . . . no definition of knowledge can be any more true than its contradictory' (p. 99). As I have already argued (pp. 181–2), the true moral of this section is that the world must have some stability: it is not just undergoing *genesis*. As Owen points out (see p. 241), this actually contradicts the two-world aspect of the theory of Forms; the things of this world have 'being' and must therefore be knowable. This is not to say that in his middle period Plato held that the things of this world are in the extreme flux he criticizes at 181c–183c: for Plato the things of this world were identifiable (thanks to Forms). That is, it is not Plato's concern in 181c–183c directly to criticize his own earlier view of the material world; it is his concern to criticize the notion that flux guarantees the infallibility of perceptions. But it is an implication of this criticism that the things of this world have enough stability to be knowable, and we also found that the objections of 181c ff. are aimed against more moderate flux theories as well – and this indicates a change of heart from the middle-period philosophy. The passage 181c–183c is part and parcel of Plato's concern throughout the discussion stemming from Theaetetus' first definition to reintroduce, in the face of Protagoreanism and Heracliteanism, the possibility of expertise about the world (see Crombie [25], pp. 27–33). Of course, it is not wholly impossible that such experts get their expertise from knowledge of Forms; but since Forms are nowhere mentioned in *Theaetetus*, it is unnecessary to bring them in. This world, Plato is implying, *can* be described in terms of 'being', not just 'becoming'.

Thirdly, in the refutation of Theaetetus' first definition (184b–186e), Cornford reckons that the 'common' terms, such as being, not being, sameness and difference, which are attributes of anything, are obviously Forms (p. 106). This is far from obvious. In the first place, there is a suggestion at 186c that we acquire such concepts gradually by education, whereas Forms are eternal and knowledge of them is acquired prenatally. Secondly, *Hippias Major* 297e–303d is worth comparing, where Plato makes considerable logical play with the same fact, that a pair can have properties which the members of the pair do not have (e.g. the properties of being two and numerically even: compare *Theaetetus* 185d–e). There is no temptation to read Forms into the *Hippias Major* passage, and there need be none here either: Plato is simply making the point that sense-perception cannot by itself acquaint us with properties such as duality. Note, in general, that the issue is not whether Plato continued to hold *a* theory of Forms – he undoubtedly did, and called such common properties Forms in *Sophist* – but whether he held the middle-period theory of Forms. And the fact that the 'common' terms are what are involved in discursive thinking about perceptible objects shows that they are not middle-period Forms. At 186a, 'goodness and badness' are even said to be relative to each other, whereas the existence of middle-period Forms is never relative, but absolute.

Cornford's general thesis, that Forms are still implicitly the objects of knowledge in *Theaetetus*, has been dealt with by Robinson [47], pp. 48–59 (see also McDowell [5], *passim*). In short, there is no reason to entertain the thesis: it blunts Occam's razor at every point. Instead of rehearsing Robinson's objections, I turn to list some features of the dialogue which tell against Cornford's thesis.

In *Theaetetus* Plato is exploring the concept of knowledge *per se*, yet in middle-period dialogues he was content to define it by reference to its objects (this approach, incidentally, is to be found in *Timaeus* and *Philebus*, both of which have been argued on other grounds to belong to Plato's middle period: see Owen [45] and Waterfield [55]). However, at 146e of our dialogue, Plato expressly denies that he wants to hear a definition of knowledge in terms of its objects (on this see Mansfeld [41], pp. 110–11). At the very least this is a big difference of approach, and one which undermines the supposition that the exclusive world of Forms is the only thing that is knowable.

Moreover, in his middle period, Plato would not even have deigned to consider the idea that knowledge is perception; yet in *Theaetetus* it is examined at great length. Similarly, the suggestion that true belief is knowledge or is a necessary condition of knowledge is taken seriously. In general, we find that belief is not sharply contrasted with knowledge; the same things are the objects of both faculties. Plato, like modern philosophers, seems now to allow more latitude in the use of the term 'know' than he would have done in his middle period.

At 201a–c it is even said that eyewitnesses have knowledge – that is, of things of this world. However, there is some doubt as to how we should interpret this feature. Hintikka, for instance, argues ([37], Chapters 1 and 3) that for Plato the eyewitness's knowledge is no more than an analogy for knowledge, which must be of eternal verities. But this begs the question of whether or not Plato continues to hold that eternal verities are the only knowables. As far as *Theaetetus* is concerned, we have no grounds for thinking that Plato was drawing any distinction akin to that between contingent and *a priori* truths and was restricting knowledge to the latter. And I wonder whether Plato would use a mere analogy as a knock-down argument, which is what the argument of 201a–c is supposed to be.

As we have seen, in his middle period, in order to sustain the separation yet knowability of Forms, Plato had posited a theory of recollection – that we have prenatal knowledge of Forms. Thus we do not acquire such knowledge by abstraction from particular instances during our lifetimes. But in the Aviary model our minds are said to be empty at birth (197e–198b); and the Wax Block is similarly a model for the acquisition of concepts. See also p. 141 on the difference between midwifery and recollection. Plato is tending towards conceptualism, which was summarily dismissed in *Parmenides* 132b–c as a possible description of the middle-period theory of Forms.

In short, not only is there no sign of middle-period Forms, but they are simply not germane either to most of the issues

Plato raises in *Theaetetus* or to his general approach. Conceivably each of the above points could be dealt with separately to show that *Theaetetus* is at least not incompatible with Plato's middle-period thought; at best, then, one would be left with a *non liquet* verdict like that of Runciman (see p. 241). Cumulatively, however, the overwhelming impression is that the middle-period theory is not just irrelevant, but also incompatible: it would have impeded the remarkable philosophy of *Theaetetus*, and to interpret *Theaetetus* in terms of Plato's earlier thought is to obscure its value. The criticisms of *Parmenides* led Plato to revise his thought: specifically, he no longer used the theory of Forms as a portmantèau theory to explain every aspect of philosophy (for two lesser, literary pieces of evidence that *Theaetetus* is later than *Parmenides*, see p. 136 and p. 85, n. 3). We have seen, I hope, that one consequence of this was not just an interesting tour around the problem of knowledge, but a breakthrough: epistemology has been freed from ontology. For even supposing that *Timaeus* and *Philebus*, with their 'middle-period' Forms, are later than *Theaetetus*; even supposing that *Parmenides* did not lead Plato to revise his views; it still remains the case that *Theaetetus* is an exploration of the concept of knowledge *per se*, without prejudging any issues as to what the objects of knowledge are. Plato is not asking, 'What do I, as a philosopher with particular metaphysical views, mean by "knowledge", when I use the term strictly?'; he is asking, 'What does anyone mean when they say that they know something?' This is precisely what makes *Theaetetus* still worth reading and studying.

BIBLIOGRAPHY

꿀

Any bibliography on a Platonic dialogue is almost infinitely extensible: one can delve backwards and forwards in time, the more thoroughly to place the dialogue in its full context. The chief restrictions I have imposed on this bibliography are to mention very few works of modern philosophy; to limit works which deal with other Platonic dialogues or Greek philosophers to those which are of central importance to some aspect of *Theaetetus*; and to mention only works written in English (though some require knowledge of Greek), and of these not the least valuable or most outdated. Even with these restrictions, the bibliography still has to be pretty long to be useful; I have accordingly starred those items which in my opinion are crucial starting-points for further study. I have also, for convenience, divided the list into sections, according to the natural divisions of the dialogue itself, and with a few preliminary sections.

A. EDITIONS AND TRANSLATIONS

[1] Campbell, L., *The Theaetetus of Plato*, 2nd ed., Oxford University Press, 1883
[2] Cornford, F. M., *Plato's Theory of Knowledge*, Routledge & Kegan Paul, 1935
[3] Levett, M. J., *The Theaetetus of Plato*, Jackson, Wylie, 1928
[4] Matthews, G., *Plato's Epistemology*, Faber and Faber, 1972
*[5] McDowell, J., *Plato, Theaetetus*, Oxford University Press, 1973

B. TEXTUAL MATTERS

Works mentioned throughout this bibliography will invariably take stands on readings of particular passages. The following articles have also been consulted and are worth mentioning.

[6] Adam, J., 'On Some Passages in the Text of Plato's *Theaetetus*', *Classical Review*, 1890, pp. 102–3

[7] Archer-Hind, R. D., 'Note on Plato, *Theaetetus* 190c', *Journal of Philology*, 1883, pp. 297–8

[8] Archer-Hind, R. D., 'Plato, *Theaetetus* 179e–180a', *Journal of Philology*, 1903, p. 15

[9] Bury, R. G., 'Plato, *Theaetetus* 188b', *Classical Review*, 1920, p. 102

[10] Cornford, F. M., 'Plato, *Theaetetus* 209d', *Classical Review*, 1930, p. 114

[11] Cornford, F. M., 'A New Fragment of Parmenides', *Classical Review*, 1935, pp. 122–3.

[12] Jackson, H., 'Plato, *Theaetetus* 190c', *Journal of Philology*, 1885, pp. 59–60

[13] Lorimer, W. L., 'Plato, *Theaetetus* 157b', *Classical Review*, 1936, p. 60

[14] Richards, H., 'Plato, *Theaetetus* 167c and 209a', *Classical Quarterly*, 1908, p. 93

[15] Rouse, W. H. D., 'Plato, *Theaetetus* 188b', *Classical Review*, 1920, pp. 63–4.

[16] Westerink, L. G., 'A Variant on Plato, *Theaetetus* 186c9', *Classical Philology*, 1970, pp. 48–9

[17] White, F. C., 'ὡς ἐπιστήμη οὖσα – A Passage of Some Elegance in the *Theaetetus*', *Phronesis*, 1972, pp. 219–26

C. GENERAL

Though several of these works home in more on some sections of *Theaetetus* than on others, their primary importance is always more widespread. I also include here some fundamental modern works on epistemology.

[18] Austin, J. L., *Sense and Sensibilia*, Oxford University Press, 1962

[19] Ayer, A. J., *The Problem of Knowledge*, Penguin, 1956

[20] Bluck, R. S., 'Knowledge by Acquaintance in Plato's *Theaetetus*', *Mind*, 1963, pp. 259–63

[21] Burnyeat, M. F., 'Aristotle on Understanding Knowledge', in E. Berti (ed.), *Aristotle on Science: 'The Posterior Analytics'*, Padua/New York, 1980, pp. 97–139

[22] Burrell, P. S., 'Man the Measure: Socrates versus Protagoras', *Philosophy*, 1932, pp. 27–41, 168–84

[23] Cherniss, H. F., 'The Relation of the *Timaeus* to Plato's Later Dialogues', *American Journal of Philology*, 1957; reprinted in R. E. Allen (ed.), *Studies in Plato's Metaphysics*, Routledge & Kegan Paul, 1965, pp. 339–78

[24] Chisholm, R. M., *Theory of Knowledge*, Prentice-Hall, 1966

*[25] Crombie, I. M., *An Examination of Plato's Doctrines*, Volume 2, Routledge & Kegan Paul, 1963

*[26] Gosling, J. C. B., *Plato*, Routledge & Kegan Paul, 1973

[27] Griffiths, A. P. (ed.), *Knowledge and Belief*, Oxford University Press, 1967

[28] Grote, G., *Plato*, Volume 3, John Murray, 1885

[29] Gulley, N., *Plato's Theory of Knowledge*, Methuen, 1962

[30] Guthrie, W. K. C., *A History of Greek Philosophy*, Volume 5, Cambridge University Press, 1978

[31] Hackforth, R., 'Platonic Forms in the *Theaetetus*', *Classical Quarterly*, 1957, pp. 53–8

[32] Hackforth, R., 'Notes on Plato's *Theaetetus*', *Mnemosyne*, 1957, pp. 128–40

[33] Hamlyn, D. W., 'The Communion of Forms and the Development of Plato's Logic', *Philosophical Quarterly*, 1955, pp. 289–302

[34] Hamlyn, D. W., 'Forms and Knowledge in Plato's *Theaetetus*', *Mind*, 1957, p. 547

[35] Hamlyn, D. W., *Sensation and Perception*, Routledge & Kegan Paul, 1961

[36] Hardie, W. F. R., *A Study in Plato*, Oxford University Press, 1936

*[37] Hintikka, J., *Knowledge and the Known*, D. Reidel, 1974

[38] Jackson, H., 'Plato's Later Theory of Ideas', *Journal of Philology*, 1885, pp. 242–72

[39] Kosman, L. A., 'Understanding, Explanation and Insight in the *Posterior Analytics*', in E. N. Lee *et al.* (eds.), *Exegesis and Argument*, Van Gorcum, 1973, pp. 374–92

[40] Lyons, J., *Structural Semantics*, Basil Blackwell, 1972

[41] Mansfeld, J., 'Notes on Some Passages in Plato's *Theaetetus* and in the "Anonymous Commentary"', in *Zetesis*, De Nederlandsche Boekhandel, 1973, pp. 108–14

[42] Moline, J., *Plato's Theory of Understanding*, University of Wisconsin Press, 1981

[43] Moravcsik, J. M. E., 'Understanding and Knowledge in Plato's Philosophy', *Neue Hefte für Philosophie*, 1979, pp. 53–69

[44] Nehamas, A., '*Episteme* and *Logos* in Plato's Later Thought', *Archiv für Geschichte der Philosophie*, 1984, pp. 11–36

[45] Owen, G. E. L., 'The Place of the *Timaeus* in Plato's Dialogues', *Classical Quarterly*, 1953; reprinted in R. E. Allen (ed.), *Studies in Plato's Metaphysics*, Routledge & Kegan Paul, 1965, pp. 313–38

*[46] Pears, D., *What is Knowledge?*, George Allen & Unwin, 1972

*[47] Robinson, R., 'Forms and Error in Plato's *Theaetetus*', *Philosophical Review*, 1950; reprinted in R. Robinson, *Essays in Greek Philosophy*, Oxford University Press, 1969, pp. 39–73

[48] Ross, W. D., *Plato's Theory of Ideas*, Oxford University Press, 1951

*[49] Runciman, W. G., *Plato's Later Epistemology*, Cambridge University Press, 1962

*[50] Russell, B., *The Problems of Philosophy*, Oxford University Press, 1912

[51] Ryle, G., 'Plato's *Parmenides*', *Mind*, 1939; reprinted in R. E. Allen (ed.), *Studies in Plato's Metaphysics*, Routledge & Kegan Paul, 1965, pp. 97–147

[52] Sayre, K. M., *Plato's Analytic Method*, University of Chicago Press, 1969

[53] Schipper, E. W., 'Perceptual Judgments and Particulars in Plato's Later Philosophy', *Phronesis*, 1961, pp. 102–9

[54] Taylor, A. E., *Plato*, Methuen, 1926

[55] Waterfield, R. A. H., 'The Place of the *Philebus* in Plato's Dialogues', *Phronesis*, 1980, pp. 270–305

[56] Watson, J., 'Plato and Protagoras', *Philosophical Review*, 1907, pp. 469–87

[57] White, N. P., *Plato on Knowledge and Reality*, Hackett, 1976

[58] Williams, B. A. O., 'Knowledge and Reasons', in G. H. von Wright (ed.), *Problems in the Theory of Knowledge*, Martinus Nijhoff, 1972, pp. 1–11

[59] Woozley, A. D., *Theory of Knowledge*, Hutchinson, 1949

❧ D. PART ONE: THEAETETUS 142a–151d ❧

[60] Brown, M. S., '*Theaetetus*: Knowledge as Continued Learning', *Journal of the History of Philosophy*, 1969, pp. 359–79

[61] Brown, M. S., 'Plato Disapproves of the Slave-boy's Answer', in M. S. Brown (ed.), *Plato's Meno*, Bobbs-Merrill, 1971, pp. 198–242

[62] Brumbaugh, R. S., *Plato's Mathematical Imagination*, Indiana University Press, 1954

*[63] Burnyeat, M. F., 'Examples in Epistemology: Socrates, Theaetetus and G. E. Moore', *Philosophy*, 1977, pp. 381–98

*[64] Burnyeat, M. F., 'Socratic Midwifery, Platonic Inspiration', *Bulletin of the Institute of Classical Studies*, 1977, pp. 7–16

*[65] Burnyeat, M. F., 'The Philosophical Sense of Theaetetus' Mathematics', *Isis*, 1978, pp. 489–513

[66] Geach, P. T., 'Plato's *Euthyphro*: Analysis and Commentary', *The Monist*, 1966, pp. 369–82

[67] Heath, T., *A History of Greek Mathematics*, Volume 1, Oxford University Press, 1921

[68] Irwin, T., *Plato's Moral Theory*, Oxford University Press, 1977

[69] Kraut, R., *Socrates and the State*, Princeton University Press, 1984

[70] Riddell, J., *The Apology of Plato*, Oxford University Press, 1867, Appendix A

[71] Robinson, R., *Plato's Earlier Dialectic*, 2nd ed., Oxford University Press, 1953

[72] Santas, G. X., *Socrates*, Routledge & Kegan Paul, 1979

[73] Vlastos, G., 'The Individual as an Object of Love in Plato', in G. Vlastos, *Platonic Studies*, 2nd ed., Princeton University Press, 1981, pp. 3–42

[74] Vlastos, G., 'Socrates' Disavowal of Knowledge', *Philosophical Quarterly*, 1985, pp. 1–31

[75] von Fritz, K., 'The Discovery of Incommensurability by Hippasus of Metapontum', *Annals of Mathematics*, 1945, pp. 242–64

[76] Wasserstein, A., 'Theaetetus and the History of the Theory of Numbers', *Classical Quarterly*, 1958, pp. 165–79

[77] Woodruff, P., *Plato, Hippias Major*, Basil Blackwell, 1982

◄✦ E. PART TWO: THEAETETUS 151d–186e ✦►

[78] Archer-Hind, R. D., 'On *Theaetetus* 158e–160a', *Journal of Philology*, 1886, pp. 149–51

[79] Arthur, E. P., 'Plato, *Theaetetus* 171a', *Mnemosyne*, 1982, pp. 335–7

[80] Barker, A. D., 'The Digression in the *Theaetetus*', *Journal of the History of Philosophy*, 1976, pp. 457–62

[81] Bluck, R. S., 'The Puzzles of Size and Number in Plato's *Theaetetus*', *Proceedings of the Cambridge Philological Society*, 1961, pp. 7–9

[82] Bolton, R., 'Plato's Distinction between Being and Becoming', *Review of Metaphysics*, 1975, pp. 66–95

*[83] Burnyeat, M. F., 'Protagoras and Self-refutation in Plato's *Theaetetus*', *Philosophical Review*, 1976, pp. 172–95

*[84] Burnyeat, M. F., 'Plato on the Grammar of Perceiving', *Classical Quarterly*, 1976, pp. 29–51

*[85] Burnyeat, M. F., 'Conflicting Appearances', *Proceedings of the British Academy*, 1979, pp. 69–111

[86] Burnyeat, M. F., 'Idealism and Greek Philosophy: What Descartes Saw and Berkeley Missed', *Philosophical Review*, 1982, pp. 3–40

*[87] Cole, A. T., 'The Apology of Protagoras', *Yale Classical Studies*, 1966, pp. 103–18

*[88] Cooper, J. M., 'Plato on Sense-perception and Knowledge (*Theaetetus* 184–186)', *Phronesis*, 1970, pp. 123–46

[89] Delacy, P., 'οὐ μᾶλλον and the Antecedents of Ancient Scepticism', *Phronesis*, 1958, pp. 59–71

[90] Digby, T., 'Plato on Instability and Knowledge', *Apeiron*, 1984, pp. 42–5

[91] Glidden, D. K., 'Protagorean Relativism and Physis', *Phronesis*, 1975, pp. 209–27

[92] Glidden, D. K., 'Protagorean Relativism and the Cyrenaics', *American Philosophical Quarterly* Monograph 9, 1975, pp. 113–40

[93] Guthrie, W. K. C., *A History of Greek Philosophy*, Volume 3, Cambridge University Press, 1969

[94] Holland, A. J., 'An Argument in Plato's *Theaetetus*: 184–6', *Philosophical Quarterly*, 1973, pp. 97–116

[95] Hussey, G. B., 'Note on Plato, *Theaetetus* 171d', *Classical Review*, 1896, p. 156

[96] Irwin, T., 'Plato's Heracleiteanism', *Philosophical Quarterly*, 1977, pp. 1–13

[97] Kerferd, G. B., 'Plato's Account of the Relativism of Protagoras', *Durham University Journal*, 1949/50, pp. 20–26

*[98] Kerferd, G. B., *The Sophistic Movement*, Cambridge University Press, 1981

[99] Kirk, G. S., *Heraclitus: The Cosmic Fragments*, Cambridge University Press, 1954

[100] Kirwan, C. A., 'Plato and Relativity', *Phronesis*, 1974, pp. 112–29

[101] Lee, E. N., '"Hoist with His Own Petard": Ironic and Comic Elements in Plato's Critique of Protagoras (*Theaetetus* 161–171)', in E. N. Lee *et al.* (eds.), *Exegesis and Argument*, Van Gorcum, 1973, pp. 225–61

[102] Levi, A., 'The Man-Measure Principle: Its Meaning and Applications', *Philosophy*, 1940, pp. 147–67

[103] Lewis, H. D., 'Naive Realism and a Passage in the *Theaetetus*', *Mind*, 1938, pp. 351–6

[104] Maguire, J. P., 'Protagoras – or Plato?', *Phronesis*, 1973, pp. 115–38

[105] Mansfeld, J., 'Protagoras on Epistemological Obstacles and Persons', in G. B. Kerferd (ed.), *The Sophists and Their Legacy*, Wiesbaden, 1981, pp. 38–53

[106] Marc-Wogau, K., 'On Protagoras' *Homomensura*-thesis in Plato's *Theaetetus*', in K. Marc-Wogau, *Philosophical Essays*, Gleerup/Munksgaard, 1967, pp. 3–20

[107] Matthen, M., 'Perception, Relativism and Truth: Reflections on Plato's *Theaetetus* 152–160', *Dialogue*, 1985, pp. 33–58

[108] Mejer, J., 'Plato, Protagoras and the Heracliteans', *Classica et Mediaevilia*, 1968, pp. 40–60

[109] Modrak, D. K., 'Perception and Judgment in the *Theaetetus*', *Phronesis*, 1981, pp. 35–54

[110] Mourelatos, A. P. D., *The Route of Parmenides*, Yale University Press, 1970

[111] Nakhnikian, G., 'Plato's Theory of Sensation', *Review of Metaphysics*, 1955/6, pp. 129–48, 306–27; 1956/7, pp. 355–6

[112] Newman, J., 'The Recoil Argument', *Apeiron*, 1982, pp. 47–52

[113] Passmore, J., *Philosophical Reasoning*, Duckworth, 1961, Chapter 4

[114] Reed, N. H., 'Plato on Flux, Perception and Language', *Proceedings of the Cambridge Philological Society*, 1972, pp. 65–77

[115] Rowe, C. J., Welbourne, M., and Williams, C. J. F., 'Knowledge, Perception and Memory: *Theaetetus* 166b', *Classical Quarterly*, 1982, pp. 304–6

[116] Shea, J., 'Judgment and Perception in *Theaetetus* 184–186', *Journal of the History of Philosophy*, 1985, pp. 1–14

[117] Sprague, R. K., *Plato's Use of Fallacy*, Routledge & Kegan Paul, 1962

[118] Tarán, L., *Parmenides*, Princeton University Press, 1965

[119] Taylor, C. C. W., *Plato, Protagoras*, Oxford University Press, 1976

[120] Tigner, S. S., 'The "Exquisite" Argument at *Theaetetus* 171a', *Mnemosyne*, 1971, pp. 366–9

[121] Vlastos, G., *Plato, Protagoras*, Bobbs-Merrill, 1956

[122] Waterlow, S., 'Protagoras and Inconsistency: *Theaetetus* 171a6–c7', *Archiv für Geschichte der Philosophie*, 1977, pp. 19–36

[123] White, F. C., 'Protagoras Unbound', *Canadian Journal of Philosophy* Supplementary Volume 1, 1974, pp. 1–9

[124] Yolton, J. W., 'The Ontological Status of Sense-data in Plato's Theory of Perception', *Review of Metaphysics*, 1949/50, pp. 21–58

[125] Xenakis, J., 'Essence, Being and Fact in Plato: An Analysis of One of Theaetetus' "Koina"', *Kant-Studien*, 1957/8, pp. 167–81

✇ F. PART THREE: THEAETETUS 187a–201c ✇

[126] Ackrill, J. L., 'Plato on False Belief: *Theaetetus* 187–200', *The Monist*, 1966, pp. 383–402

[127] Barnes, J., 'Socrates and the Jury: Paradoxes in Plato's Distinction between Knowledge and True Belief', *Proceedings of the Aristotelian Society* Supplementary Volume 54, 1980, pp. 193–206

[128] Bogen, J., 'Comments on Lewis', in J. M. E. Moravcsik (ed.), *Patterns in Plato's Thought*, D. Reidel, 1973, pp. 150–57

[129] Bondeson, W. B., 'Perception, True Opinion and Knowledge in Plato's *Theaetetus*', *Phronesis*, 1969, pp. 111–22

*[130] Burnyeat, M. F., 'Socrates and the Jury: Paradoxes in Plato's Distinction between Knowledge and True Belief', *Proceedings of the Aristotelian Society* Supplementary Volume 54, 1980, pp. 173–92

*[131] Fine, G., 'False Belief in the *Theaetetus*', *Phronesis*, 1979, pp. 70–80

[132] Hackforth, R., 'The Aviary Theory in the *Theaetetus*', *Classical Quarterly*, 1938, pp. 27–9

[133] Lee, H. D. P., 'The Aviary Simile in the *Theaetetus*', *Classical Quarterly*, 1939, pp. 208–11

*[134] Lewis, F. A., 'Two Paradoxes in the *Theaetetus*', in J. M. E. Moravcsik (ed.), *Patterns in Plato's Thought*, D. Reidel, 1973, pp. 123–49

*[135] Lewis, F. A., 'Foul Play in Plato's Aviary: *Theaetetus* 195bff.', in E. N. Lee *et al.* (eds.), *Exegesis and Argument*, Van Gorcum, 1973, pp. 262–84

[136] McDowell, J., 'Identity Mistakes: Plato and the Logical Atomists', *Proceedings of the Aristotelian Society*, 1970, pp. 181–95

[137] Rist, J. M., 'The Aviary Model in the *Theaetetus*', *Dialogue*, 1962, pp. 406–9

[138] Williams, C. J. F., 'Referential Opacity and False Belief in the *Theaetetus*', *Philosophical Quarterly*, 1972, pp. 289–302

ᥟᥳ G. PART FOUR: THEAETETUS 201c–210d ᥳᥟ

*[139] Annas, J., 'Knowledge and Language: The *Theaetetus* and *Cratylus*', in M. Schofield and M. Nussbaum (eds.), *Language and Logos*, Cambridge University Press, 1982, pp. 95–114

[140] Bondeson, W. B., 'The "Dream" of Socrates and the Conclusion of the *Theaetetus*', *Apeiron*, 1969, pp. 1–13

*[141] Burnyeat, M. F., 'The Material and Sources of Plato's Dream', *Phronesis*, 1970, pp. 101–22

[142] Centore, F. F., 'Atomism and Plato's *Theaetetus*', *Philosophical Forum*, 1974, pp. 475–85

[143] Cross, R. C., 'Logos and Forms in Plato', *Mind*, 1954; reprinted in R. E. Allen (ed.), *Studies in Plato's Metaphysics*, Routledge & Kegan Paul, 1965, pp. 13–31

[144] Desjardins, R., 'The Horns of Dilemma: Dreaming and Waking Vision in the *Theaetetus*', *Ancient Philosophy*, 1981, pp. 109–26

*[145] Fine, G., 'Knowledge and *Logos* in the *Theaetetus*', *Philosophical Review*, 1979, pp. 366–97

[146] Galligan, E. M., 'Logos in the *Theaetetus* and the *Sophist*', in J. P. Anton and A. Preus (eds.), *Essays in Ancient Greek Philosophy*, Volume 2, State University of New York Press, 1983, pp. 264–78

[147] Gallop, D., 'Plato and the Alphabet', *Philosophical Review*, 1963, pp. 364–76

[148] Gillespie, C. M., 'The Logic of Antisthenes', *Archiv für Geschichte der Philosophie*, 1912/13, pp. 479–500; 1913/14, pp. 17–38

[149] Haring, E. S., 'The *Theaetetus* Ends Well', *Review of Metaphysics*, 1982, pp. 509–28

[150] Hicken, W., 'Knowledge and Forms in Plato's *Theaetetus*', *Journal of Hellenic Studies*, 1957; reprinted in R. E. Allen (ed.), *Studies in Plato's Metaphysics*, Routledge & Kegan Paul, 1965, pp. 185–98

[151] Hicken, W., 'The Character and Provenance of Socrates' "Dream" in the *Theaetetus*', *Phronesis*, 1958, pp. 126–45

[152] Lesher, J. H., '*Gnosis* and *Episteme* in Socrates' Dream in the *Theaetetus*', *Journal of Hellenic Studies*, 1969, pp. 72–8

[153] Meyerhoff, H., 'Socrates' "Dream" in the *Theaetetus*', *Classical Quarterly*, 1958, pp. 131–8

[154] Morrow, G. R., 'Plato and the Mathematicians: An Interpretation of Socrates' Dream in the *Theaetetus* (201e–206c)', *Philosophical Review*, 1970, pp. 309–33

[155] Rorty, A. O., 'A Speculative Note on Some Dramatic Elements in the *Theaetetus*', *Phronesis*, 1972, pp. 227–38

[156] Ryle, G., 'Letters and Syllables in Plato', *Philosophical Review*, 1960, pp. 431–51

[157] Yoh, M., 'On the Third Attempted Definition of Knowledge: *Theaetetus* 201c–210b', *Dialogue*, 1975, pp. 420–42